MEMOIRS AND LETTERS

OF

JAMES KENT

MEMOIRS AND LETTERS

OF

JAMES KENT

BY WILLIAM KENT

DA CAPO PRESS · NEW YORK · 1970

A Da Capo Press Reprint Edition

This Da Capo Press edition of
Memoirs and Letters of James Kent
is an unabridged republication of the
first edition published in Boston in 1898.

Library of Congress Catalog Card Number 78-99481
SBN 306-71847-2

Published by Da Capo Press
A Division of Plenum Publishing Corporation
227 West 17th Street, New York, N.Y. 10011

MEMOIRS AND LETTERS

OF

JAMES KENT, LL.D.

MEMOIRS AND LETTERS

OF

JAMES KENT, LL.D.

Late Chancellor of the State of New York.

AUTHOR OF

"COMMENTARIES ON AMERICAN LAW," Etc.

BY HIS GREAT-GRANDSON,

WILLIAM KENT,

OF THE NEW YORK BAR.

BOSTON:
LITTLE, BROWN, AND COMPANY.
1898.

University Press:
John Wilson and Son, Cambridge, U. S. A.

TO

MARY KENT STONE,

This Memoir of Her Father,

JAMES KENT,

IS AFFECTIONATELY DEDICATED.

PREFACE

ONE of the peculiarities of letters, as a form of literature, is that the writer cannot superintend their publication; and the duty which therefore falls upon a literary executor is complex.

It should be his aim to present to the reader a concise, true, and attractive selection from the material at hand, yet at the same time neither to dwarf nor magnify his subject out of true proportion.

Light and shadow, as they inevitably come into the life of every man, are necessary to give true perspective, and, as Mr. Froude has said, "the sharpest scrutiny is the condition of enduring fame."

To this end has this Memoir been written, in which there has been nothing to hide, nothing to extenuate.

It has been the Editor's aim to tell the simple story of the life of this painstaking, industrious, and conscientious student, in his own words; and the narrative is chiefly interesting as we note the method by which he became the embodiment of such a vast store of legal erudition.

The fire of the Revolution had burned fiercely, destroying the traditions, institutions, and usages which the colonists had transplanted from the mother country.

To James Kent came the duty of reconstruction; and at this day, fifty years after his death, it can be truly said that it is due to his life's work, more than to that of any other man, that the United States, from ocean to ocean, is controlled by the same system of jurisprudence, founded upon those principles of law and equity which he enunciated.

Early in his professional career he grasped the thought that he was free to reconstruct, with no one to controvert; and from the writings of the great sages and civilians of antiquity, he enriched, beautified, and enlarged the commercial laws of his country, and dignified for all time the profession to which he belonged.

Much of the material for this Memoir was collected by Judge William Kent shortly after the death of his father.

It is much to be regretted that he could not carry out his intention to write a biography; the failure to do which was largely caused by the weakening effect of disease, which brought about his death a few years later.

The assistance of Mr. Edmund J. Carpenter, of Boston, in preparing this book for the press in its present form, is thankfully acknowledged, and the work submitted to the indulgence of the public. The frontispiece is from the portrait by Rembrandt Peale, painted in 1843, and in the possession of the family at Tuxedo Park.

TUXEDO, N. Y., *January, 1898.*

CONTENTS

Memoirs of Chancellor Kent

I

JAMES KENT, LL.D., Chancellor of the State of
New York, and the author of " Kent's Commentaries on American Law," was of pure New England
descent. His father, Moss Kent, a lawyer in Dutchess
— now Putnam — County, was the son of the Rev.
Elisha Kent, D. D., a graduate of Yale College, and
himself the great-grandson of Thomas Kent, a resident of Gloucester, Massachusetts, in 1644.

On the distaff side, his grandfather was the celebrated Dr. Uriah Rogers, of Norwalk, Connecticut,
— Mr. Kent deriving his lineage through the Moss,
Russell, Dudley, and other sturdy New England stock,
for the most part substantial farmers, with a strong
infusion of Presbyterian clergymen.

The Rev. Elisha Kent, D. D., was one of the
Presbyterian clergymen of the olden days. Graduated at Yale College in 1728, he studied divinity, and
for several years preached at Newtown, Connecticut.
Comparatively early in life he removed to the precinct of Fredericksburgh, — now the town of South
East, — Dutchess County, New York, where he was
settled for many years over a parish still — or until

recently — known as "·Kent's Parish." Dr. Kent died in the year 1776, at the age of seventy-two years.

Rev. Elisha Kent lived in the quiet discharge of his pastoral duties in the secluded valley of the Croton for many years, and during his life had the happiness of having his children prosperously settled around him. His son, Moss Kent, the father of the Chancellor, was graduated at Yale College in 1752. He studied law for some time in Norwalk, Connecticut, under Lieutenant-Governor Fitch, and subsequently at Poughkeepsie, in the State of New York, under Mr. Cranny. He was married in 1760, and established himself, partly as a lawyer and partly as a farmer, in the neighborhood of his father and in the precinct of Fredericksburgh. Within a very few miles were settled his three sisters. One of them, Sybil, was married to Mr. John Kane, an Irish Protestant, who was the progenitor of the widespread and distinguished family in the State of New York, of which family Dr. Elisha Kent Kane, the famous leader of the Grinnell Arctic expeditions in search of Sir John Franklin, was a member. A second sister, Lucy, was married to Mr. Cullen, a Scotchman; a third sister was married to Mr. Malcolm Morrison, also a native of Scotland; and a fourth sister was the wife of Mr. Alexander Grant, a lieutenant in the 42d Highland Regiment, who perished with his family in a shipwreck on the coast of Nova Scotia.

Here the old minister held unbounded sway, visiting his children and guiding his parishioners. His grandson so well remembered the rigidness of the

Puritan regimen that it seems to have inspired him through life with a strong distaste of the severity and asceticism of the sect, while he rivalled in every relation of life the purity of its morals. Yet his grandfather, though a man severe and stern to view, seems to have had mingled with his professional strictness a strong dash of humor. His grandson used to tell one or two anecdotes illustrative of this feature of his character. On one occasion, while pacing on horseback the roads of his parish, he saw a collection at a farm-house of young men and girls quite symptomatic of a dancing party, — for even in 1760, and in this secluded Presbyterian valley, this fascinating temptation was not unknown. The old gentleman immediately fastened his horse among the pillioned and saddled steeds of the company, and presented himself to the circle of young folks, to whom his white wig and portly presence were never more unwelcome. Yet he was received with great respect, and assiduously furnished with a chair, and his pipe was officiously filled and lighted. After smoking he smiled complacently upon the assembly, and, observing such a fine assembly of young people, proposed a hymn. A good long one was sung with melancholy cadence. After a little while the old gentleman condescended to smoke another pipe, and, that furnished, he set another hymn; and he continued smoking and singing till one young settler after another stole away with his horse, taking his sweetheart behind him on the pillion, and the evil spirit of the dance was effectually exorcised. The old minister then took his leave of the family, with a grave congratulation on the pleasant and profitable evening which had been passed. He died, as has been mentioned, in 1776, happily before the utter dispersion of his children by the War of Independence. The actual presence of the enemy was seen but little in the valley of the Upper Croton, but the entire breaking up and permanent separation of the near relatives, whose names have been mentioned, is a striking exhibition of the wide-spread consequences and effects of civil war.

The tender age of James Kent would have prevented, even if his inclinations had pointed in that direction, his personal participation in the War of Independence. He frequently stated to his children that he vividly remembered the outbreak of the War and the Declaration of Independence, which was signed when he was thirteen years of age; and he used to recount many incidents of the times, the most striking of which was a slight adventure which happened to him when the British made their attack on Danbury in 1777. On this occasion the future Chancellor was for the first and only time under fire.

The English troops landed in the neighborhood of Saugatuck and advanced on Greenfarms in force. Brigadier-General Gold F. Silliman, then a colonel (the grandfather of Benjamin D. Silliman, of New York), collecting the militia, hurried to Greenfarms to check the advance. Young Kent, noting the excitement of the villagers as the militia was gathering, followed the troops as they marched out to oppose the attack. The posse occupied the highway a little in advance of a fork of the road, at which point was standing a school or meeting house, having a chimney on the side facing the main highway. A barricade of fence-rails had been hastily thrown across the road and preparations were made to dispute the passage.

Young Kent, eager to see what was going on, climbed to the roof of the house, and, edging his way along the ridgepole, ensconced himself behind the wide chimney, in a place of comparative safety, and from which he could watch the proceedings below. His interest in the matter did not last long, however. The attacking party, having unlimbered a small field-piece, fired a round shot at the barricade, which, flying high, struck the chimney, behind which Kent was sitting, with considerable force. Naturally thinking that he had been discovered, and that the British were firing directly at him, he deemed prudence the better part, and scrambling down from his perch made his way back to his father's farm. Many years afterward, when on a visit to this locality, he pointed out the building, which was still standing, behind the chimney of which he had hidden during this encounter.

It must be remembered that when Kent came to early manhood, the war had drifted into the Southern States, except for occasional raids along the north shore of Long Island Sound. It is doubtful if his instincts would have led him to embrace the calling of a soldier, except at the stern demand of duty to his country; still, we find his commission, dated October 24, 1786, signed by George Clinton, whereby he was appointed Paymaster No. 1 of a militia regiment of Dutchess County, of which Elias van Banschoter,

Esquire, was lieutenant-colonel commander; and Kent duly qualified for and acted in his appointed place.   Later in life he followed with deep interest the progress of the great wars in Europe, and numerous manuscript volumes testify to his interest and devotion to the subject.

Shortly after his elevation to the Supreme Court Bench, Judge Kent prepared a series of memoranda of his life and experiences, in which he gave a very clear idea of the methods of study which were the means by which he gained success in life. He speaks but briefly of his family, simply noting that his grandfather " was distinguished for a strong and lively mind, and for wit and humor and a talent to command," and speaking in equally affectionate terms of his father. He notes his father's marriage to his mother, Miss Hannah Rogers, the eldest daughter of Dr. Uriah Rogers, of Norwalk, Connecticut, and states that " he lived in great conjugal felicity, for she was a woman of great prudence and discretion, until her death, the 30th Dec'r, 1770."   The latter portion of the father's life was marked by vicissitudes.   His property was several times devastated and plundered during the War of the Revolution by British troops and Tories. He imprudently sold his farm, the proceeds of which sale, being invested in the colonial currency of the day, were lost or greatly reduced by depreciation. Later in life he was disabled and finally rendered totally helpless by repeated strokes of palsy, and died at the home of his son, in the city of New York, February 4, 1794, at the age of sixty-one years.

Mr. Kent, in the memoranda to which allusion has

been made, records some of his recollections of early childhood. After fixing the date of his birth as July 31, 1763, in the precinct of Fredericksburgh, in the county of Dutchess, New York, he continues: —

"After I had begun to read (and I well recollect the first evening that I essayed to read in the spelling-book the paragraph, 'Hold fast in the Lord,' etc., and what joy I gave to my mother), I was sent to Norwalk to school about the age of five years, and here I lived with my grandfather Rogers till the spring of 1772, and passed nearly four years at an English School, and in innocent and youthful sports. The government of my grandfather was pretty strict, and his family, after the manner of the day, was orderly, quiet, and religious. On the 28th of July, 1772, I went to study under Mr. Kalna, at my Uncle Kane's in Pawling Precinct, and here I commenced the study of Cordery and the Latin tongue. I remained here until April, 1773, and then was sent to Danbury to a Latin School under the Rev'd Ebenezer Baldwin, a very respectable scholar, and a worthy and distinguished preacher.

"Such was the progress of the first ten years of my life; and I well recollect I was then as fond of activity and play as other boys, yet I had discovered an aptitude to learn, and an emulation to understand my lesson well. At Danbury I remained under Mr. Baldwin till his death in Sept'r or October, 1776, and had read Eutropius, Justin, and Cornelius Nepos and Virgil, and had made progress in Latin exercises. I boarded in Danbury at the house of Deacon Knapp, a worthy, pious, illiterate farmer, whom I used to

revere as a grandfather.   After the death of Mr. Baldwin I continued my studies under Mr. Ebenezer White,
at Danbury, Mr. Ross, at Stratfield, and again with
Mr. White at Newtown, until I entered New Haven
College, September, 1777.

"During this continual residence abroad, the seasons with me of unbounded transport and romantic
felicity were my periodical visits at home, at my father's
house, either at Fredericksburg or at Compo, in Fair-
field.   Nothing could equal the delightful pleasures
of such periods, when I was freed from restraints and
books and tasks, and could roam with my brother
from one juvenile play or amusement to another, in
rapid activity.   Perhaps these incidents of life are not
so much noticed as they ought to be, but I can from
experience declare that these home visits were the
most joyful, and my returns from thence to my
studies, for a little while, the most distressing periods
of my youthful life.   And this passion for home lasted
till I left for college; then the impression grew fainter,
and my return (to college at least) ceased to be painful and grew to be pleasant.

"My four years' residence at New Haven College
were distinguished by nothing material in the memoranda of my life.   I had the reputation of being quick
to learn, and of being industrious and full of emulation.   I surpassed most of my class in historical and
belles-lettres learning, and was full of youthful vivacity and ardor; I was amazingly regular, decorous, and
industrious, and, in my last year, received a large
share of the esteem and approbation of the President and tutors.   I left New Haven September, 1781,

clothed with college honors, and a very promising reputation."

James Kent was graduated September 22, 1781, with the degree of Bachelor of Arts. Sixty-seven years later, in February, 1848, one of his classmates, Mr. Simeon Baldwin, in a letter addressed to Hon. William Kent, the son of the Chancellor, supplied an admirable and interesting account of the Chancellor's college life, which he himself, in his "memoranda," dismissed with such brief description. Says Mr. Baldwin : —

" I was introduced to James Kent on the first Monday in May, 1773, at Danbury. He had that day come to town, to go to school to my brother, the Rev'd Mr. Baldwin, the clergyman of the parish, who had opened a school for a few boys, to fit them for college. Danbury was then quite an isolated country town (N. B. On a vague rumor of the Bunker Hill battle I was sent an express to New Milford, sixteen miles, to obtain a newspaper containing the particulars), its inhabitants plain in their manners, and Deacon Knapp and his wife, with whom he was placed to board, like most of the people, were Puritans of the old school. [After the death of Mr. Baldwin, Danbury was made a military depot; the consequent intercourse with the army materially changed the habits and manners of the inhabitants.] He was then about ten years of age, the youngest of the school, a friendly, social, innocently playful boy, beloved by all who knew little Jimmy Kent, as he was familiarly called. He was studious and attentive to all the rules of the school, and a good scholar in all the branches

taught.   He became a favorite of his instructor, and,
guided by his influence, and the guardian care of the
worthy family where he lived, I do not recollect that
his conduct ever required reprimand or censure.   He
continued in that school until the death of Mr. Baldwin on the 5th of October, 1776.

"We were then separated one year, and met as
freshmen of Yale College in 1777.   Our class was
small, consisting of young men grown up, most of
them much older than either of us.   He, I think, was
the youngest in the class, but was better fitted for his
standing than most of them.   While we were members of college the students were often dispersed and
their studies interrupted in consequence of the war,
but he still kept his standing in the class, and, to say
the least, in all the classical studies, he ranked among
the best.   In history, in the belles-lettres studies,
and in reading generally, he excelled them all.   His
attention to what he read was strict, and his memory
was uncommonly retentive.   It was the common remark of his companions that they could generally tell
the author he last read, by the style and matter of his
next composition.

"He wrote his compositions with great care, and
in a pleasing, flowing style.   But the rapid flow of
his ideas often embarrassed him in public speaking,
whether extempore or memoriter.   When preparing for public speaking, he has often requested me
to hear him rehearse, and, by signal, to check him
when speaking too rapidly, as he generally would,
without knowing it, when he felt the spirit of the
subject.   On these occasions, when often checked, I

have known him to sit down and weep; but he would try again and again, and by repeated trials, did learn, in a great measure, to regulate the rapidity of his speech, which, without attention, would, at times, be unintelligible.

" He left college universally beloved by his class and ranked as a scholar among the first. During President Stiles' administration, the Bachelors had a public exhibition connected with the examination for their degrees in July. Their cliosophic and valedictory orations were then pronounced, and the class dismissed till Commencement, when the Bachelors occupied the forenoon, and the valedictory by the Masters closed the exercises of the day. From the year 1798, the valedictory of the Bachelors has been transferred to Commencement, and the Masters do not now take part in the exercises of Commencement. I find by President Stiles' diary that at the July examination of our class, Kent had the most honorable appointment; namely, the cliosophic oration, for which, from his extensive reading, he was the best qualified of any in the class. Gridley had the valedictory in Latin. There was also a dispute and a dialogue. At Commencement, Baldwin had the salutatory oration in Latin; Perkins, oration in Greek on Greek Literature; Hinckley, oration in English. There was a dispute on the question whether the modern surpasses the ancient literature, in which Gridley and Kent maintained the affirmative, and Channing and Stebbins the negative. These, with sundry syllogistic disputes, occupied the forenoon. In the afternoon the Masters exhibited a poem by Barlow, orations by

Webster and Wolcott, and the valedictory by Tutor
Meigs.

"When we took our degree as Masters (in 1784),
Kent was appointed to deliver an oration. He accepted the appointment, but was prevented from
attending, and sent an apology to the President.
Baldwin also delivered an oration in English, and
Channing delivered the valedictory. No others of
the class took part in the exercises. It will be remembered we were in college during part of the
Revolutionary War, and all the classes were for a
time convened for safety in separate country towns,
in the centre of the State. James Kent and myself
joined the class in Glastenbury, under the care of
Professor Strong as tutor, and continued together until the January vacation; were then dismissed, and
not called together again until June of the next year.
We then met at New Haven and Doctor Stiles was
inaugurated President. Mr. Atwater was appointed
tutor of our class, — a meek, modest, unassuming
man, a good scholar in the languages taught, a
preacher by profession, not much of an orator or
belles-lettres scholar, but peculiarly affectionate, kind,
and conscientiously devoted to the faithful discharge
of his official duties. We continued under his faithful
care and instruction till we became seniors. The
President then became our instructor.

"On the 5th of July, 1779, the British troops took
possession of New Haven, and the students were
again scattered. They were not called to return till
the end of the fall vacation, about 1st of November
following. The winter of 1779–80 was severe, and

the quantity of snow from successive and continued storms was seldom, if ever, equalled; in consequence of which the steward of college informed the President that he could no longer furnish commons for the students. College was of course dismissed, a fortnight before the usual January vacation, and did not convene again until the next summer. Our class were then juniors. From that time we pursued our studies without further interruption; but it will be perceived that a large portion of valuable term time was lost by those various interruptions; and when together, our means of instruction and of obtaining information were very much limited, — the college library then consisting of little more than three thousand volumes, most of them valuable for their antiquity and much of the time kept out of the town for safety; and the Society libraries, the Linonian and the Brothers', then consisted of about one hundred and sixty volumes each, — now over nine thousand volumes. The faculty of college then consisted of the President, one professor, and three tutors, — a very limited establishment compared with what it is now. The classical studies were proportionally limited.

"The only Latin authors then studied classically were Virgil, Cicero's Orations and his treatise on oratory, and some parts of Horace. The Greek Testament was the only book read in that language. The Hebrew language was taught by the President, to the very few who volunteered. A few, — generally two or three in each class, — to qualify themselves for the Dean's County, so called, made themselves acquainted with Homer and Xenophon and a few other classical

books; but this was optional. Perkins and Channing
were the Dean scholars in our class. It was then the
duty of the tutors to give all the instruction which the
pupils received during the first three years, not only
in the languages, in mathematics, natural philosophy,
and astronomy, but in grammar, rhetoric, logic, composition, oratory, history, geography, and the belles
lettres generally. Chemistry, mineralogy, and geol-
ogy were then little known and not studied; and no
stated lectures were then delivered on any literary
subjects.

"Considering these things, I have often viewed
with wonder the roll of distinguished men found
among our college contemporaries, as may be seen
particularly in a note to Chancellor Kent's oration
before the Phi Beta Kappa Society, in 1831. Some
of them, doubtless, owe their distinction to the circumstances of the times in which they came forward
into active life, but many of them have exhibited a
laudable improvement upon the imperfect foundations thus acquired at college. Among the distinguished men of this description is the illustrious
subject of this memoir. Although a distinguished
scholar in his class, he acquired nothing at college,
and nothing in the circumstances of the times, which,
without great personal effort, could make him the
most eminent of the jurists of his time.

"When we left college, I, having no dependence
for further support, took a school in New Haven for
the first year. The second year, by the recommendation of the faculty of Yale College, I (in connection
with Mr. Lovett) took charge of the Academy in

Albany, then under the patronage of the mayor and aldermen of the city, and continued there until appointed tutor in Yale College. I remained in that office three years, and, during that time, studied law and was admitted to practice. James Kent was more fortunate. He immediately entered the office of Mr. Benson,[1] and continued a faithful, uninterrupted student for three years, and was then examined and honorably admitted to practice.

"When I resided in Albany and he in Poughkeepsie, our correspondence commenced and has continued ever since. That correspondence is peculiarly interesting to me, not merely from the warm expressions of friendly attachment, which I never doubted, but as they pointed out the course he meant to pursue, and did pursue, to attain the eminence to which he aspired. In a letter dated Sept. 15, 1782, the first of our regular correspondence, after some general remarks, he writes: —

The time, sir, has arrived when we must think seriously of coming forth upon the stage of human life. . . . It is a matter of perfect indifference what profession we are delegated to follow, . . . since all our labors and pursuits ought uniformly to center in this one great object, the glory of our Creator and the general interest of mankind. These ought to be in all, and they are in the Christian and the Patriot, the governing principles of life, and the great efficacious springs of action. *Nam non nobis ipsis nati sumus, sed partim patriæ, partim amicis.*

"In his letter of Oct. 10, 1782, he writes: —

[1] Hon. Egbert Benson, born 1746, died 1833.

at gale ?

The study of the law has absorbed my principal attention for the last twelve months.   Law, I must frankly confess, is a field which is uninteresting and boundless.   Notwithstanding, it leads forward to the first stations in the State.   The study is so encumbered with voluminous rubbish and the baggage of folios that it requires uncommon assiduity and patience to manage so unwieldy a work.   Yet this adage often serves to steel my courage and smooth the rugged moments of despair: "The harder the conflict the more glorious the triumph."

" In his letter of June 16, 1783, in answer to mine, proposing a solitary retirement from the busy world, etc., he answers: —

We are all subject to ebbs and flows of the ocean of ambition.   When you wrote, it was probably low tide with you; but, sir, had we not better first step forward into the scenes of public life, discharge our duty to our friends and to our country, like true patriots, and benevolent Christians; assist in forming the heart by precept and in subduing it by example; in guarding our political constitution as the most sacred rampart of national independence and freedom; in asserting the rights of individuals by laws and an equitable administration of justice; in being noble in our motives and diffusive in our exertions, and aim at the lustre, the merit, and the utility of fixed stars in the firmament of the Commonwealth?   Then, my friend, in the afternoon of life, when the hand of time and the load of meritorious burden shall weigh us down and apprise us of the season to retire, an approving conscience and an applauding country will render a retreat honorable, and make us happy neighbors and companions in your rural hermitage.

" In answer to my letter, informing him of his appointment by the faculty to deliver an oration at

Commencement, when a candidate for the degree of Master of Arts, he acknowledges the honor done him by the appointment, and writes: —

I shall endeavor to discharge the part honorably to myself, and I could wish not inconsistent with the President's judgment and the reputation of the university.

" In his letter of the 8th of September, 1784, he writes : —

I am yet a poor clerk to an attorney, and all my property is confined to my chest; but I have a thirst for knowledge and a determination to put in a claim for some of those honors which imprint immortality on characters; and this thirst and this determination, I trust, under providence, will lead me forward to some of those good and generous actions, and that sacred integrity of conduct and principle, which will render me not a dishonorable object to the few who love me.

" In the year 1794, after he removed to New York and became professor of law in Columbia College I had the pleasure of visiting him and found that, with a view of enlarging the field and opening new sources of obtaining useful knowledge, he had determined to revise and extend his knowledge of the ancient languages, and to that end adhered rigidly to a systematic division of his time between the languages, his profession, and the belles lettres; and hearing him lament the want of a full collection of the works of Cicero, I had the pleasure, soon after, to present him with a set, which I received from my brother's library, and which I believed he would use to better advantage than I had, or could. It consisted, I think,

of ten or twelve volumes.   In his acknowledgment he
says : —

These, with a little volume I had, complete the entire remains of the greatest philosopher, scholar, and orator, take
him all in all, of the ancient world.

" I might extend similar extracts from his interesting correspondence, but these are sufficient to show
that he was prompted by a laudable ambition for
distinguished usefulness, to be attained by honorable
means. He early, from conviction, became a Federalist, of the Washington school, and conscientiously so
continued through life, without regarding the changes
or influence of political parties.   Whether in other
respects he followed the honorable rules of action he
prescribed for himself in early life to guide him in his
ambitious career, is better known to his contemporaries, in the same field, of his after life."

Mr. Kent's own estimate of his early attainments
was modest, for he records, in his " Memoranda : "

" I stood as well as any of my class, but the test of
scholarship at that day was contemptible.   I was
only a very inferior classical scholar, and we were not
required, and I had never looked into any Greek book
but the New Testament. My favorite studies were
geography, history, poetry, belles lettres, etc.   When
the college was broken up and dispersed in July, 1779,
by the British, I retired to a country village, and,
finding Blackstone's Commentaries, I read the four
volumes.   Parts of the work struck my taste, and the
work inspired me, at the age of 15, with awe, and I
fondly determined to be a lawyer.

"In November, 1781, I was placed by my father with Mr. (now called Judge) Benson, who was then Attorney-General, at Poughkeepsie, on the banks of the Hudson, and in my native county of Dutchess. There I entered on law, and was the most modest, steady, industrious student that such a place ever saw. I read, the following winter, Grotius and Puffendorf, in huge folios, and made copious extracts. My fellow students, who were more gay and gallant, thought me very odd and dull in my taste, but out of five of them, four died in middle life, drunkards. I was free from all dissipations; I had never danced, played cards, or sported with a gun, or drunk anything but water. In 1782 I read Smollett's History of England, and procured at a farmer's house where I boarded, Rapin's History[1] (a huge folio), and read it through; and I found during the course of the last summer, among my papers, my MS. abridgment of Rapin's dissertation on the laws and customs of the Anglo-Saxons. I abridged Hale's 'History of the Common Laws,' and the old Books of Practice, and read parts of Blackstone again and again. The same year I procured Hume's History, and his profound reflections and admirable eloquence struck most deeply on my youthful mind. I extracted the most admired parts, and made several volumes of MSS."

In a letter written in the year 1847 to William B. Reed, the Chancellor recalls these days passed as a law student in the office of Attorney-General Benson. "In 1781," he wrote, "I left college and was placed

---

[1] Paul de Rapin (1661–1725), author of *L'Histoire d'Angleterre*. Translated into English by Tindal. 2 vols. 1725-31.

as a law student at Poughkeepsie, in the office of Mr. Benson, then Attorney-General of the State, and there I saw, and from time to time listened to, the great men that visited there, such as George Clinton, Washington, Hamilton, Lawrence, Schuyler, Duer, Duche, etc., and imbibed the utmost veneration for such characters."

Still earlier than this, in an anniversary discourse, as president of the New York Historical Society, delivered December 6, 1828, Chancellor Kent said of Egbert Benson: —

"Egbert Benson rendered eminent service to this State (New York) throughout the whole period of the American War. He was zealous, firm, active, and extremely useful, from the very beginning of the contest. In 1777 he was appointed Attorney-General, and in that office, in the Legislature, and in Congress, his devotion to the public interest was unremitted. The value of his services as a member of the Legislature, throughout the War, was beyond all price, and in the able, constant, accurate, and faithful discharge of the duties of that station he has scarcely an equal in the legislative annals of the State."

Judge Benson died in the year 1833. Upon the occurrence of that event Judge William Kent, the son of the Chancellor, in a private note thus characterized this extraordinary man: —

"By his long retirement from the labors of professional and political life, he had gradually disappeared from the public observation; yet there are many persons living to whom his name will bring up agreeable association and recollection. He was to the last a very handsome old man. His mind was vigorous and active to the day of his death, while his untiring vivacity, his fund of anecdote, his power of narration, his love of argument, his humor, and his various points of eccentricity and quaintness gave him an individuality and interest which it was amusing to observe and it is pleasing to recall. He remained through life an invincible bachelor, but there was nothing morose nor ascetic about him. No one was more fond of society; no one enjoyed more, but always in an innocent and decorous degree, the pleasures of the table. It was a jubilee to the children and a pleasure to the parents when, on a summer afternoon, the Judge was seen to drive up to the door of a friend, — like Mr. Van Schaak at Kinderhook, or the Patroon, or the Chancellor at Albany, announcing his intention of passing a few days, and carefully dislodging from his carriage a fine fish, or a pair of canvas-back ducks, or some other epicurean rarity, which he delivered over to the cook, with some skillful suggestions as to the dressing. Then would follow a season of liveliness and gayety, — of thronging visitors, disputations, dinners, conversations, in which the old gentleman would display all his peculiarities, all his pertinacity and disputatiousness; keep the table in a roar, while he never for a moment forgot that he was a Federalist and a gentleman. Woe to the man who crossed his path and interfered with his hobbies! William Cobbett was not a more determined enemy of the potato, and luckless was the agriculturalist who ventured to assert that there was any nutriment in this much discussed

esculent.   More zealous still he was for the Dutch
Reformed Church and the Heidelberg Catechism;
and he anticipated the times of Oxford tracts and
Puseyite theology in his denunciations of the papistical
tendencies of the Episcopal Church.   But his pleni-
tude of zeal and constancy was reserved for his
Dutch brethren in America, on whose behalf he was
ready to do battle at all times and against the hostile
world.

"'What, Mr. Benson,' asked the late Dr. Dwight,
'are the peculiar vices of the Dutch?'   'Vices, sir,'
was the reply,—'they have none!'   The Doctor, a
little embarrassed, changed his question: 'Tell me,
then, their peculiar virtues.'   'Virtues,' said the Judge,
—'they have all the virtues!'   He never forgave
Washington Irving's 'History of New York;' and his
criticism of 'Irving's Wife,' a very amusing specimen
of dry special pleading, applied to poetic diction and
imaginative romance, was the production of a feeling
which approached nearly to malice.   Irving's retort,
however, was good-humored, when he made one of
his heroes die in the arms of 'Justus Benson, an
ancient and honored poet of the Manhattoes.'   And
yet the Judge ate the potatoes he despised, admired
the liturgy of the church he attacked, and selected
some of his chosen friends from among the Yankees,
the hereditary enemies of his blood and race."

To return to Chancellor Kent's memoranda after
this digression: "I was admitted to the Bar of the
Supreme Court in January, 1785," he records, "at
the age of twenty-one, and then married, without one
cent of property; for my education exhausted all my

kind father's resources and left me in debt four hundred dollars, which took me two or three years to discharge. Why did I marry? I answer that, at the farmer's house where I boarded, one of his daughters, a little, modest, lovely girl of fourteen, gradually caught my attention and insensibly stole upon my affections, and, before I thought of love or knew what it was, I was most violently affected. I was twenty-one and my wife sixteen when we married, and that charming and lovely girl has been the idol and solace of my life, and is now with me in my office, unconscious that I am writing this concerning her. We have both had uniform health and the most perfect and unalloyed domestic happiness, and are both as well now, and in as good spirits, as when we married.

"On the 12th of April, 1785, I entered into partnership with Gilbert Livingston, for twelve years, with liberty to remove out of Dutchess at any time after six years. The great and established run of business which he then had and my embarrassments and poverty rendered the connection necessary and advisable. I had now reached the age of twenty-one and the marriage state. I soon felt the salutary effects of business, and after boarding a year and a half at my father-in-law's, I had purchased and repaired and fitted a snug dwelling-house in town, to which I moved and began housekeeping the 10th of October, 1786."

In the autumn of 1839, after the marriage of the youngest of his children, the Chancellor thus wrote in his diary: —

We are reduced at present to the primitive state in which we began housekeeping in October, 1786. We had then no person with us but my brother and a servant girl, at fourteen shillings a month, and a little boy; now our children are all gone.   Mary is settled in Boston and Eliza is with her daughter in Philadelphia and expects to be there until near December.   But in 1786 we were young and buoyant and full of hopes and joys and love.   Our house was very small and our furniture very scanty, but it was new and charmed us as elegant for that day, and my brother was a good helpmate and was willing and able to do anything. We lived neat and simple and snug, and so I want to live now, with a cheaper establishment and a house of less size.

"My reflections soon began to recall," the memoranda continue, "the memory of my classic studies, which I had most improperly and totally neglected ever since I left college in 1781.   I had never looked into a Latin or Greek book since that time, and I had lost in a great degree the Latin, and had forgotten even how to read the Greek, language.

"At the June circuit, in 1786, I saw Edward Livingston (afterwards the codifier for Louisiana), and he had a pocket Horace and read some passages to me, and pointed out their beauties, assuming that I well understood Horace.   I said nothing, but was stung with shame and mortification.   I purchased immediately Horace and Virgil, a dictionary and grammar, and a Greek lexicon and grammar, and the Testament, and formed my resolution, promptly and decidedly, to recover the lost languages.   I studied in my little cottage mornings, and devoted an hour to Greek and another to Latin daily.   I soon increased it to two for each tongue in the twenty-four hours.   My acquaintance with the languages increased rapidly.

"After I had read Horace and Virgil, I ventured upon Livy for the first time in my life; and, after I had construed the Greek Testament, I took up the Iliad, and I can hardly describe at this day the enthusiasm with which I perseveringly read and studied, in the originals, Livy and the Iliad. It gave me inspiration. I purchased a French dictionary and grammar, and began French, and gave an hour to that language daily. I appropriated the business part of the day to law, and read Coke on Littleton and made copious notes. I devoted evenings to English literature in company with my wife.

"The English classics I, however, had not neglected. They had been constantly cultivated, and I devoted, from the time of my marriage, a great many happy hours to communicate a knowledge of and taste for polite English authors to my wife. She inherited, not only a sound and vigorous mind, but the principles of correct taste, and soon perceived the beauties and felt a relish for the pleasures of pure and elegant learning. I began early to form a select and chosen library, and that object I have ever since kept steadily in view, and I have always found my library to constitute a great and essential source of felicity. It has been my mentor, my guardian genius, and has cherished in me a passion for letters which has literally grown with my growth and strengthened with my strength. But to return to my classic studies which I had undertaken to revive.

"I purchased Smart's Horace and in January, 1787, set apart an hour every morning to read it. My brother, who then boarded with me, was a much

more recent and better classic scholar than myself,
and assisted me in my first and feeble efforts.
Horace was then so forbidding, and my disrelish of
the language so great, that it was not till January,
1789 (the space of two years), that I finished the
reading of Horace with a translation. I began
Davidson's Virgil and finished that in November,
1789, and by the 28th March, 1790, I had read
Ovid's Metamorphoses and Horace again.

"On the 30th March, 1790, I ventured on Cicero de
Oratore without a translation, and concluded him by
6th September, 1790, and my subsequent rapid and
ardent progress in the Latin classics was as follows:
From 6 September, to 20 October, 1790, Sallust;
20 October, 1790, to 7 October, 1791, Jacoby; 16
October, 1791, to 27 July, 1792, Livy; August, 1792,
to 24 October, 1792, Cæsar; 25 March, 1793, to
August 4, Cicero's Select Orations; August 5, 1793,
to September 9, Cicero de Officiis; September 11,
1793, to October 19, Q. Curtius; October 19, 1793,
to November 17, Bynkershoeck's Quotations Publici
Juris; January 7, 1794, Quinctilian; June, 1794,
Suetonius and Florus.

"In December, 1788, I purchased a Greek grammar
and learned the letters and grammar, and in January
following I began the Testament; and after slow and
dull progress till November, 1789, I opened and read a
part of Lucian's Dialogues. May 5, 1790, I began
Homer's Iliad, and read and finished it with great
delight by August 3, 1791. In three months after, I
read Xenophon's Cyropædia. In the course of the
summer and autumn of 1793 I read part of Demos-

thenes and Hesiod, and with them I terminated, and
probably forever, my pursuits in Grecian literature;
for I find my subsequent neglect has effaced in a
great degree the knowledge of the language, and
the books are too scarce and the type too fine to
render the more thorough attainment of the language
a very desirable thing. I must, however, observe that
the sublimity and pathos of the fierce and barbarous
scenes of the Iliad were so powerful and impressive
as to render the reading of Homer a rich compensation for all my pains.

"The *French* I began in 1789 and read Télémaque;
In 1790, Corneille's Select Plays, Marmontel's Tales;
1791, Sully's Memoirs; 1792, Sévigné's Letters,
Montesquieu; 1793, Belisaire, DeRoby's Memoirs,
Rousseau's Éloïse; 1794, Anacharsis. In short, by
the year 1793 I had become a master of the Latin
and French languages and read the authors with
facility. Few persons ever pursued classic studies
with more pleasure and ardor than I did. They
opened to me a world of learning, of happiness, and of
fame, and I flattered myself I had discovered the true
time of my most solid happiness and honor. I
gradually adopted a method of dividing my time, and
adhered to it with the exactest punctuality. In the
morning till half after eight I read Latin, then Greek
until ten. Then I gave myself up to law or business
until the afternoon, and, after two hours' attention to
French, I concluded the rest of the day with some
English author. This division of time has ripened
with me into habit, and I adhere to it in a great
degree still. It enables me to do more reading than

I otherwise could.   No sooner does the mind grow weary with one department but it is instantly relieved by introduction to another.   Variety seems to refresh and to animate it.

" But I recall my recollections back to the period at which I commenced the independent and happy station of lord of my own fireside.   Our house was small, but neat and convenient.   It impressed all who entered it with the image of domestic taste and felicity.   I suspect that few persons have ever lived with more satisfaction than I did in my simple, snug, and classic style at Poughkeepsie from October, 1786, to my removal to New York on the 27th of April, 1793."

II

THE young lawyer was now fairly committed to his career. He had been admitted to the Bar. He had married in April, 1785, Miss Elizabeth Bailey, daughter of Col. John Bailey, of Poughkeepsie, New York, a young lady a few years his junior. Both were young, and both were poor. As one eulogist[1] has said: " His industry and learning, his intellectual powers, and his unblemished character were all the capital he possessed, and the only dowry of the bride were her personal charms, her firm principles and excellent judgment, the sweetness of her temper, and the purity of her heart. It is true, then, that they were poor — exceedingly poor; but it is also true that, in their poverty, they were exceedingly rich; for, in addition to the riches I have named, their mutual affection was disinterested and sincere, and their trust in Providence unlimited and unwavering." Although his legal practice had not become so large as to yield him any considerable income, his studious and dignified manner, his thorough conscientiousness in the preparation, and care in the conduct of the business committed to his charge, soon won for him an enviable position at the bar. He had not been long in practice when an event occurred in which he took the

[1] Hon. John Duer, Discourse before the Bar of New York, April 12, 1848.

deepest interest, and which was of the last importance in the political history of the United States. This was the assembling, at Poughkeepsie, of the convention of the State of New York, convened in the summer of 1788 to consider the ratification of the Constitution of the United States, which had been adopted by the Federal Convention, at Philadelphia, in the September previous. Kent thoroughly comprehended the grave and important nature of this convention, and listened to its deliberations with the deepest interest. In a letter written to Robert Troup, Esq., of New York, June 10, 1788, he details the opening of the convention by the Chancellor, and gives an abstract of his speech. In conclusion he states: —

As to the result, I can only say I look forward to it with anxious uncertainty. I do not abandon hope. I think the opposition discover great embarrassment. I believe they do not know what to do. Some of them, I am told, have said that they will not vote against it. The decision of Hamptshire and Virginia we are flattering ourselves will be favorable, and that they will give energy to the debate on one side and confusion if not absolute despair to the other side.

Many years after, in an address delivered before the Law Association of the City of New York, October 21, 1836, he thus alluded to this important historic gathering: " The intense interest with which the meeting of the convention was anticipated and regarded can hardly be conceived at this day, and, much less, adequately described. I was enabled and induced to attend the convention as a spectator, daily and steadily during the entire six weeks of the session."

Of the opposition, Governor George Clinton was recognized as the leader. His chief opponent was Alexander Hamilton, for whom young Kent conceived an admiration which was deep and lasting. He followed, with the utmost eagerness, the arguments of this brilliant statesman. Hamilton, he perceived, "generally spoke with great earnestness and energy, and with considerable, and sometimes vehement, gesture. His language was clear, nervous, and classical. He went to the foundation and reason of every doctrine which he examined, and he brought to the debate a mind richly adorned with all the learning that was applicable."

Here it will be interesting to quote further from this address, Chancellor Kent's characterizations of the two men who were, at this period, at the zenith of their powers, and whose names are indissolubly linked together, in the history of our country, by the tragedy of fate.

"After the peace of 1783," said the Chancellor, "a few gentlemen of the colonial school resumed their ancient practice ; but the Bar was chiefly supplied by a number of ambitious and high-spirited young men, who had returned from the field of arms with honorable distinction, and by extraordinary application, they soon became qualified to commence their career at the Bar with distinguished reputation. . . . Colonel Burr was acute, quick, terse, polished, sententious, and sometimes sarcastic in his forensic discussions. He seemed to disdain illustration and expansion, and confined himself with stringency to the point in debate. . . . But among all his brethren Colonel

Hamilton was indisputably pre-eminent. This was universally conceded. He rose at once to the loftiest heights of professional eminence by his profound penetration, his power of analysis, the comprehensive grasp and strength of his understanding, and the firmness, frankness, and integrity of his character."

So long as Alexander Hamilton lived, Mr. Kent, whether as the humble law student at Poughkeepsie, or as a justice of the Supreme Court of his native State, entertained for him the highest regard and admiration. Hamilton was Mr. Kent's senior by about seven years, and it was but natural that the rising young lawyer should have sought the friendship of so distinguished a soldier and statesman.

Upon the elevation of Mr. Kent to the bench of the Supreme Court, as was the custom of the day, the judge, together with many of the lawyers, rode the circuit together, in which journeys intimacy would quickly ripen, under the stress of the hardships of travel. Many and delightful must have been the gatherings about the hospitable board of the inn, at which the homely fare and rude hospitality of the innkeeper were dispensed for judge, lawyer, and client alike; and many reminiscences of joyous times and hearty discussion must have clustered about those meetings, when battles were fought over again, and anecdotes of "circuit" freely discussed.

Such an intimacy can now scarcely be appreciated, and the friendly, anxious interest with which the members of these gatherings regarded each other may be illustrated by the following incident.

On one of the circuits, upon which Judge Kent and General Hamilton were together, the judge had retired early, alleging some slight indisposition, and the party broke up, perhaps a little earlier than was its wont, being deprived of its chief. The night was cold and tempestuous, and the kindly nature of Hamilton was evidently disturbed by the indisposition of his friend. On his retiring, he entered Judge Kent's room armed with an extra blanket, which he insisted on tucking carefully about the recumbent figure, saying: "Sleep warm, little Judge, and get well. What should we do if anything should happen to you?"

In a bound volume of newspapers in Chancellor Kent's library, which contain all the published accounts of the death of Hamilton and of the duel with Burr, the Chancellor noted only this simple memorandum: "General Hamilton killed in a duel with Col. Burr." Only this brief reference to that tragic event has been found among Chancellor Kent's papers, — a circumstance which is regarded as somewhat remarkable, since the cause of the duel was undoubtedly a conversation between General Hamilton and Judge Kent, as fully appears in the correspondence published at the time. The bitterness which had been growing in the personal relations of General Hamilton and Colonel Burr came to a head in June, 1804, when Colonel Burr demanded an explanation for a statement contained in a letter signed "Doctor Charles D. Cooper," in which it is stated that "General Hamilton and Judge Kent have declared, in substance, that they looked upon Mr. Burr to be a dangerous man, and one who ought not to be trusted with the reins of government."

Hamilton, in his reply, attempted to evade the issue which Burr would press upon him, and upon which Burr insisted in no very courteous manner. In the interview and consultations and letters which followed, it is evident that, without receding from the position in which he unfortunately found himself, Hamilton never for an instant attempted to shift the blame from his shoulders to that of Judge Kent, who, it cannot be denied, was equally responsible with General Hamilton for the expression of opinion. During this time Judge Kent was at Albany, or its vicinity, attending to the duties of his professional position, and there is every reason to believe that he had no knowledge of the transactions, or of the claims made by Burr, until after the duel.[1]

In the collection of newspapers of July and August, 1804, the full account of all transactions and proceedings, so far as they were known to the public, are fully detailed, and in some of them are sketches of the life and writings of General Hamilton, which, although unsigned, bear strong internal evidence of having been from the pen of Judge Kent. Endorsed on the fly-leaf of this volume of newspapers is found a sketch of Burr's life from Judge Kent's pen: —

"The melancholy instability of human influence and popularity is strongly exemplified in the case of Colonel Burr, who in March, 1804, was a candidate

---

[1] The duel occurred July 11, 1804, the same day that the Commission of Judge Kent, as Chief-Justice, reached the Secretary of State's Office.

for Governor in the State of New York, and generally and zealously supported by the Federalists; and in 1807 his fall and disgrace are sufficiently exemplified by the publication of an extract stating his passage through Fredericksburgh on March 26 under a guard of soldiers. In the summer of 1807 (only three years after the duel) he was indicted and tried for high treason at Richmond, in Virginia, before Chief-Justice Marshall, and acquitted, for that the crime (if any) was not committed in Virginia. Colonel Burr was then recognized to appear at the circuit in Ohio on a charge of misdemeanor. He did not appear, but forfeited his recognizance, and, after wandering for a time incognito, he in the month of June, 1808, embarked in a British packet, off Sandy Hook, for England.

"In April, 1809, Aaron Burr resided in London in obscurity and poverty, and, upon the representation of the minister of the Spanish Junta, he was ordered by the British government to leave the kingdom. He denied being engaged in any enterprise against the Spanish government, declared that he was too poor to remove, and declared that he was a British subject and disclaimed being an American citizen. All would not do, and he was compelled to depart to Gothenburg in Sweden. October 15th, 1809, he left Gothenburg on his return from Stockholm to Paris, by the way of Copenhagen. In the year 1810 down to the summer of 1811, Colonel Burr was in Paris, living in obscurity and poverty and covered with spleen, melancholy, and disgrace. He lodged in an upper story of some common hotel in an obscure street, was very meanly clad, and scarcely commanded the comforts of life.   In August, 1812, Colonel Burr appeared in the ' Supreme Court in Albany and resumed business in New York.' "

Before closing this digression, the following story, current in family traditions, is deserving of place. Mr. Kent, although in early life a supporter and believer in Burr, never forgave him for the death of General Hamilton, and always asserted his willingness to maintain all that he and General Hamilton had said, which had led to the celebrated duel. Chancing one day, sometime after Burr's return, to see him in Nassau Street, in New York, although on the opposite side of the street, the Chancellor could not restrain his impetuosity, but rushing across shook his cane in Burr's face and exclaimed, with a voice choked with passion, "You are a scoundrel, sir! — a scoundrel!"   Burr flushed at the epithet, and was about to make a hasty answer; but time and misfortune had dulled the keenness of his temper; and, checking himself, as he paused to consider the age and dignity of his adversary, he contented himself with raising his hat, and, making a sweeping bow, exclaimed, "The opinions of the learned Chancellor are always entitled to the highest consideration."   He then passed on, leaving the Chancellor somewhat surprised and mortified.

In dismissing the episode of the friendship of James Kent and Alexander Hamilton, it should be added that the latter excelled in the knowledge of French literature, and it is probable that the attention of his younger friend was thus first directed to the study of the French jurists, a study from which he derived important and lasting benefit.

In returning to the narrative of the early professional life of James Kent, and in studying this era in his career, one cannot resist the impression that it was his close attendance upon, and his deep interest in, the deliberations of this convention that impressed upon his mind an interest in political affairs. Less than two years after its close James Kent made his entrance upon public life. On the 26th of May, 1790, he was elected a member of the New York Assembly for Dutchess County. At this time was begun an intimate correspondence with his brother, Moss Kent, a correspondence which was continued until the time when, many years after, it was interrupted by death.

Moss Kent was his brother's junior by a little over two years, having been born April 3, 1766. The brothers were devotedly attached to each other, and, although they resided for many years in different parts of the country, nothing could exceed the devoted tenderness of their letters and their constant attention to each other. The character of Moss Kent was by no means as powerful and energetic as that of his more celebrated brother; still, he played his part in the political history of his country with credit to himself and his family. He never married, the male line of this branch of the Kent family being derived only through James Kent.

There is nothing in this correspondence nor in his letters to his brother-in-law, Theodorus Bailey, that indicates that James Kent was particularly pleased at

his election to office; on the contrary, he seems to
have begrudged the time it took and the restriction
placed upon his leisure and the pleasures of study
and literary pursuits.   He writes of the social life in
New York, where the Assembly then convened, a
life which was remarkable for its brilliancy, and yet,
although a new experience, it does not appear to
have had decided charms for him.   "Dinners multiply upon me," he writes to Mr. Bailey, "like the
hydra's head.   I am engaged to-day.   I have dined
already with Burr and N. Lawrence.   Hughes is preparing me for dinner at J. Ogden Hoffman's."   And
again: "I conceive hospitality and politeness as characteristic virtues of this city.   I dined on Friday with
Mrs. King.   I breakfasted on Saturday with Mr. Burr,
and dined the same day, or yesterday, with Macomb,
who is a very clever, plain man, and lives in a house
the most splendid I ever saw in its structure and
furniture."

The interest of this legislative session was largely
centered on the election of a United States Senator
to fill the vacancy caused by the expiration of the
term of General Schuyler, on March 4, 1791.   The
canvass, in which General Schuyler and Mr. Burr
were opponents, was exceedingly bitter, and resulted
in the election of Mr. Burr.   The defeat of the
former was attributed partly to the unprepossessing
austerity of General Schuyler's manner, and partly to
the influence which was supposed to be exerted over
him by General Hamilton and the ultra wing of the
Federal party.[1]   Mr. Kent's record of this memorable

[1] Vide Jenkins' Political History, p. 65.

canvass and of its result is found in his letters to Mr. Bailey. Under date of January 16, 1791, he writes:

This week we expect to choose the Congressional Senator. It will lie between Schuyler and Burr. The event is very dubious, and, as far as I can judge, their interests are nearly balanced. It will be in some measure a question of Northern and Southern interests. I have dined and again breakfasted with Mr. Burr, and have received great attention and politeness from him. The insinuation of his manners is equal to the refinement of his taste and the activity of his mind. But I apprehend that I shall vote differently from what you would wish. My companion, Colonel Van Ness, and I, tho' we harmonize in every other point, will vote opposite to each other on this occasion. I take it for granted that not a single member from the middle district, in either House, will vote with me but McBarker. I believe you may depend on this calculation. I rather think things look auspicious for Mr. Burr. I shall not be grieved either way. But I have made up my mind as to the prudence and expediency and political wisdom of the measure, and I conceive my moral reputation would require me to adhere to those determinations with firmness.

On the 27th of January, 1791, he again writes to Mr. Bailey: —

You have heard of Mr. Burr's election. I congratulate you because I know it is agreeable to your wishes. I was of the minority. The objection of Schuyler's being related to the Secretary had weight with me, and I should have preferred another man equally attached to the administration of the government, if we could have found him, and could have united on him. The objection, however, is by no means so strong as was that to Doctor Tappen, because the council of appointment is so small that one individual is of

great consequence, and because it was created expressly
as a check to the Governor. And it is only a general
theoretic maxim that the legislative and executive departments should be distinct. They are not perfectly distinct
anywhere in any government in the world. In this instance
the objection was with me borne down by opposite objections of a more powerful nature. I saw the administration
of Hamilton, which I conceive essential to the prosperity
of the nation, violently opposed. North Carolina may be
deemed in a state of rebellion; Virginia and Pennsylvania
make the most alarming encroachments, and interfere with
great intemperance in matters perfectly and exclusively and
unequivocally vested in Congress, and subject to their
deliberations. To send a character, then, who has always
been regarded as unfriendly to the government and its
administration, and who was brought forward by persons
always hostile to it, and who himself possessed talents that
might be exerted in a powerful degree, was with me to
contradict the most obvious dictates of good policy, and
of faithful attachment to the success of the Constitution. I
therefore voted from the conviction of my judgment.

The matter of national moment, at this time under
discussion in the country, was the bill, introduced
into Congress, to charter the Bank of the United
States. " In 1791, in most of the States, a bank-bill
had never been seen. Beyond the mountains, in the
districts of Kentucky and Tennessee, military war-
rants and guard certificates, horses and cows, oxen,
cow-bells, and acres of land, constituted the money
with which the people paid their debts and in which
they expressed their wealth. In western Pennsylvania whiskey was the circulating medium. In the
South, every merchant and planter so fortunate as to

have coin kept it securely locked in strong-boxes in his own home, and when a note was brought told down the joes and Spanish dollars with his own hand." [1]

It was from the anti-Federalists in the House of Representatives that the opposition to the passage of the bill came. It had passed the Senate, in January, 1791, with scarcely a dissenting vote. In the House, it had already passed to its third reading, when a note of opposition was sounded from the delegation from South Carolina. A warm debate followed, which was continued for a week, but the bill at length passed the House by a handsome majority. It was sent to the President with all possible speed, for it was now the eighth of February, and Congress would rise on the fourth of March. Washington withheld his signature until the Constitutional period of ten days had nearly passed. Attorney-General Randolph and Secretary of State Jefferson advised him to return the bill to Congress without his signature. Jefferson, in a written opinion, was bitter in his opposition; but the influence of Hamilton prevailed with President Washington, and the bill became a law Feb. 21, 1791. Immediately a bill to incorporate a State Bank was introduced into the New York Assembly. On the 27th of February, 1791, Mr. Kent, who was an ardent Federalist, wrote to Mr. Bailey:

The Bank Bill will be taken up to-morrow, and most probably will be successful. The National Bank Bill has at last received the approbation of the President, and new and

[1] McMaster, ii. 29.

strong reasons on the ground of expediency now appear, which have not existed before. It is as requisite to have a State Bank to control the influence of a National Bank as of a State government to control the influence of the general government. Besides, our money will be carried to a great degree to Philadelphia, a rival city, unless we incorporate our bank. These reasons have determined Jones Lawrence, John Smith, and some others to favor the bill, who are in general opposed to the thing in the abstract. I favor it on both grounds, — on the ground of expediency, and from a conviction of the utility of banks on general principles. The writings of Adam Smith, and particularly the report of the Secretary, which is drawn with his usual precision and discernment (and which, by the way, I recommend you to buy as a curious and ingenious treatise), have served to confirm my general habits of thinking on the subject.

Somewhat contrary to his wishes and expectations, Mr. Kent was re-elected a member of the Assembly for Dutchess County in May, 1792. The position which he took in regard to the contested returns, whereby Governor Clinton was declared elected, and Mr. Jay was wrongfully deprived of his election, was calculated considerably to alienate him from many of his Democratic friends and family connections; and his subsequent defeat by his brother-in-law Theodorus Bailey, when nominated for Congress, was the cause of his removing from Poughkeepsie and settling in New York. The result of this defeat, and of the subsequent support of Mr. Jay, into which he entered with heart and soul, was probably his appointment as Recorder a few years later; the first step in the judicial career which was destined to render his name famous. It is doubtful if, as a politician or

legislator, his mind would have found an opening
which was suited to his capacity. His strong partisan
feeling, quick and impatient temper, hasty, energetic,
and upright bearing, scorned those devious methods
which keep in action the strings upon which hang
political preferment, and made the pursuit of politics
unsuited to his mind and method; while the close
attention to study, and the calm deliberation of the
judicial situation, coupled with its responsibility, were
eminently calculated to bring to the front those characteristics which would tend to polish and round out
his character.

It was a matter local in its nature, which was considered at this session of the Assembly, in which
James Kent was most deeply interested, and in the
discussion of which he bore a notable part. An intense adherent of the Federal party, he had watched
the canvass preliminary to the gubernatorial election
in New York with an almost painful interest. At the
critical moment, when the success of his party hung
in the balance, he wrote to his brother: "I am very
solicitous to hear of the result of the election. I shall
feel signally devout to Providence for his goodness if
he has but permitted us, this time, to remove so corrupt a man as Clinton from the administration of the
government." Governor Clinton's opponent in this
closely contested election was Hon. John Jay, then
Chief-Justice of the United States. He was enthusi-
astically supported by Mr. Kent, whose opposition
to the re-election of Governor Clinton, as has been
seen by the extract just quoted, was bitterly intense.
The result was, to Mr. Kent, a sad disappointment.

who was William Kent?

A letter to his brother, under date of June 15, 1792, details his understanding of the affair, and is likewise a rebuke to those who regard our country as politically debased in these modern times, far below its condition in the days of our fathers: —

James Kent to Moss Kent, Jr.

DEAR BROTHER, — Before this reaches you the news will have arrived of the re-election of Governor Clinton. This event, tho' it would have been melancholy if it had been the voice of the people, yet is rendered deeply afflicting from the consideration that it takes place to the violation of law and of justice. I apprehend I can give you more full information than you can otherwise obtain. The counties of Clinton, Otsego, and Tioga were not canvassed. The first was rejected, I believe, because D. Platt, who carried down the votes, was not deputed in writing nor qualified. I don't precisely know the ground on which the votes of Tioga were refused; but the votes of Otsego were lost because Richard R. Smith was not deemed to have been at the time, in contemplation of law, sheriff of the county. This decision is repugnant to the clearest principles of law and right. . . . If all the votes had been canvassed, Jay would have been elected by a majority of at least 400. What indignation must it have provoked to find then the People deprived of their constitutional rights by the violence of unprincipled men.

The progress of the business has been this. The Senate and Assembly each chose six canvassers. The Senate did as they ought to do; they chose three friends to Jay: Jones, Roosevelt, and Gansevoort; and three friends of Clinton: Gelston, Joshua Sands, and Tillotson. The Assembly chose six devoted Clintonians, to wit: Jonathan N. Havens, M. Smith, John D. Coe, Pierre Van Cortlandt, Junior, Daniel

Graham, and David McCarty. This I deem to have been a corrupt thing in the Assembly. These canvassers form a court of the highest importance, a court to decide on the validity of elections without appeal. They ought at least to have been equally biassed. I believe a more partial tribunal cannot be found in the annals of freedom. No sooner had they met than anonymous publications appeared against the Otsego votes, and indeed against all the boxes returned by deputies. . . .

On the final question respecting Otsego there were seven to four. These four have refused to sign the certificate and have protested. Previous to the decision the canvassers referred the question to King and Burr, and they differed. King was for the canvassing, and Burr for rejecting them. The latter has shamefully prostituted his talents to serve a desperate and abandoned party. He is the only lawyer who has publicly avowed in writing an opinion on that side. . . . But tho' most cruelly oppressed, I know of no constitutional remedy; we must submit. It is to me a most unpalatable cup. I have at least as solid a conviction and as keen an indignation against the corrupt administration of Clinton, the corruption of his party, the outrage done to justice, as is compatible with a due respect to order and law.

If one may judge from the tone of Mr. Kent's letters during the ensuing few months, the action of the board of canvassers met with bitter denunciation by many throughout the State. "I take it for granted," he writes, "that we must acquiesce in the decision, and that no legal remedy can be obtained. The people, in their original character, can, no doubt, rectify the grievance, but I don't see that the ordinary legislatures have jurisdiction over a contested election to the chief magistracy. The peace of the community requires an ultimate decision somewhere, and if we attempt to declare the chair vacant, we must assume the powers of the convention parliament in 1688, and if the Governor would claim his office under the certificate and the law, I see no peaceable way to accommodate. My idea is that we ought, from consideration of peace and prudence, to acquiesce in the authority of the decision. It is highly proper, however, that the people should reprobate the atrocious insult and injury, and pursue with recrimination and punishment the authors of the wrong, as far as the law will tolerate them."

Later, he writes of the passage of Mr. Jay through Poughkeepsie, on his way to New York, and of a banquet given by his friends in his honor. He has reconsidered his opinion, as stated in the epistle last quoted, and suggests a remedy for what he regarded as a gross wrong.

James Kent to Moss Kent, Jr.

July 11, 1792.

I have, since my last letter, revolved in my mind a mode of redress now in contemplation, and I warmly advocate it. It is that a convention be called under the recommendation of our legislature, to take the decision into review and to ratify or annul it and order a new election, as they shall deem proper. This mode is wise, benign, orderly, and republican, and no application can be made to it of the harsh and forbidding name of faction and sedition. I shall espouse it, and I believe firmly it will succeed. I hope therefore what I wrote before will be no check to your ardent hopes of redress.   Be assured that the atrocious injury will be redressed. . . .

The appointment of Burr as one of the judges of the Supreme Court of New York, by Governor Clinton, presumably as a reward for his political services in the Governor's behalf in the contest of the canvassers, filled Mr. Kent with disgust and indignation. This feeling was in nowise lessened by the fact that his old preceptor, Mr. Benson, for whom he always entertained the highest admiration, was the unsuccessful nominee in the Governor's council for the position.   "The review of this transaction alone," he wrote, "is enough to make us tremble with astonishment at the violence and partiality of our administration.   The Governor can, at least, be said to have faithfully fulfilled his obligations to Burr, for his opinion to the canvassers, but he has surpassed example in the contempt of appearances and public opinion."

At the convening of the Assembly, in the winter of 1792, Mr. Kent entered with great ardor into the investigation of the election contest.   In November of that year he wrote to his father, Moss Kent, Senior:

James Kent to Moss Kent, Senior.

MY DEAR FATHER, — . . . The Assembly have entered seriously into the investigation of the transactions of the last canvass.   We have examined the Secretary and his deputy, and shall probably examine several other witnesses.   We shall get all the material facts on the Journals so that our constituents may know the grounds of our ultimate decision.   We shall then attempt to carry some resolutions expressive of our disapprobation of the business, and there I believe the thing

will end.   Whether we can carry anything is very doubtful.
Nothing but the force of opinions out of doors will prevail
on many to go with us.   Mr. Burr has taken great pains to
procure opinions in support of his, and he has obtained
more of Edwards and Randolph.   A number of opinions in
condemnation have also been procured from very respectable men.   The lawyers in this city have also published a
very elaborate opinion on the subject.   It is by far the best
thing I have seen, and I deem it perfectly conclusive.

The friends of Judge Jay in the Assembly were not
successful, however, in reversing the decision of the
canvassers, although various expedients were tried.
Of the contest, Mr. Kent wrote to his brother:

James Kent to Moss Kent, Jr.

The great question which was raised by the other party
before we had half finished the inquiry was, whether the
canvassers were impeachable.   They decided in the negative.   Two speeches of mine in favor of the impeachability
of the canvassers have been published in the " Daily Adver-
tiser," and I flatter myself we have suffered no disgrace on
that question.   After the decision we then contended that
the business should be dismissed, that we had no jurisdiction over the conduct of men unless deduced from the
power of impeachment, and that since they by resolution
referred the persons aggrieved to the courts of law, they
ought not to prejudge the question by giving an extra-judi-
cial opinion.   Here we failed.   They first brought forward
a resolution that the canvassers were not guilty of mal or
corrupt conduct.   They then changed that as not being
favorable enough and substituted " no impropriety."   After
two days' debate they grew ashamed of this and resorted to
" no mal or corrupt conduct," and that they carried, and so

ended the business. Hoffman's and my speeches on this question are also published. Sometime or other I hope to let you see them.

The part maintained by Mr. Kent in these proceedings, although it could not fail to draw attention to his learning and legal attainments, deeply offended his family and friends, who were warm supporters of Governor Clinton. The strong family influence of the Baileys, through the Livingstons, and other kindred connections, made itself felt in opposition to his further political advance, by placing in nomination against him, for the office of Congressman, his brother-in-law, Mr. Theodorus Bailey. Mr. Kent's nomination was made while he was in New York, attending the session of the Legislature, and it is quite certain that he never sought nor desired the office. His failure at the polls, at which Mr. Bailey was his successful opponent, did not weigh heavily upon his mind. To his brother he wrote, March 14, 1793 : —

James Kent to Moss Kent, Jr.

DEAR BROTHER, — I am extremely impatient to get rid of this public situation and to return to the pure pleasures of a domestic and literary life. Mr. Bailey carried his election by a majority of 132 votes. The evil reports circulated on the eve of the election in the newspapers, relative to the expense of the inquiry into the canvassers' conduct, and of my capital agency in it, contributed greatly to this event. Besides, the interest and exertions of Mr. Bailey, and family of Judge Platt, the Hoffmans, etc., in Poughkeepsie, were great. That town never gave so many votes before. Every elector turned out. Dowe had 214 in that town alone.

I am not grieved at the result. My interest and happiness will be promoted by it; I only feel indignant at the hypocritical and impure exertions made use of by a profligate party, pretending to be real Republicans of the State. We have, however, been successful in the State at large. Seven out of ten are Jayites and Federalists. I shall move here [New York] either in May or July, and I have confidence of meeting with success.

A few days later he writes from Poughkeepsie : —

I am busy in arrangements to move to New York the first of May. I have already sold my chaise and cow, and am settling my business. This town has discovered so little confidence in me on a recent occasion, and some principal men, such as Judge Platt, Mr. G. Livingston, and T. Bailey, have either been instrumental, or willingly connived in such gross tales of calumny and hypocrisy to injure my reputation, that I shall leave this place with much less regret than might otherwise have arisen. I feel strong, tho' I hope no presumptuous confidence in meeting with success in my profession at New York. If I should fail eventually, I must retreat to Otsego and live with you. . . .

Mr. Kent's own entry of these events, made in his " memoranda," a few years later, and of the occurrences following his removal to New York, is both interesting and pathetic.

" While I was at New York in 1793," he wrote, " attending to my duties in the Assembly, I was nominated and supported as a candidate for Congress; but my brother-in-law, Mr. Bailey, was my successful competitor, by a majority of 132 votes. The partnership with Mr. Livingston had by this time become a

heavy and mortifying burden, and this was my principal inducement to quit Poughkeepsie and remove to
New York, the last of April, 1793. I carried with
me to New York my wife, then in the splendor of
her personal accomplishments; a lovely and precious
little daughter of upwards of two years of age, and
whose great debility and sickness during the summer
of 1792 had riveted the affections and awakened the
most painful anxieties of her parents; a small, well-
chosen library, scanty furniture, and £100 in cash;
leaving real property behind to the value of £200;
and this was the total result of my eight years' settlement at Poughkeepsie.

"But I owed nothing and came to the city with good
character and with a scholar's reputation. My newspaper writings and speeches in the Assembly had
given me some notoriety. I do not believe any
human being ever lived with more pure and perfect
domestic repose and simplicity and happiness than
I did for these eight years."

Dr. Edward Jenner, in England, was even then
pursuing his series of investigations, which resulted a
few years later in his beneficent discovery, by which
mankind has been delivered from its greatest scourge.
At this time, however, thoughtful and judicious persons sought to avert its most hideous results, by
resort to the heroic method of inoculation. So fearful were her parents that this much loved child might
become a victim to this dread disease that it was
determined to resort to this device. The result may
best be told in the Chancellor's own words: —

"Upon my arrival at New York I was under the

necessity of inoculating my daughter for the small-pox, and she had scarcely recovered when she was unexpectedly swept off by a fever on the 26th of May, 1793. No event in my life had ever before taught me the genuine agonies of grief. My whole soul seemed to be buried in my child. I loved it with excessive tenderness. I think of the lovely babe to this day with pathetic and melancholy emotions. My excellent and most interesting wife divided with me all the pain and anxiety of our disconsolate condition."

On his removal to New York Mr. Kent was admitted, May 18, 1793, attorney and counsellor in the Mayor's Court, his commission being signed by Richard Varrick, then mayor. It was at that time, and continued for some years to be the practice to admit to each court separately, the younger members of the Bar being admitted from time to time, on motion, as their business required, the fees payable on admission being a matter of considerable importance to the struggling practitioner.

"My first summer in New York," continued the Chancellor's memoranda, " was very gloomy. I was poor and had but little business and lived in a narrow, dirty street, and a thousand times recalled with eagerness the country beauties and domestic pleasures of the preceding year. In November, 1793, my father was brought to my house by my brother. He was then bedridden with the palsy, and, to add to my uneasiness, my brother then informed me of his failure in trade in Otsego County, and of the apprehensions of his ruin."

In the darkest period of this year, when money was at the lowest ebb, and the hope of obtaining any faint indeed, Mrs. Kent was appalled one morning by a wheel-barrow stopping at the door, literally full of books. They were the works of De Thou, the French jurist, for which her husband, in an enthusiastic and reckless hour, had given an order some months before. The bill presented with the books was $40! Years afterwards, they used to recall with amusement the terrified looks of the busy housekeeper, which, in this instance, were reflected by her husband. He extricated himself from his difficulty with unusual adroitness. He met in the street his friend Edward Livingston, the well known author of the Louisiana Code of Laws, with whom he preserved an intimate acquaintance during a long life. Mr. Livingston was then a trustee of the Society Library. "Are you aware, Livingston," asked Mr. Kent, "that you have not in the Society Library any of the works of the great Thuamus?" However familiar Mr. Livingston may subsequently have become with the historians and civilians of the Continent, he was obviously not very clear as to the identity of this Thuamus, though he agreed with great gravity that the absence of his works caused a sad chasm in the shelves of the library. Mr. Kent informed him that a copy could be procured in New York, and that he would even charge himself with the office of sending it to the library. The offer was gratefully accepted. Another wheel-barrow was speedily obtained, the works of the great Thuamus (with the bill) were carried to the library; and debt went away from, and smiles again lighted

up, the humble but happy household of Marketfield
Street.

This was the period of low tide in the fortunes of
James Kent. He greatly missed the pleasures and
beauties of country life, and so reduced did he become in his circumstances that pecuniary assistance
rendered by his brother was received with the deepest gratitude. " Nothing," he wrote in acknowledgment, " could have come more seasonably. My great
and uncommon expenses since I have been here, and
the total stop to business which my removal occasioned, rendered me quite dependent. . . . Your letter
gave me great satisfaction and consolation. I place
every reliance on your love and attachment. I hope
I shall be able to prosper myself. Tho' my afflictions
have been most painful and my spirits depressed,
I have entered with determined zeal on the studies of
my profession, and I am sure it will be in my power
to merit, if I cannot attain, the highest honors of the
Bar."

Again, in October, 1793, he wrote to his brother:

James Kent to Moss Kent, Jr.

. . . I am very healthy, but my business comes on
slowly and living is very high. The beef in market is
7*d.*, 8*d.*, and 9*d.* a pound, and other things in proportion.
But the most serious of all our expenses is wood. It is
now 18*s.* a load at the wharf, and four loads make a cord.
The expense of riding, sawing, etc., is about 3*s.*; so that
every load of nut wood, which is the only wood brought
here that will burn, costs me 21*s.* a load. This extraordinary
dearness of wood is owing partly to the great influx of people from the West Indies, etc., but principally because last

winter was open, and there was no sledding to bring the wood down to the landings up the river. I endeavor to keep up my spirits all I can, but low spirits and discouragements frequently press so hard upon me as to retard my studies. However, I will try a year or two yet, and if it will not do here, I must go into the woods somewhere, as you have done.

But brighter days were soon to dawn for Mr. Kent and his devoted wife. At a meeting of the trustees of Columbia College, held at the house of John Simmons, innkeeper, in the city of New York, on Monday, the 2d of December, 1793, it was resolved that a professorship of Law be established in Columbia College, with a salary of £200 per annum, to be paid out of the funds allowed this college by the Legislature. Dr. Bard then nominated James Kent, Esquire, for the Professor of Law. At a subsequent meeting of the trustees held on Tuesday, the 24th of December, 1793, he was unanimously elected.

A retrospect of his early professional life, written by Chancellor Kent, for the information of his children and grandchildren, in March, 1847, gives an excellent idea, not only of his own days of small things, but of the jurisprudence of our country a century ago. "When settled as a lawyer in Poughkeepsie in 1785," he wrote, "I remained in practice until I removed to New York in May, 1793. I was then a young and married housekeeper. I owned one acre of ground and fitted up, in neat style for that day, a snug and endearing little cottage, and I cultivated an excellent garden, and my income by practice did not reach on an average above $500

a year. My wife was my young housekeeper, with
only a servant girl for cook, and everything else and
all my furniture might have cost about $250; but
we lived as creditably and attractively as any persons in the village.   My brother was my inmate and
helpmate for the three years that he was a clerk in
my office. He was admitted to the Bar in 1789,
and went and settled on the Mohawk, in the town
of Canajoharie. After he left me, Smith Thompson
took his place as my clerk, and served me faithfully for three years, or until about the time I
removed to New York. He had been nominally
educated at Princeton College, and he kept an English school at Poughkeepsie before he joined my
office. He was a plain, modest, sensible, ignorant
young man, with narrow views and anti-Federal politics. His mind did not expand, and his principles
became liberal but very slowly. The Federal Convention, and the new Constitution, and the discussions
therein, gave amazing impulse to my feelings, and
with an intensity of ardor I embarked in Federal
politics, and quite gained an ascendant in the local
proceedings and discussions. I had General Bailey,
who lived next door to me, and my partner G.
Livingston, and Thompson my clerk, as controversial
antagonists, and Judge Benson, then living at Poughkeepsie, as my patron and coadjutor. Jacob Radcliff,
who studied with Judge Benson and settled as a lawyer at Red Hook, was a correct, sensible, and respectable young lawyer, and he and I became great
political and professional friends; and this lasted
until after he became a judge. There were no other

lawyers from 1789 to 1793, in Dutchess County, that were worth notice. Silas Marsh was only a County Court lawyer and quite illiterate, but a man of wit, and irregularity, and poverty; and he tormented me exceedingly, he was so dilatory and ignorant in his County Court practice. I did very little business in the Supreme Court while I remained at Poughkeepsie. My practice was almost confined to County Court practice, and to issuing writs to collect debts, and to entering up judgments in the Supreme Court. I was not admitted into the Court of Chancery until after I removed to New York. My great occupation for the eight years of my settlement at Poughkeepsie was studying the classics, attending to quite inconsiderable county practice and conveyancing, and studying Federal politics, and reading all the histories and travels and poetry that I could lay my hands on, and in devoting my leisure to my garden, to my lovely wife, and to the nurturing and tending the blessed little daughter that I had at Poughkeepsie, and carried with her mother to New York in 1793, where she died within four weeks after I got there, to my inexpressible grief. Hamilton became my idol very early in life. His two letters of Phocion were published in 1784, against the intemperance of the Whigs in trying to persecute the Tories, contrary to the spirit of the treaty of 1783. They were much admired, and frustrated the puny pamphlet of Dr. Ledyard and the illiberal and narrow construction given to the treaty by the anti Federal Whigs of that day.

"It was a great blessing to me at Poughkeepsie to live adjoining Theodorus Bailey, for he had much better country patronage and practice, and he got an ambitious desire to buy books, and such as I recommended, and I, in that way, got access to the best English authors and translations. While at Poughkeepsie my Federal celebrity procured my acquaintance and friendship with several distinguished men in New York, such as Chief-Justice Jay, Judge Hobart, of the Supreme Court, and Colonel Troup and Edward Livingston. It was the character I had insensibly acquired as a scholar and a Federalist and a presumed (though it was not true) well-read lawyer that the very first year that I removed to New York I was appointed a Professor of Law in Columbia College. The influence of Dr. S. Bard, of Judge Hobart, of B. Livingston, Edward Livingston, and probably of Chief-Justice Jay, procured me the appointment.

"The progress of jurisprudence was nothing in this State (New York) prior to the year 1793. There were no decisions of any of the courts published. There were none that contained any investigation. In the city of New York, Hamilton, Harrison, Burr, Cozine, and perhaps John Lawrence and old Samuel Jones (then deemed and known as the oracle of the law) began to introduce the knowledge and cultivation of the law, which was confined of course to Coke, Littleton, and the reporters, down to Burrow. Hamilton brought a writ of right in a Waddell cause in this city (New York) which made quite a sensation and created much puzzle in the courts. The judges of the Supreme Court (Morris, Yates, and Hobart) were very illiterate as lawyers, and the addition of John Lansing, in 1790, was supposed to be a great im-

provement to the bench, merely because he appeared
to have studied more the King's Bench Practice, and
was more diligent, exact, and formal in attending to
cases and enforcing rules of practice. The country
Circuit Courts were chiefly occupied in plain ejectment suits and in trying criminals in the Courts of
Oyer and Terminer. In short, our jurisprudence was
a blank when Hamilton and Harrison first began by
their forensic discussions to introduce principles and
to pour light and learning upon the science of law."

III

DURING December, 1793, and January, 1794, Mr. Kent made a journey from New York to Washington, on the Potomac, as the post road runs, a distance of two hundred and fifty-seven miles, in the public stage, accompanied by Mr. James Greenleaf and Mr. Charles Lagarenne, a Frenchman. In a letter to his brother, this tour is minutely described. Especially interesting is his narrative of his visit at Philadelphia, then the seat of the Federal government.

James Kent to Moss Kent, Jr.

. . . The Philadelphians have not great gayety in their dress. The Quakers, who compose a large part of the city, have probably given a tincture to the manners. Their obstinacy and bigotry were very manifest on the present occasion. They kept their shops all open on the day of public humiliation appointed by the government, in consequence of the late distress. [A scourge of fever which had decimated the population of the city.] I visited the celebrated Museum of Peale ; the principal live curiosities were a baboon, monkey, a white owl, a white-head eagle, a hawk, a rattlesnake, and the cow with five legs. I was much pleased with his interesting collection of portrait paintings of the first Congress in 1774 and of several generals in our late army. I visited also Pine's Cabinet of Paintings. The colors were coarse, but some of the pictures striking, particularly the allegorical piece representing America ;

those representing Garrick and others in some of Shake-speare's plays ; Mrs. Yates in the character of Medea and Jason, Macbeth, etc.

I visited the President at one of his public levees. They are every Tuesday from three to four o'clock P. M. You enter, make a bow ; the President and company all stand with their hats in their hands, and after exchanging a few words retire *sans cérémonie*. I saw Mr. Adams, the British Minister Mr. Hammond, and several members of Congress. The President was dressed in a suit of plain cloth of a snuff color, with silk stockings, and a sword by his side. His manners were easy, but distant and reserved. His eye was expressive of mildness and reflection. His person was tall and full of dignity. No person can approach him without being penetrated with respect and reverence. Without the brilliancy of Cæsar's talents, or the daring exertions of Frederick, such has been his steadiness, discretion, good sense, and integrity that no man ever attained a greater ascendency over free minds or ever reigned so long and so completely in the hearts of a sober and intelligent people.

. . . .

This journey, though performed in the month of De-cember, was highly agreeable and comfortable. I travelled in the public stages, and found the stages and stage-houses in good accommodation. I shall ever remember with pleasure the intimate introduction that was given me to the knowledge of some of the Southern States and particu-larly of the Potowmac Country, which has a city so admira-ble in its plan and noble in its object beginning to discover the marks of industry, genius, and freedom, and to rear itself on its banks.

Upon his return from this journey Mr. Kent found a new era opening before him. He had, as already related, been elected to the recently established chair of Law in Columbia College. The salary, it is true, was not munificent, being only £200 a year; but there were perquisites attached to the position which amounted to as much more. " I conclude the appointment," he wrote to his brother, " not only honorable and profitable, but it will even aid my professional practice at the bar. You can easily judge how forcibly I am now led to professional pursuits and historical inquiries." Although he was elected to this professorship in December, 1793, it was not until November, 1794, that his duties actually began. The preparation of the introductory lecture gave zest to deeper legal researches. He read, in the original, Bynkershoeck, Quintilian, and Cicero's rhetorical works, besides English reports and digests.

In February, 1794, his father died, at the house of his son in New York, after a long and afflicting illness. " He survived," wrote Mr. Kent, " not only the use of his feet, but, in a great degree, the powers of his understanding. During the year 1794," he continues, " I removed to a more desirable situation in Liberty Street, my business increased, and in the summer of that year I devoted myself with great zeal and industry to the compilation of my law lectures."

" I read a course in 1794–95," he recorded in his Memoranda, " to about forty gentlemen of the first rank in the city. They were very well received, but I have long since discovered them to have been slight and trashy productions. I wanted judicial labors to teach me precision. I soon became considerably

involved in business, but was never fond of, nor much
distinguished in, the contentions of the Bar."

Chancellor Kent's slight estimate of the legal value
of his first efforts as a teacher and expounder of
the law does not appear to have been shared by his
friends and admirers.   Hon. John Duer, in his discourse delivered before the Bar of the city and State
of New York, in April, 1848, to which allusion has
already been made,[1] describes the introductory lecture
as "written with great vigor of style and compass of
thought," and "the views that it unfolds of the true
nature and province of the law, and of the advantages
to be derived from its study," as "judicious, discrim-
inating, and comprehensive."   The introductory law
lecture was printed for private distribution by the
trustees of Columbia College, in 1794, by Francis
Childs of New York.   This was followed, the following
year, by a pamphlet called : "Dissertations, Being the
preliminary part of a course of Law lectures by James
Kent, printed by George Forman of No. 156 Front
St., New York, for the Author in 1795."

These "dissertations" consisted of three lectures :
the first on the "Theory, History, and Duties of Civil
Government;" the second, "Of the History of the
American Union;" and the third, "Of the Law of
Nations."   This volume was published at the expense
of the author, and, as Mr. Kent noted later, never
returned him the cost of publication.   A distinguished
fate, however, awaited this maiden effort.   In Brown's
Treatise on Civil and Admiralty Law, published in
England shortly afterwards, this pamphlet is cited,

[1] *Supra*, page 29.

and it is believed that this is the first reference made to an American law publication by a transatlantic writer.

Among the papers of Chancellor Kent, found after his death, are copies of three letters in criticism of the introductory law lecture of Mr. Kent, written by John Adams, then Vice-President of the United States, to his son Charles Adams. The packet containing these interesting documents bears this indorsement, in the handwriting of the Chancellor: "Copies of three letters left with me by Charles Adams, Esq.,[1] Feb'y 25, 1795." These letters here follow: —

I

John Adams to his Son, Charles Adams.

PHILADELPHIA, February 14, 1795.

DEAR CHARLES, — As you seem to wish to know my sentiments of Mr. Kent's Lecture, I will give you a few hints to assist your own reflections and inquiries, but as they may be liable to misconstruction and misrepresentation, they must be in confidence between you and me.

I am much pleased with the Lecture and esteem the talents and Character of the Professor; indeed I wish you to consider whatever I may write upon the subject as queries proposed for your research, rather than as opinions of mine, much less as Lessons didactically inculcated by a Father upon a Son.

I can scarcely say with Mr. Kent on the first and second Page that "the attention of mankind is thoroughly engaged in speculations on the Principles of public Policy." I see a general Dissolution of Society, a general absence of Prin-

---

[1] Charles Adams, born May, 1770, died in New York, December, 1800, leaving no male descendants.

ciple, a general scramble of factions for Power, but the sincere Inquirers after Truth, the Impartial Investigators of Principles are yet to appear, and after they shall appear, miracles must be wrought for what I see, before Mankind will respect and adopt their Discoveries.

"The human mind," says Mr. Kent, "which has been so long degraded by the fetters of feudal and Papal Tyranny, has *begun to free herself from Bondage*." When we speak of the human mind, we mean commonly in Europe : and there, it is true, feudal and papal tyranny have declined. I shall say nothing of popery at present, having chiefly in view the curt part of our Subject. | Feudal Tyranny has declined, but it may still be a question whether the human mind has proportionally freed itself from Bondage. Instead of feudal Tyranny, the Tyranny of national Debts, Taxes, and funds and Stocks were substituted, and it has been sometimes a serious Question which was worse. Are the standing armies of Europe, which have created the Debts and Taxes, freer men than the Retainers and Tenants of the feudal Barons? I trow not. Are not the People now universally tributary to the holders of Stock, the public creditors, — obliged to labor as much, to pay them, as they did formerly to pay their landlords? It must be confessed that the funding Systems have been more friendly to Arts, Sciences, Agriculture, Commerce, Manufactures, and Industry than the feudal System. They have also promoted more corruption and Luxury and the Destruction of all Principle. They may have converted an ardor for honor and military glory into universal avarice. | One passion is exchanged for another, one Tyranny is substituted for another; but it is not yet quite clear that the "human Mind has ever begun to free herself from Bondage," or if it has begun it has made little Progress. |

The funding system and standing armies have grown to

such an height of Tyranny and oppression that mankind can bear them no longer, and they are shaking their shoulders to throw them off, and in the struggle are increasing the Evil, by doubling both Debts, Taxes, and Armies. Are they nearer freeing themselves from Bondage?

They have now substituted a new Species of Bondage without destroying the old one. In France they have destroyed monarchy and nobility, but have they prohibited a Tyranny of Clubs and Majorities, which for the time has been the worst Tyranny that ever existed among men? They have committed more cruelties in one night than the whole House of Bourbons ever committed from the accession of Henry IV. to the Death of Louis XVI. Instead of being " thoroughly engaged in Speculations on the Principles," instead of freeing themselves from Bondage, Mankind seem to have broken to pieces the feudal Bondage and Destroyed funding Systems only to bow their necks to mere Popularity, a Tyranny as terrible as either; it is the Tyranny of Hurricanes and Tornadoes or the raging waves of the Sea. All freedom of thought, speech, writing, and Printing shrink themselves before it, as if it were made up of Pretorian Bands or Turkish Janizaries.

There may be a few Instances of men who have examined the Theory of Government with a liberal Spirit: but I really know not who they are. But certainly they have not been attended to. Those who have taught for Doctrines the Commandments of Faction, and the impervious Dogmas of Popularity are the only ones who have attracted the public attention.

You may preserve my Letters, if you think them deserving any notice, and fifty years hence, compare them with the Times. I am, my Dear Sir,

Your affectionate Father,

JOHN ADAMS.

CHARLES ADAMS, ESQ.

II

John Adams to his son, Charles Adams.

PHILADELPHIA, February 14, 1795.

DEAR CHARLES, — Our amiable Professor in the 5th Page informs us that " the free Commonwealth of the United States, which in all its ties, relations, and dependencies, is animated with the pure spirit of popular representation, offers the highest rewards to a successful cultivation of the law and the utmost encouragement to Genius."

I scarcely have the courage, my dear son, to write even to you my candid, free, and independent thoughts upon this passage. Would to God it were true in any reasonable construction of the words. Is it animated with the pure spirit of popular representation? And what is the pure spirit of popular representation? I know of no other answer which can be given to this last question than this, viz. : a spirit in Election, of Candor, Truth, Justice, and public affection : in contradistinction and opposition to all Partiality, falsehood, party-spirit, Intrigue or other species of corruption.

Is the Commonwealth of the U. S. animated with such a pure Spirit? Recollect the first Election of President and Vice-President. There were no Bribes received or offered. But were there not Intrigues of an unwarrantable nature, wholly inconsistent with the pure spirit we have Described? Recollect the second Election of the same Officers. Collect together the newspapers in all the States, and see what a monstrous mass of lies you will have before you. Recollect the pure Spirit of Clintonian Cabal, of Virginia Artifice, of Kentucky delusion, and then say whether all this is pure Spirit.

Examine and see whether you find this pure Spirit in the Election of Senators of U. S. — I shall not descend into minute details : But in general, my son, enquire whether the Elections of Senators are not too often determined by Party Spirit and even by factions meeting in the Legislatures of the States, and whether there is not danger that such an evil will increase.

But I have a more serious question still to ask: whether the pure Spirit of popular representation when Elections are so frequent, of the executives, as well as of the Senate, is consistent with Liberty. The purest Spirit of popular Representation will forever elect Representatives of the majority in number. Education, property, honor, will not be proportionately represented, consequently Education, Property, and Honor will not be secure. Moreover, if the pure Spirit of Popularity is to give the Tone to everything, why see the President and Vice-President chosen by Electors instead of the People? Why are Senators chosen by another description of Electors and not by the People? The Answer is obvious, the pure Spirit of Popularity is not always and in all things to be trusted.

We are told further that "the free Commonwealth of the U. S. offers the highest rewards to a successful cultivation of the Law, and the utmost encouragement to Genius." Whether this is true or not and in what degree it is true, or otherwise, deserves your serious consideration. The purest Spirit of Popularity that we have in this Country is adulterated if not poisoned with ancient mawkish prejudices against the Profession and Professors of Law, which it is difficult to overcome. It deserves your consideration whether the highest Rewards are given to the cultivation of the law or not. Whether they are not given too often to a successful cultivation of popular Prejudices; to an assiduous fomentation of contracted notions; to a Party Spirit, and to vulgar Sophistry. To an abuse of words? Read Mr. Locke's chapter on the abuse of words, and see if the Frauds and knaveries there described do not too often decide the Spirit of popular representation and bestow the highest rewards. I am afraid the encouragement to Genius will as little bear examination. Genius with Integrity appears to be very little encouraged and Genius without Integrity had better not be encouraged at all. Genius is too much encouraged to affect Popularity; to flatter the people; to excite prejudices, to associate with Clubs, but not enough to study and pursue the public good in the plain Path of virtue, Honor, and Knowledge.

Tell me, Charles, is this croaking? At all Events you must keep it to yourself, and not expose yourself or your

Affte Father,

JOHN ADAMS.

CHARLES ADAMS, ESQ.

III

John Adams to his son, Charles Adams.

PHILADELPHIA, February 15, 1795.

DEAR CHARLES, — Be not surprised if, in considering the Lecture, I lay hold of particular Expressions which appear to me exceptionable, though they may be in paragraphs I love and admire. " Our political Fabrics and Systems of Jurisprudence have been reared with great Pains and perfected with much wisdom." (Page 6.)

Our systems of Jurisprudence, relative to the administration of civil and criminal Justice, are derived from our ancestors, and have indeed been perfected with much wisdom. Our political fabrics, too, have been reared with great pains, but I cannot yet say they have been perfected at all; much remains to be done, and I much fear that Mr. Kent and you will have a hard labor to perfect them in the whole course of your lives, be they even as long as I wish them.

Pages 8 and 9 : " Many of the fundamental Doctrines of their (British) Government and axioms of their Jurisprudence are utterly subversive of Equality of rights." Our learned Lecturer has not descended to particulars, nor quoted Instances ; we are, therefore, left to conjecture. I own I know of no such Doctrines or axioms, and I am sorry to see our Professor indulging and inculcating prejudices against a constitutional code of laws which have reconciled right to power, and liberty to wealth and numbers more effectively and for a longer period of time than ever was before effected upon this globe. If I were to conjecture the sense of Mr. Kent, I should suppose that he alluded to the rights of Primogeniture in the descent of real estates, and especially in the Descent of Titles of Nobility, Seats in the Senate, and above all of the Crown.

Now I contend that the laws from our own Country, and every other Country where the hereditary Descent of real Estates is established, is as utterly subversive of Equality as the Descent of the whole of real estate to the first born, or of a Lordship in Parliament, or of the Crown itself. All laws which establish Property are inconsistent with Equality in one sense. The very idea of Property is inconsistent with equality. Property is an exclusive privilege. Rousseau acknowledges this when he says in his " Origin of Inequalities among Mankind " that the first man who marked out a cabbage yard and said, " It is mine," ought to have been put to Death. The descent of real Estate is not by the law of Nature, but by municipal law alone ; a real Estate is a public Trust as much as any public office, and many real Estates are public Trusts often times of more Importance to the People than many public offices are. If the interests or Policy of the Nation finds it necessary that an heir apparent should be educated and prepared for the management of an Estate, or the exercise of the Trust, it has a right, and it is its duty, to do it. If the nation finds it necessary to keep lands together in such quantities as may support a family, instead of having them split into shreds only to corrupt the younger children and do mischief in the neighborhood, it has a right to do it. And although this may not be thought consistent with the equality and Independence of Nature, it is consistent with an equality of civil and Political rights as much as any establishment of Property whatever.

It is the establishment of Property and of marriage which introduce the great Inequalities in fact, but no Inequalities of right. The ancient Legislator Plato particularly, and every other great man who has reflected deeply on the subject, has been aware of this, and has accordingly insisted on a Community of Goods and of wives. Of goods that there might be no Property, and of wives that there might be no families. All the wild ravings of Rousseau, imparted to the world by his enchanting Eloquence, and all the grave whinings of De Mably, in his deliberative and didactic Style, amount to the same thing. Property! Property is their great enemy; both of them saw that if you admit Property their whole Systems are Demolished. I may one day find leisure to write you some strictures on Rousseau and De Mably, especially his principles of Legislation, where you will plainly perceive that their theories are altogether chimerical, without a community of goods and wives and children, or no goods at all. The imperious and supercilious frown of Popularity in these arbitrary times forbids me to communicate anything to the public, and this I do not regret. But I will not be intimidated from communicating to my children the objections and reflections of a long life of much public experience, as well as some private reading, which I know to be founded on Truth, and essential to their Happiness and Safety.

The Judges, Charles, have estates for Life in their offices in this Country. The Judges, then, are a privileged order; would Mr. Kent annihilate this privileged order? Will Mr. Kent say that this privileged order is utterly subversive of an equality of rights? A Senate is essential to a republic, — a senate solid, permanent, and independent enough to defend the Constitution and the rights of men both against Power and Popularity. Our Senators have Estates in their offices for six years. Is this subversive of an equality of rights? Suppose the time should come when increasing Intrigues and corruption in elections should make it necessary to introduce in a regular, legal, and constitutional way, a prolongation of those Estates to twelve years, would that be subversive of equality of rights? Suppose, again, 20, 30, 40, or 50 years more of increasing venality, Bribery, Intrigues, and corruption, as well as additional wealth and numbers should make it necessary for the people to give the Senators Estates for Life in their offices, as the judges now have, would that amendment to the constitution be utterly subversive of equality of rights?

One supposition more : suppose Elections of Senators should become, by the acknowledgment of all the world, a source of evil, and no good in any case, and better men would come by Inheritance than by choice, and consequently a seat in Senate should be made up by the people themselves an Estate of Inheritance, would this be a total subversion of Equality of rights? So far otherwise that it would be the only chance for preserving equal laws and equal rights to all or any of the people.

The Judges are made independent that they may be upright, — under no temptation to be partial arising from a Desire of keeping, or a fear of losing, their Places or appointment. Is it not as necessary that the Senators should be upright, impartial, above fear, favor, affection, or hope of reward, or fear of punishment? Are not the lives, liberties, characters, Property of Individuals, parties, and indeed the whole People, as much in the Power of a Senator as a Judge? Is it not, then, as necessary that he should be independent?

This reasoning has prevailed in England to establish an hereditary House of Lords, and it may prevail in America to establish a Senate for more years, for Life, or for an hereditary Perpetuity, and in neither case be subversive of any equality of rights at all.   No republic ever existed without a Senate, and in rich, powerful, populous, commercial Nations, the Senate must not be blown about with every wind of popular Breath or Doctrine.   Tell me what you think of these things.

Your affete Father,

JOHN ADAMS.

CHARLES ADAMS, ESQ.

The series of lectures thus auspiciously begun was continued throughout the winter of 1794–95, closing about March 1.   They were well received, served to quicken an interest in jurisprudence, especially among members of the Bar, and served also, no doubt, to increase Mr. Kent's private practice.   His pecuniary affairs prospered and the period of depression for him had finally passed.   As early as 1794 his circumstances had already begun to improve.   In June of that year he wrote to his brother: —

. . . Your happiness and success are my highest wishes and anxiety.   Our interests are inseparably conjoined and our profits shall be also.   If either succeeds in pecuniary matters and the other does not, he will still be provided for.   I sold my Poughkeepsie lot in April for 400 Pounds. This discharged my 200 Pounds I owed still on it, and the residue I had for use.   I owe nobody now, and I have 200 Pounds loaned on interest.   So you see I have some resource yet, and my resources are yours also.

A few months later we find him a real estate owner of the city of New York.

James Kent to Moss Kent.

February 4th, 1795.

Since I wrote to you last I have purchased a very genteel house in King Street,[1] for £1475, and shall move into it in May. The payments are easy, but as I have sold my right in a township in Ontario for £1000 clear profit payable in one year I expect to be able to pay for the house much sooner than I engaged.

In the early spring of 1795 Mr. Kent completed his first course of law lectures. His plan of the course, as designed and as finally executed, is set forth in an epistle to his brother, Moss Kent: —

James Kent to Moss Kent.

March 1, 1795.

On Friday last I closed my lectures at college and I feel now restored to my ancient freedom. Twenty-six lectures have been delivered, extending not only through the Constitution and Jurisprudence of the Union, the Constitution of this and the other States, but our doctrine of real property. My first plan was to examine law of personal property, including the commercial branches, and the system of our criminal code. But I found myself absolutely unable to complete the whole, and was obliged to leave this first course imperfect. It will be an easy thing to make these additions, and review and improve the whole by next November. I am satisfied that my lectures have been well received, and that my expectations are answered. When I recollect what I have done in point of labor and researches for a year past, I am astonished at the extent of the effort, and I should not have had courage to undertake

1 Now Pine Street.

it had I fully anticipated the pains which have been bestowed.

My time now is once more my own. I have accordingly begun Cicero's works in the morning and also Homer and the French authors. My friend S. Baldwin, Esq., of New Haven, sent me this last fall a complete set of Cicero's works. It is in ten volumes, and I expect a rich store of pleasure in perusing them.[1] In May I move into our new house in Pine Street, and your sister and I are flattering ourselves with much happiness and neatness under our new roof. I am very considerably engaged in new land speculations. This, however, is a circumstance to be kept private. You know of the success of my former ones, by means of which I was enabled to clear as much as the value of my house and lot. I expect great profit from what I am now concerned in. If I am lucky I shall be able in two or three years to retire into the country. If they do not turn out well I think I cannot lose by them, for I can at all events pay the consideration moneys by my own resources. To look back about sixteen months, when you brought our good old father down here, and when you and I were in the depths of despondency and very poor, and to contrast that state with my present independent and flattering condition, excites emotions of wonder and amazement. You are now also in independence, and God grant we may both take care to remain so. It is a great consolation to converse in this way of our mutual prosperity. . . .

In the succeeding winter a second course of lectures was begun, but, for some reason unexplained, they met with little encouragement, and after a further trial the following winter, they were abandoned, although he retained the nominal professor-

[1] *Supra*, page 17.

ship until the year 1798. Early in the year 1796 he
wrote thus to his brother: —

James Kent to Moss Kent.

January 4, 1796.

The small encouragement with which my lectures have
been received by the public this year has cooled and dulled
my ardor for finishing and perfecting them. I have never
had but two scholars and of course read the lectures in my
office, and feel little ambition about them. I hope soon to
enter on my old classical career, and then I shall be happy
again. Nothing is so miserable as irresolution and want of
vigorous and animated application. All my wishes are to
realize property enough to retire into the country, and live
in retirement near you. There is a probability that I shall
be able ere long to do it, *sed multum abludit imago.*[1]

A passage in this, and another in the last preceding
letter as well as in subsequent epistles, betray a phase
in Mr. Kent's character, — his longing for the time
when he, too, might retire to some Sabine farm, there
to enjoy *otium cum dignitate;* a longing strangely inconsistent with the active energy of his life. Still he
clung to this fond illusion, never to be accomplished,
until his life's work was ended. For him there could
be no rest, no lingering by the wayside, no rural retreat, until the door of the temple of fame should
have opened to receive the tribute of his life.

Upon the fly-leaf of Mr. Kent's own copy of his
first law lectures, as published, is found this note: —

This work was published in December, 1794, at the request of the trustees. I was appointed Professor of Law

[1] Cf. Horace, Sat. ii. 3, 320.

in Columbia College, Dec. 24, 1793. On the 17th of November, 1794, I commenced the reading of a course of Lectures in the College Hall and delivered the introductory lecture. I read that season twenty-six lectures (two a week) and was honored by the attendance throughout the course of seven students and thirty-six gentlemen, chiefly lawyers and law students who did not belong to the college. During my second course, commencing November, 1795, I read thirty-one lectures, in my office, and had only two students besides my clerks. The next season I attempted another course, but no students offering to attend, I dismissed the business, and, in May, 1797, sent a letter of resignation to the trustees. This was not accepted, and in the winter of 1797 and 1798, in my office, I read lectures to six or eight students, and in April, 1798, I finally resigned the office. I published the ensuing dissertations in December, 1795, and they form the first three of the thirty-one lectures I have composed.

In May, 1797, as above noted by himself, Mr. Kent tendered his resignation of his professorship of Law in Columbia College. His letter of resignation was in these words: —

COLUMBIA COLLEGE, May 2, 1797.

GENTLEMEN, — I take the liberty of communicating to you my wish to resign the appointment of Professor of Law in Columbia College, which I have had the honor to hold from you for upwards of three years past; and it is with sincere regret I mention that the institution has not been attended with all the success which you had intended and which I have endeavored to produce. My first course consisted of twenty-six lectures, commenced in November, 1794, and received a very flattering encouragement and steady attention of forty students and several other gentlemen of the city, equally distinguished for their literary accomplishments, and their zeal for the knowledge and improvement of our municipal law. The second course, in a more correct state, and with several additional lectures, commanded only two students. I then supposed that a more general acquaintance with the plan I had delineated, and the manner in which it was executed, might possibly conduce to the benefit of the establishment, and accordingly published, in the early part of that course, the three preliminary lectures, together with a summary of the entire course, which I had prepared, and which formed the completion of my original plan. In this expectation I was disappointed. The commencement of a third annual course, in November, was duly announced in the public print, but no student appeared to countenance the attempt, and the trial was abandoned.

Having thus acquitted myself to the best of my ability, in the discharge of a duty which I accepted with diffidence, my resignation becomes proper and necessary. I cannot, however, take my leave of the college without returning to you, gentlemen, my grateful and respectful acknowledgments (and which I shall always owe) for the very honorable confidence you have placed in me ; and be pleased to accept my cordial wishes that the general principles of our constitution and laws may still be academically taught, and that the institution which you have so liberally established may hereafter, under abler professors, and in more auspicious times, be crowned with happier success.

I have the honor to be, gentlemen, with perfect respect,
Your humble servant,

JAMES KENT.

The Trustees of Columbia College.

Mr. Kent's copy of this letter was found inserted in the volume of his lectures, in connection with the note above quoted.   Appended to the letter are these memoranda : —

At the annual commencement in Columbia College, May 3, 1797 [being the day after the above letter was written], I was honored by the Trustees by the Degree of Doctor of Laws.

Wednesday evening, April 18, 1838. — I attended, in the Chapel of the University of New York, and heard my son William Kent deliver his introductory law lecture, as one of the professors of law in that University, being forty-three years and five months since I delivered the annexed lecture. I was thirty-one years and four months, and my son thirty-five years six months old, when we delivered our respective introductory lectures.

"The summer of 1795 was oppressively hot," writes Chancellor Kent, in his " Memoranda," " and I took at that time a most settled disgust to a summer residence in town.   The yellow fever made its appearance the latter part of the season, and soon after a pleasant little ride that I had with my friend Boyd to River Head on Long Island, I was compelled by the alarm of disease to flee with my family on the 17th of September to Poughkeepsie, and there I spent six weeks in Mr. Bailey's library, devoting myself with pleasure and ardor to polite reading.   Business, politics, and law studies had for so long a time occupied my attention that I entered with uncommon zest upon the perusal of history, voyages, and travels, and I shall long remember the force of my returning passion for *belles-lettres* pursuits.

"In February, 1796, I was appointed a Master in

Chancery. This office promised me a more steady supply of pecuniary aid (of which I stood in need), and it enabled me in a degree to relinquish the practice of an attorney, which I always extremely hated. | My diffidence, or perhaps pride, was a principal cause of this disgust, since I found that I had not the requisite talents for a popular and shining advocate at the Bar.|

"In 1796 I began my career of official life. It came upon me entirely unsolicited and unexpected. In February, 1796, Governor Jay wrote me a letter, stating that the office of Master in Chancery was vacant, and wished to know, confidentially, whether I would accept. I wrote a very respectful, but very laconic, answer. It was that 'I was content to accept of the office if appointed.' The same day I received the appointment, and was astonished to learn that there were sixteen professed applicants, all disappointed. This office gave me nearly the monopoly of the business of that office, for there was but one other master in New York. The office kept me very busy in petty details, and outdoor concerns, but was profitable."

To his brother Mr. Kent wrote, on the twenty-second of June, 1796: —

. . . . I have made large additions to my books since you were here, but the new office of Master in Chancery, which I hold, is exceedingly perplexing, by its avocations, and almost entirely cuts me off from my old classical companions, such as Cicero, Homer, and Voltaire. It will be impossible ever to read and reflect much while I am confined to business in town, and equally impossible to partake of much contentment in summer seasons in a noisy, hateful city. It is Hope, which, on the opening of Pandora's Box, so kindly lingered for our consolation, that keeps up my cheerfulness and spirits, — the hope, I mean, of quitting this city, at some future day, and living nearer you in the country, surrounded by quiet, books, fields, gardens, and my lovely wife and daughter.

This last allusion discloses the fact that the terrible loss of three years before, which had overwhelmed Mr. Kent and his wife with grief, had now, in some measure, been repaired. On the 23d of March, 1796, he wrote to his brother : —

DEAR BROTHER, — My little babe is now five weeks old, and a most sweet, divine little thing. She is very fair and flourishing, and I feel as if my former loss was almost wholly made up. I hope to see you in April and in November also. I am doing a little business and getting along as well as I can. I hope in a year or two to wind up worth something, and retreat into the country.

Three months later he again wrote to the same correspondent : —

I am now alone here at home. I expect my wife, however, next Saturday, and my little babe, which you may be assured is extremely engaging and lovely. It is the universal assent of my acquaintance that my little child equals any of its age in sprightliness, health, and beauty.

This child was his daughter Elizabeth, bearing her mother's name. Later in life she was known as Eliza, and married Mr. Isaac S. Hone of Philadelphia.

IV

PUBLIC honors, with James Kent, now began to
multiply. Within less than a year after his
appointment as Master in Chancery he was elected a
member of the Assembly from the city of New York,
and very soon thereafter he received from Governor
Jay, without his own solicitation, or previous knowledge, an appointment to the office of Recorder, a
minor judicial office of the city of New York, at that
time confined, in its scope, to civil causes.   He himself thus recorded this experience : —

" I had commenced in 1786 to be a zealous Federalist.   I read everything in politics.   I got the Federalist almost by heart, and became intimate with
Hamilton.   I entered with ardor into the Federal politics against France in 1793, and my hostility to the
French democracy and to French power beat with
strong pulsation down to the Battle of Waterloo.

" In the spring of 1796 I was elected a member
of Assembly of New York, and by this time, or in
the space of three years, I had attained to standing,
influence, and competent support in the city of New
York.   The office of Master in Chancery was attended
to in all its little outdoor duties with unceasing and
punctual attention, and I found it alone nearly adequate to my support.   After spending the months of

January and February, 1797, at Albany, with the
Legislature, I no sooner returned home than I was,
very unexpectedly for myself, appointed Recorder of
the City of New York. This was done at Albany, and
without my knowledge that the office was vacant or
was expected to be. The first I heard of it was the
appointment announced in the papers. This was
very gratifying to me, because it was a judicial office,
and I thought that it would relieve me from the
drudgery of practice, and give me way of displaying what I knew, and of being useful, and to my taste.
I pursued my studies with increased appetite, and
enlarged my law library very much. But I was overwhelmed with office business, for the Governor allowed
me to retain the other office also, and with these joint
duties, and counsel business in the Supreme Court, I
made a great deal of money that year. I was able
to renounce all my professional business except a
little occasional employment as counsel in the Supreme Court. I devoted that year most zealously and
promptly to the duties of my respective offices,
and I found myself at this era advanced to an easy
and independent support, to public estimation, and to
complete and joyful emancipation from all pecuniary
engagements."

Upon his commission as Recorder of the City of
New York, which was signed by John Jay, Governor,
Chancellor Kent made this endorsement: —

At the time of taking the above oath I was admitted a
freeman of the City, and took the oath accordingly, and was
also at the same time appointed Attorney and Counsel to
the Corporation.

This institution of freeman was a direct derivation from the old English form of government, and refers to the rights of certain classes only to vote for candidates for municipal positions. To entitle a man to these privileges of citizenship, that of voting or being voted for, he was obliged to be a "freeman" or a "freeholder" in the strict English sense. The "freeholder" in New York was one who was the owner of an interest in land, of the value of forty shillings annually. The census of 1795 shows New York to have had a population of 30,000, while it had only 1209 freeholders, holding real property of the value of £100 and upwards, 1221 of £20, and 2661 of forty shillings. The "freemen" were not so numerous as the "freeholders," and also did not consist of such a select body, since they were, for the most part, recruited from the upper artisan class, with few merchants and professional men. The fee for admission varied from five pounds to twenty shillings, not including a number of smaller fees payable to the mayor, clerk, bell-ringer, and other city officials, who at that date were dependent upon their fees and perquisites for their salaries.

If one might judge wholly from his correspondence, the conclusion would be reached that, although Mr. Kent consented for a third time to occupy a seat in the State legislature, an active participation in political life had now for him few charms. "I was a candidate for the Assembly in this city," he wrote to his brother, in May, 1796, "very much against my inclination. I am probably elected, and it will be for the last time; for to attain to a plain but independent and active literary life will be the consummation of my wishes. . . . My office in Chancery keeps me very much occupied, and I believe is alone equal to my support. In every respect I have no reason to be dissatisfied with my situation and prospects." Again, to Theodorus Bailey he writes : —

I set off to-morrow for Albany, and I dread the unpleasantness of the campaign, and regret the sacrifice of business I make. It is a scrape in which I shall not find myself very soon again, and if you are not re-elected, as your Dutchess opponents assert, I think there is not much reason for regret.

The matters of prime importance before the Assembly which convened this year were the election of a United States Senator to succeed Burr, and the choice of electors for President and Vice-President of the United States. Even these important matters appear not to have engrossed his attention to a considerable extent. An election of President of the United States was impending, but even to this his correspondence shows but slight reference. " We are greatly apprehensive," he wrote to his brother on the 13th of November, 1796, " that Jefferson will be President." The political antagonism of his brother-in-law, Theodorus Bailey, does not appear to have shaken the personal friendship of the two, for a month later he wrote again to Mr. Bailey, then a member of Congress : " Our anxiety for news of the result of the election for President has been on tiptoe for several days, but if the accounts of yesterday from Virginia are true I take it for granted Mr. Adams will be President. It is a fact, too, highly honorable to the

Virginian character that amidst all their party zeal they have so completely abandoned Burr."

President Washington, in his eighth and last annual message to Congress, December 7, 1796, recommended to the United States " to look to the means and set about the gradual creation of a navy." He also proposed " to the consideration of Congress the expediency of establishing a national university and also a military academy."   " The desirableness of both these institutions," he said, " has so constantly increased with every new view I have taken of the subject that I cannot omit the opportunity of once for all recalling your attention to them."

President Washington in this message also considered our relations with the French Republic in these words : —

" Our trade has suffered and is suffering extensive injuries in the West Indies from the cruisers and agents of the French Republic, and communications have been received from its minister here which indicate the danger of a further disturbance of our commerce by its authority, and which are in other respects far from agreeable. . . . I cannot forget what is due to the character of our government and nation, or to a full and entire confidence in the good sense, patriotism, self-respect, and fortitude of my countrymen." [1]

On receipt of a copy of this important State paper, sent him by his brother-in-law, Mr. Bailey, Mr. Kent writes : —

[1] Vide Richardson's " Compilation of the Messages and Papers of the Presidents," i. 201, 202, 203.

James Kent to Theodorus Bailey.

December 17, 1796.

I received yours inclosing the President's speech. All his writings discover much experimental knowledge, great reflection, and anxious solicitude and love for his country. I have, however, my doubts on the policy of naval armaments and military academies. They are apt to lead by gradual steps to heavy expenses, and to encourage a propensity to war. But I highly approve of the remarks concerning the attitude of the French Government in relation to us. Their treatment of the United States through the medium of their ministers has, from the beginning of the war, according to my impression of things, been extremely insolent and unjust.

The election of John Adams to the Presidency of the United States, in defeat of Jefferson, was, as has been seen, exceedingly gratifying to Mr. Kent. Both were ardent Federalists, and Mr. Adams's opinions, as indicated by Mr. Kent's careful preservation of the copies given him of the letters of the Vice-President to his son Charles,[1] were held by him in great respect. Mr. Kent was not, however, so ardent an admirer of any man that he deemed him to be beyond criticism. In July, 1791, he had written to his brother: —

"I enclose to you a couple of our Poughkeepsie papers, by which you will see that I have employed some of my leisure moments in other vocations than the classics. I thought, and think still, that Mr. Adams is propagating a passion for monarchy. I think he is vulnerable and deserves reprehension."

[1] *Supra*, pp. 64–73.

The publication to which Mr. Kent refers appeared in the issue of the " Poughkeepsie Journal " for May 21, 1791, and will be read with interest, in connection with Mr. Adams's critiques, already presented, of Mr. Kent's law lectures, delivered four years later. The publication, it will be seen, is in form of a letter addressed to a young student of political science.

DEAR SIR, — I have just now received yours of the 10th inst., and I thank you for the remarks on the work you have lately read. It appears to answer in your mind the recommendations I gave it in a former letter. Nothing gives me more pleasure at my time of life than to be imparting the little fruits of my knowledge and experience to the generation which is coming after me. Tho' I have but a few moments' leisure, I shall endeavor, tho' imperfectly, to comply with your request and give you my thoughts on the writings of Mr. Adams, the Vice-President, on which you tell me you are about to enter. As you are on a course of political studies, which I hope hereafter will render you a wise, a useful, and above all an honored patriot, I would have you always bear in mind that you cannot imbibe too deep an acquaintance with nor cultivate too high an attachment to the general or local Constitutions of the United States.

The Federalist, tho' written in haste and on the spur of the occasion, is, as I have observed to you before, one of the best publications on the former. It is full of correct method, sound sense, and luminous principles of liberty, from beginning to end, and I have no doubt that the commentary will be coeval in point of time with the text.

But the writings of Mr. Adams must be read with some grain of allowance. There is a great deal of learning and a great deal of wise principle of government brought into view, but he appears to me to be attached to aristocratical and monarchical principles. My belief is founded on an attentive examination of his writings. This great master of politics is frequently and pretty directly inculcating a scepticism as to the goodness of Republican government, and a belief of the utility of hereditary monarchy, in terms which cannot but excite in the best of those who are attached to the one, and who despise the other, a painful regret and a lively indignation.

I wish to make a firm stand against such pernicious tenets. They are as directly in the face of our institutions and manners as they are repugnant to our feelings and happiness. Besides, it is against moral fitness, no less than political duty, to be constantly instilling distrust and diffidence as to the Constitution of our country. An unshaken confidence, a reverential attachment to our established system, ought rather to be the lesson of the schools.

In vol. i., letter 20, of his defence of the American Constitution he observes: " The Americans have not made their first magistrates hereditary, nor their Senators; here they differ from the English constitution and with great propriety. Land is so equally divided among the people that they would not endure a hereditary king and nobility; or at least, if created, they would be entirely subservient to the Commons, in whom nineteen twentieths of the property would reside. In future ages if the States become great nations, rich, powerful, and luxurious, their own feelings and good sense will dictate to them what to do. They may make transition by a fresh convention, without the smallest interruption of liberty. But they will never become necessary until great quantities of property get into few hands."

Here Mr. Adams speaks of hereditary monarchy and aristocracy as not advisable in this country, as yet; we are not quite ripe for them, because of our too great equality of property. Hereafter the natural progress of things will render them necessary, and they may exist without the smallest interruption of liberty. If this change should be thought proper, Mr. Adams informs us we have an aristocracy already formed for our purpose by the kind hand of nature. In letter 25 of same volume he observes : —

" There are sources of inequality in every society, and in Massachusetts as well as in others : 1. Inequality of wealth; 2. Of birth; 3. Of merit ; and 4. All these advantages of birth, fortune and fame united. These sources of inequality can never be altered by any people, because they are founded on the constitution of nature. This natural aristocracy among mankind is a body of men which contains the greatest collection of virtues and ability in a free government."

Fame and fortune may be and frequently are hereditary, but this is the first time I ever heard a grave philosopher pronounce virtue and ability to be so.

In the 3d volume of his defence, and which contains a very ingenious and useful criticism on Mr. Needham's "Theory of a Commonwealth," he observes (Letter 6) that: "We have adopted in America one idea of Needham's, in making a succession in our Senate and Governors.   It is still, however, problematical whether the succession will be the grand preservative against corruption, or the grand inlet to it.   There is room to hope and grounds to fear.   The experiment is made, and it will have fair play.   If corruption breaks in a remedy must be provided, and what that remedy must be is well known to every man who thinks. . . . In what manner annual elections of Governors and Senators will operate in America remains to be ascertained.   It should always be remembered that this is not the first experiment that was ever made in the world, of the election of great officers of State.   How they have hitherto operated in every great nation, and what has been the end, is very well known.   Mankind has universally discovered that chance is preferable to a corrupt choice, and has trusted Providence rather than itself.   Thank Heaven! Americans understand calling conventions, and if time should come, as it very probably may, when hereditary descent shall become a less evil than fraud and violence, such a convention may still prevent the first magistrate from becoming absolute as well as hereditary.   This hazardous experiment we have tried, and if elections are soberly made, it may answer well; if not, the people must again have recourse to convention and find a remedy."

The prevailing bent of Mr. Adams in favor of hereditary government seems to have acquired new force as he proceeded in his writings. In first volume he speaks of it as a thing desirable only at some future period and not suited to our present condition. Here he declares himself much more emphatically in its favor, considers elective governments as of hazardous experiment and of doubtful issue, and, in a strain of exultation and devotion, thanks Heaven that America can assume with ease an hereditary monarchy. Mr. Adams has lately obliged the public with a number of periodical pieces, entitled "Discourses on Davila," and which, like all his other writings, discover extensive learning and superior capacity, and are calculated, like his former volumes, to point out the necessity of a balanced government. These discourses, however, are constantly interrupted with the remarks on the natural love for family and distinctions and property and rank, and that aristocracy and monarchy have their foundation in the original constitution of our nature.

In No. 12 he observes: " But it shall be left to the contemplation of our state physicians to discover the causes and the remedy of that fever whereof our power is sick. One question shall be respectfully insinuated: whether equal laws, the result only of balanced government, can ever be obtained, without some sign or other of distinction and degree." In No. 15, after many arguments on the unextinguishable passion for title and distinction, he breaks out into the following apostrophe: " Americans, rejoice that from experience you have learned wisdom, and instead of a whimsical and fantastic project, you have adopted a promising essay towards a well ordered government."

Mr. Adams has now begun a discourse on Stephen Boetius,[1] which will probably be the same thing as a second edition of his commentary on Needham. It would be easy for me to proceed with quotations of similar import, but I trust I have sufficiently proved the truth of my assertion and the justness of my belief in the beginning of this letter, that Mr. Adams was attached to monarchical, aristocratical principles. In saying this I do not desire, if I had the power, to derogate from the general reputation of his work. I only wish that the false doctrines they contain may be separated from the salutary counsels with which they are attended.

His writings have profoundly developed and placed in all its variety of attitude to the world one excellent truth, long before known, recognized, and adopted by his countrymen in their political systems, and that is, the necessity of a division of the legislative, executive, and judicial powers, and the partition of the former into three independent parts, in order to control the spirit of rivalship inherent in the minds of men. But his writings have also inculcated, cherished, and propagated one abominable heresy, and that is, that hereditary monarchy and aristocracy are compatible with permanent freedom, and probably effectual to a wise, happy, and perfectly balanced constitution.

[1] Stephen Boetius lived in the reign of Charles IX. of France, and was one of the King's counsellors in the Court of the Parliament of Bordeaux, and the friend and contemporary of Montaigne. He died young, at the age of thirty-two years, leaving behind him a most excellent reputation.

It is well worth observing that Mr. Adams has undergone, since his residence in Europe, a very great change in his political principles. He wrote a letter to Mr. Wythe, of Virginia, and which has been recently published. In that letter he says that there is no good government but what is republican; that the only valuable part of the British Constitution is so; that the legislature should be divided into two branches, and that the executive should have a negative in both; but that the executive, as well as both branches of the legislature, ought to be annually elective, there not being, in the whole circle of science, a maxim more infallible than this : Where annual elections end, there tyranny begins. "These great men in this respect," says Mr. Adams, "should be elected once a year.

> ' As bubbles on the sea of matter form,
>   They rise, they break, and to that sea return.'

This will teach them the great political virtues of humility, patience, and moderation, without which every man in power becomes a ravenous beast of prey."

Mr. Adams ought to show us whether human nature has altered since the year 1776, and what there is at this day, more than there was at that day, to prevent a man who holds his seat by hereditary right, or (as Mr. Burke says the king holds his crown) "in contempt of the people and who is not responsible for his conduct," from becoming a ravenous beast of prey. Whereas, the great leading maxim in all his writing is that mankind is just as imperfect as formerly, in America as in Europe, in this century as in ten centuries ago.

But it is the fate of Mr. Adams, in many places, to
be as inconsistent with himself as some of his doctrines are inconsistent with the genius of his country.
The English government is the perfect model to which
his observations are directed. "It is [says he] the
most stupendous fabric of modern invention, both for
the adjustment of the balance and the prevention of
its vibrations." But the furious wars of the two Roses,
the constant tyranny of the Tudors, the constant tyranny and convulsions under the Stuarts, the two
rebellions against the house of Hanover, are rather
bad precedents in favor of hereditary succession. At
present there is not, indeed, the avowed oppression of
former times. But the constitutional tyranny (if I
may so express myself) of the hereditary part has
changed its color, not its nature. It has laid aside its
fierce visage and assumed the livery of Venus and
the Graces. Henry VIII. was a despot, with the iron
rod of prerogative. George III. is a despot also, with
the courtly sceptre of corruption. I sincerely believe
the English administration to be as much under the
influence of corruption as that of any government in
Europe. The House of Commons, chosen once in
seven years, is a mere mockery of representation.
The English nation would have, if justice were done
them, their Commons fairly chosen by upwards of
400,000 electors, and yet a ninth part of the English
representatives are chosen by 364 votes and a majority of the representation by 5,723 electors, most of
whom have no property. The House of Commons,
thus wretchedly constituted, has not been able (as we
might well suppose) to preserve its equipoise in the

system, and has submitted itself implicitly to the corrupt influence of the hereditary despotism.

Nothing but the independence of their judiciary and pride and honor of their judges preserves the remnants of their liberty. The Roman civilians and judges in like manner preserved their integrity and good sense long after Tiberius, Nero, and Domitian had infused their government with the most accursed of all tyrannies. Mr. Hume, some years ago, predicted (and he predicted right) that the tide of power in England was running to the monarchical side and that absolute monarchy was the true euthanasia of the British Constitution. This government, however, is held up to us as a model of wisdom and imitation. Mr. Adams has devoted the labor of years to point out the evils to which free governments are incident, and to warn mankind against them. I thank him for his learned labors. But I wish he would also warn us against the dangers of the opposite course, to which he is steering our political vessel; together with his commentaries on Machiavel, Needham, and Stephen Boetius, would also give us his commentaries on the reign of Tiberius, as delineated by the masterly hand of Tacitus. His writings have certainly the tendency (whatever may be his intention) to make people weary of republican government, and to sigh for the monarchy of England.

To inculcate the doctrine that men are not fit to choose their own rulers; that frequent elections are dangerous; that distinctions, not of virtue and talents, but of birth and fortune, are essential to the order of government; that riches and family should be the

titles to preferment, and poverty the object of contempt, — such doctrines I deem heresy in American
politics.

As already narrated, Mr. Kent, in March, 1797, received from Governor Jay an appointment as Recorder
of the City of New York. It was the first judicial
office which he had occupied, and was much in ac-
cordance with his tastes and habits of thought. It
was his first impression, on learning of his appointment, that this office and that of Master in Chancery
would be incompatible, and that he would be obliged
either to decline the one or to resign the other. In
May, 1797, he wrote to his brother : —

James Kent to Moss Kent.

May 18, 1797.

DEAR BROTHER, — I have, as you suggest, as much as I
can do with my several offices at present. But I am no
monopolizer in principle, and I never shall indulge any intemperate avidity for wealth. Before I knew I was Recorder, the Council had adjourned, and I suppose will not
meet again till next January. I cannot resign till they meet,
and then I intend to resign either the office of Recorder, or
Master in Chancery. I take it for granted I shall retain the
office of Recorder, tho' upon the whole less lucrative than
the other, but it amply makes up that deficiency in respecta-
bility. The office of Onondaga Commissioner I resigned as
soon as the Governor returned from Albany. It required
too long an absence from home to be agreeable, or profitable, or consistent with requisite attention to other duties.

He soon discovered, however, that it was the intent
of Governor Jay that he should fill both offices, and

that such an arrangement would be entirely feasible soon became apparent.

Soon after the death of Chancellor Kent, in 1847, his son, Judge William Kent, received from the hand of Hon. Robert Morris extended memorabilia, covering many of his life experiences. Much of this matter, although of interest, and of great historical value, has no relevancy to the present narrative. A paragraph, however, relates to the appointment of James Kent as Recorder, and is itself its own explanation: —

In the year 1796 or 97, I do not remember which, I was chosen a member of the Council of appointment, consisting of Judge Spencer, Mr. Onderdonk, Mr. Gansevoort, and myself. By this council the late Chancellor Kent was made Recorder of the City of New York. The circumstances relating to his appointment were as follows: —

Governor Jay nominated in the first instance Mr. Cozine. Judge Spencer and myself voted against this nomination, not for any particular objection to the individual proposed by the Governor, but from a desire that the place should be filled by Mr. Kent, then a Master in Chancery in New York. Governor Jay expressed the highest opinions of Mr. Kent, but was induced to nominate Cozine, on the ground of seniority, Mr. Kent being at that time by many years his junior, both in point of age and standing at the Bar. Mr. Spencer and myself, however, persisting in our opposition, the Governor nominated Mr. Kent, who was appointed unanimously. This appointment was no sooner announced than the then Mr., now Judge, Spencer, with the vehemence for which he was at the time noted, inquired of the Governor whom he meant to nominate as Master in Chancery, in the place of Mr. Kent. To his great mortification the

Governor replied that there was no incompatibility between the two offices, and that Mr. Kent's appointment to that of Recorder did not disqualify him from holding also that of Master in Chancery. At this annunciation Spencer became very indignant, for he was not friendly at the time to Mr. Kent, but was actuated in promoting him to the situation of Recorder by advice to procure for his friend the late Cadwallader D. Colden the situation of Master in Chancery. The Governor having taken the opinion of the members of the Council on this subject, we all, excepting Judge Spencer, concurred in opinion with him.

The emoluments of the two positions combined produced for Mr. Kent a yearly income entirely adequate to his support, and enabled him not only to add extensively to his rapidly increasing library, but to invest considerable sums of money. A letter to his brother, written at about this period, shows not only that he had now become, in a modest way, a capitalist, but touches also upon a phase of social life then but little considered, but which, later in the history of our country, like an impenetrable cloud, obscured the brightness of our political sun.

James Kent to Moss Kent.

June 13, 1797.

. . . You may ask what I do with all my money, as I make a great deal. I can tell you. I paid the first of last May, £349, being the third instalment on my house here. I paid in May £65 for a wench I purchased. I have to pay, the third of July next, £833, being the remainder of moneys I owe on the Phelps contract. That is all I now owe, and by this means I shall be able to meet the July payment, as I have all to within £40, and that I hope to re-

ceive by my business by that time.   So you see what full
occasion I have for my money.   But after the third of July
next I shall be one of the most independent of men.   Not
a note against me except the last instalment of £400 on my
house payable by bond.   Next May I shall not owe any-
body on earth.   In the fall, therefore, if you want, call
on me.

An anecdote related of him at this period well
illustrates his broad research, and also the remarkable
powers of his memory.   A case was tried before him
in which Alexander Hamilton and Richard Harrison
were opposing counsel.   A nice point was involved,
and there was an impression on the minds of both that
some old reporter had recorded a case, in which a
similar point was involved; but neither of these eminent counsel was able to give the reference.   After
counsel had closed, Mr. Recorder Kent gave the title
of this old case, the proper reference, the page of the
report, and the names of the barristers engaged.   He
even quoted the words of the presiding Justice who
delivered the opinion.

Some years later, one of the members of the New
York Bar, and an intimate friend of Mr. Kent, asked
him if he recalled the incident, and why his memory
had been so correct.   In reply, Mr. Kent said that
he well remembered the circumstance, and explained
it by saying that on one occasion, when he was making a journey to his home at Poughkeepsie on a
sloop, — a trip which usually occupied about a day,
— by repeated calms and head winds he had been
eight days in reaching his home.   By some curious circumstance he found, in the cabin of the sloop,

a volume of the reporter in question, and that being the only book on the vessel, he had read and re-read every portion of it, until he had almost committed the entire volume to memory.

The same gentleman, in speaking of the incident, said that Mr. Kent's memory for detail was surprisingly accurate, even as to incidents which were outside of the limits of his profession. He related that when he was a student at law, in Mr. Kent's office, after he had retired from his office of Chancellor, Mr. Kent was visited one day by a lawyer from Poughkeepsie, who made inquiry if a certain man, a soldier, and a resident of Poughkeepsie, was alive at a certain time, shortly after the close of the Revolution.

Mr. Kent recalled the man at once, said that he was alive at the time in question, and lived in a certain house, just outside the village. He recalled an afternoon drive he had taken with his wife, passing the house, which stood close to the road, and seeing over the lower half of a Dutch door a soldier's cap and coat hanging upon the wall, together with other minute details of the drive.

His duties as Recorder were occasionally varied by presiding in the Mayor's Court, in the absence of that functionary, as appears by a letter addressed to his brother in August, 1797: —

James Kent to Moss Kent.

The Mayor has been absent from the city for four weeks past, and I have had, as presiding magistrate in his absence, my hands full of business, respecting the Police of the City, and the Cause of Justice. I held one Mayor's Court entirely alone, and at which seventy-four causes were noticed for trial. It has become time for me to have a little relaxation. The great thing I have to regret is the omission of literary pursuits, impossible in the hurry, and amidst the avocations which press upon me. This makes me long, ardently long for a more retired and tranquil life. This I can never expect in town; and perhaps while one is at business it is best to have as much as you can do, so as to have it sooner at an end.

His increased professional cares did not prevent his continued attention to classical and polite literature. Early in this narrative was shown the care and system with which he apportioned his time, and the zeal with which he devoted himself to the study of the ancient classics. This habit, then formed, was not discontinued, although labors multiplied upon him. It was in the summer of 1786 that his resolve was made that he would revive and continue his study of the classics. Four years later he wrote to his brother:—

James Kent to Moss Kent, Jr.

I have finished second Coke in law, and begun a course of Chancery studies. I have finished the two volumes of Télémaque[1] in French, and am beginning Corneille. I think I have acquired the language with great facility, and can read it with some degree of fluency. I have finished Ovid in Latin, and am near through the second volume of Horace again. Greek is the most difficult. I apprehend Lucian to be harder than Homer, but I have read about half of him, and shall arrive with joy to the end by April, and with anxiety to pay my respects to the Mantuan Bard.[2]

[1] Fénelon.
[2] " Mantua me genuit: Calabri rapuere: tenet nunc
Parthenope; cecini pascua, rura, duces."

Such has been my progress in classical studies since your departure. I am not ashamed to acknowledge to you the extent of my progress, and I contemplate the rich and extensive field that it opens, and the pure and honorable pleasure that it yields with great satisfaction.

A few months later he again writes : —

I have read Sallust's history of Catiline's conspiracy. He, Livy, and Tacitus are the three greatest historians in the Roman history, and all three have been mutilated by time, or the more cruel depredations of superstition, and are only presented to us in fragments. Sallust is vastly concise and he appears, in some measure, to make war on grammar and orthography, as you will find when you come to peruse him. He uses the infinitive mood for the indicative, and he had a mode of spelling which was obsolete in the Augustan Age.

I have read Buffon's Natural History, a great and magnificent work, and not more distinguished for penetration and novelty of thought than for elegance of expression. I wish I had time to send you the heads of it. I should be exceedingly fond of reading so eloquent and engaging a writer in the original. I am on the eighth Iliad, where the Greeks begin to feel the necessity of Achilles, and to yield to the inevitable progress of Hector.

In July, 1791, he wrote : —

I have pursued routine of studies as usual, I have just received from Rivington the Letters of Madame de Sévigné, in eight volumes, and also Xenophon's Cyropædia, by which you may judge of my progress in Greek and French.

In March, 1792, he again wrote to his brother, Moss Kent : —

If you are then reading the Orations of Demosthenes, you have the consolation of reading the most perfect production, according to Hume, in the most perfect language, according to Blair, and all other celebrated critics.   I have just been reading a second time Smith's Inquiry,[1] and Warburton's Legation,[2] two of the ablest system writers of any age or nation.   The latter is a most singular performance.   He enters, as you know, minutely and most deeply into the knowledge, with an exuberant profusion.   He is too fond, however, of allegorizing all the ancient poets, thereby obscuring the most valuable attribute, simplicity.

In the autumn of the year 1795, it will be recalled, Mr. Kent was obliged to leave New York, with his family, and seek refuge in Poughkeepsie, on account of the prevalence of the yellow fever in the metropolis.[3]   The time of his absence was profitably employed in reading, and he made a minute record of the manner in which this enforced vacation was passed.

Memoranda of my absence from New York in the Autumn of 1795, on account of the Yellow Fever.

" I left New York, with my family, on account of the prevailing epidemic of bilious fever, September 17, 1795, and went to Poughkeepsie, and boarded with T. Bailey, Esq., and returned again to the city, October 31, 1795.   During my exile I spent my time most happily in reading, and in little country excursions, as to Sharon, and to my friends in the neigh-

---

[1] Adam Smith, *Inquiry into the Nature and Causes of the Wealth of Nations.*

[2] William Warburton, *The Divine Legation of Moses Demonstrated on the Principles of a Religious Deist.*

[3] *Supra*, p. 79.

borhood of Poughkeepsie. I read, or ran over in that time, Whittaker's History of Manchester; Bruce's Travels; Cook's Third, or Last, Voyage; Savary's Letters on Greece; Voltaire's Essay on General History; Voltaire's Miscellaneous Historical Tracts; Russell's Modern Europe; Dr. Aiken's Letters to his Son; Ferguson's Essay on Civil Society; Beattie's Moral Essays; Sir W. Temple's Works.

" I mention this catalogue as evidence of the immense resource, the pure and delightful amusement, that books afford to those who have taste or fondness for them in the leisure of country retirement. And it fortunately happened that most of the authors, and especially Whittaker, Bruce, Cook, Voltaire's General History, and the History of the Buccaneers, and Temple, were to me works not only new, but extremely instructive and interesting.

" During my absence from New York, five hundred and sixty-eight persons died of the fever, according to the reports of the Health Committee. The three days before I left it, forty-three persons were reported to have died, and I conclude that, from the first of August to the first of November, about seven hundred persons fell a sacrifice to the sickness in New York, and the reports of the Health Committee were about that number. Several, however, who took it in New York died in the country, and were not included in the reports of the Health Committee, and many people suppose that a great many died in the city and were not reported by the committee. The fever began about the first of August, and ceased about the first of November. The summer had been

the most remarkably and oppressively hot of any
within my remembrance.   The heat continued almost
to October.   In September the city was also miserably afflicted with mosquitoes.   Very few of the citizens of any note died.   Those who died were chiefly
new immigrants from Ireland and obscure young
people.   I suppose one half of the city fled into the
country.   The terror for a few weeks was very great.
All intercourse between the city and Philadelphia, on
the one hand, and New Haven, on the other, was prohibited by those cities."

In July, 1796, as was frequently his custom, he reported to his brother his progress in study and in the
collection of books.

James Kent to Moss Kent.

July 17, 1796.

I keep making daily additions to my library, which I
regard as the repository of my happiest pursuits.   I long
to see the New American Register for 1795, and to see
in one condensed view the History, Politics, and Literature
of Europe.   I own Voltaire complete, in French, in 92
vols. ; Mably complete, in 13 vols. ; European Magazine
complete, in 25 vols. ; New American Register, in 15 vols.
Here you see what a store of learning I have (besides the
Encyclopædia, which is a library by itself) collected in
those single sets.   I got the other day President Gognet's
Origin of Laws, Arts, etc., a most learned and interesting
work ; the History of Louisiana, which contains a great deal
of curious learning respecting the Mississippi country, and
the best novels of Fielding and Richardson, the classics in
romance.

In February, 1798, he again reports : —

. . . To inform you of my literary history since your departure, be it known that I have finished Sallust, and was this morning near half thro' the 3d book of the Annals of Tacitus. I have this day finished the perusal of all my mighty and voluminous law collections. Perhaps I have glanced over also a couple of volumes of the European Magazine. Your sister and I have spent some most happy evenings alone by the fire in various and desultory reading, but generally it is my lot to have somebody almost every night to smoke a pipe, or drink a glass of wine, and chat on the news and politics of the day.

V

"IN February, 1798," writes Chancellor Kent, in
his "Memoranda," "I was appointed to the
office of a Judge of the Supreme Court. This was
the grand object of my ambition for several years
past. It appeared to me to be the true situation for
the display of my knowledge, talents, and virtue,
the happy mean of placing me beyond the crowd
and pestilence of the city, of giving me opportunities
to travel, and to follow literary pursuits, — a taste for
which is, after all, the most solid and permanent of
all sublunary enjoyments. By the acceptance of this
office I renounced all my offices in New York, with
all their accumulated income, and all my prospects
of wealth, for a moderate but permanent support,
for leisure to study, for more rural enjoyments, and
for a more dignified reputation. Whether or no I
judged well for my happiness must be left to the
event to decide, and this depends also in a great degree upon my own taste and disposition. This is
certain, that the mere men of business and of pleasure, who estimate happiness by income, and by the
splendid luxuries of the city life, all condemned my
choice as mad and absurd. But men of patriotism
and reflection, who thought less of riches and more
of character, if they did not approve, were yet more

slow to condemn.   My present impression is so unfavorable to public liberality and public justice, and
to the belief of the eventual success and credit of firm
and upright government, that I think it questionable
whether I calculated well or ill when I abandoned
the offices of Recorder and Master and took that of
Judge.

"In April, 1798, I removed to Poughkeepsie and
found myself upon my ancient ground, after an absence of five years.   But so great and so rapid a
change in so short a space of time few persons have
met with.   I went to New York poor, without patronage, and had a most gloomy and distressing introduction to the city life.   In five years I had run
through several honorable offices and attained one
of the highest respect in the community.   I had
collected not only a large and valuable library, and a
neat and valuable stock of furniture, but I returned say
at least £1000 richer than when I went.   I brought
back with me a little daughter about the age of the
one that I carried down and lost, and my wife had,
by her city life, greatly enlarged her mind, corrected
and cultivated her taste, and, without perceptible dim-
inution of her personal charms, had added exceedingly to her various and elegant accomplishments.

"No sooner had I settled myself at Poughkeepsie
than I resumed my long lost acquaintance with the
classic writers.   In the summer of 1798 I performed
the Western and Southern Circuits; I found means
between May and January to read Horace and Virgil, Vertot's Malta, De Pan on the Greeks, Brown,
Vezey, Ambler, Anstruther, 2d vol. Black's Reports,

Fonblanque's Equity and a great variety of miscellaneous reading. I perceived, this year, my love of home and my vivid and exclusive fondness and esteem for my wife to have received strength and addition.

" I find myself now in the middle of life, and a sense of its value and rapidity to be greatly increased in my reflections. This urges upon me constantly the necessity of improving time with the utmost diligence, and constantly to make it subservient to all the noble purposes of social and domestic happiness, of public and private duty."

The commission of James Kent as Justice of the Supreme Court of the State of New York, signed by John Jay, Governor, bears date June 16, 1798. The appointment had been presaged by his brother, as appears by a letter bearing date of January 18, 1798.

Moss Kent to James Kent.

I observe by the Albany papers that Judge Hobart is elected a Senator. I conclude therefore that he will immediately resign his seat on the Bench. There will be two vacancies in our Supreme Court in a few weeks, and you will undoubtedly have the offer of one of the appointments, as Governor Jay has a Council that will unanimously concur in his nomination. I hope and believe that you will accept; though the salary will be less than the income of your present business, you will have vastly more leisure for study, and you will be enabled to choose any place of residence within the State that shall be most agreeable to your taste. I think it likely that I shall be elected one of the Senators of this district next spring, and one very great inducement to me to wish it is that I should, in that case, have the pleasure of spending the winters with you in Albany, as you would be obliged to attend there as one of the Council of Revision should you be appointed a Judge; this is, however, between ourselves. . . .

Further personal record of this event, marking so important an era in his life, is found in a letter from James Kent to his brother, under date of February 25, 1798.

James Kent to Moss Kent.

. . . You have heard of my appointment to the Bench of the Supreme Court. It is an office agreeable to me, and I have accordingly sold my house and hired one at Pough-keepsie for a year, whither I shall remove early in April. Where I shall permanently settle is uncertain. The city will be left by me with satisfaction; a country residence has infinitely more charms and conduces to a more tranquil and literary life. Your little niece grows finely. She is fat and sweet and full of play and prattle. . . .

I am reading to-day, during the cessation of business, the description of Germany given in a late tour, and the "History of the Knights of Malta" by the Abbé Vertot, a most lively and agreeable historian. The third Tuesday in April I shall of course be in Albany, where you will proba-bly hear from me, and learn the Spring Circuit that will be assigned to me.

James Kent, when he reached the height toward which his ambition had long impelled him, was not quite thirty-five years of age. In a discourse on the life, character, and public services of James Kent, de-livered before the judiciary and Bar of the city and

State of New York, in April, 1848, by Hon. John
Duer, to which reference has already been made,[1] that
eminent member of the judiciary characterized the Supreme Court of the State, at the time when the subject
of his eulogy ascended the Bench, in these words: —

"The condition of the Supreme Court at the time
of his accession to the Bench was probably much
the same as it had been, with little variation, from
the close of the Revolution. It was not a condition that reflected credit on the jurisprudence of
the State; it was not such as the character and the
honor of the State and the interests of the public
demanded. The judges, although not distinguished
by any marked superiority, were by no means deficient in learning or ability; but it was in a very imperfect and unsatisfactory manner that their duties
were discharged. There was not only a great delay
in the determination of causes, — a delay not at all
excused by the multiplicity of business, — but the decisions, when pronounced, were far from supplying the
requisite proof of a mature consideration. It was
evident that they were not the fruit of that careful
and laborious investigation which is essential to the
proper discharge of the judicial functions; and the
authority they might otherwise have claimed was
greatly impaired by those frequent differences in
opinion that are the necessary result of imperfect examination and study. It was seldom that the opinions
of the judges, even in the most important cases, were
reduced to writing, and as no reports were then published, and no records preserved of the grounds on

[1] *Supra*, p. 29.

which their decisions were placed, the cases were numerous in which they had no rules to direct, no precedents to govern them.

" Of this state of things the inevitable consequences were vacillation, contradictions, confusion, and uncertainty. It is hardly necessary to add that this defective administration of the law had a most unfavorable influence on the character and pursuits of the Bar; for when cases are slightly examined and rashly decided by the judges, the principal motives for a diligent preparation on the part of counsel cease to exist. No further observations can be requisite to show that, in order to redeem the character of the Bench and of the Bar, and the honor of the State, a great revolution was necessary to be effected; and it was effected, mainly by the efforts and by the example of the man who, at the early age of thirty-five, was now raised to the Bench.

" As soon as his seat was taken, his determination was made that he would examine for himself every case not decided on the hearing; and in such examination would not confine himself to the cases and authorities cited on the argument, but would embrace in his researches all the law justly applicable to the questions to be determined; and that in each case he would embody the result of his examination in a written opinion. Accordingly, at the second term that followed his appointment, in his first meeting for consultation with his brethren, and to their great astonishment, he produced a written opinion in every case that had been reserved for decision; and as these opinions were carefully prepared, were clear in style,

forcible in reasoning, and well sustained by a reference to authorities, his brethren, even when they dis-
sented from his conclusions, were in no condition to
controvert and oppose them. Hence they at once
understood and felt that their own position was
materially changed. It was evident that they must
either surrender to their junior brother — their junior
in station and far their junior in years — the effective
control and administration of all the important business of the court, or if at all solicitous to maintain
their own character and dignity, must follow his
example.

" Fortunately for themselves and the public, it was
upon the latter course that they resolved. From that
time there was a constant and most honorable emulation in the discharge of their weighty duties, and the
result was that, in the space of a few years, the Supreme Court of this State was placed on an elevation
— an elevation of influence, dignity, and authority —
that from that day to the present, with a just pride we
may affirm, it has continued to maintain. . . .

" Although his brethren on the Bench, during this
period, emulated his diligence, and contributed by
their efforts to advance or sustain the reputation of
the court, yet it is not to be denied that the opinions
that he delivered were distinguished by qualities that
in those of his brethren were rarely displayed, or displayed only in an inferior degree. There was a clearly
defined and marked superiority that he was soon admitted to possess, and which he retained without dispute, during the whole period of his continuance on
the Bench. . . . What, then, are the causes to which

his superiority over his brethren must be attributed ?
. . . He had cultivated his mind in all its powers and
faculties — imaginative and moral, as well as purely
intellectual — with far greater care and assiduity.
His studies had not only been more extensive and
various, but more thorough, systematic, and profound.
His learning not only embraced a larger compass in
its subjects, but was firmer in its principles and more
scientific in its arrangement.

"From his far greater intimacy with the classic
writers of antiquity and with the great masters of
composition in our own language, he derived eminent
advantages.   To this intimacy, the justness, elevation,
and purity of his taste must be attributed ; it was this
intimacy that had endowed him with a command and
mastery of language that enabled him to express his
thoughts, on every subject to which they were directed,
with such remarkable facility, precision, perspicuity,
and force.   It was this intimacy that gave choice and
variety, and occasionally splendor to his diction, and
enriched his style with apt and varied illustrations.
In short, it was the intrinsic and peculiar excellence
of his opinions, in matter and style, that gave to them
a paramount authority, and to their author his wide-
spread and rapidly increasing reputation."

This extended quotation from the record of a contemporary of Judge Kent has been made, not so much
because the words uttered are the words of a eulogist,
but chiefly because of their historic interest, and because they bear the evidence of a sincere and unbiased
consideration of the effect which this man's elevation
to the Bench produced upon the judicial system of his
State.

In September, 1828, Thomas Washington, of Nashville, Tennessee, a distinguished member of the Bar, and introduced by Governor Carroll, of that State, addressed a letter to Chancellor Kent, in which he begged to be told the secret of his success in life. The Chancellor, after repeated requests, made an extended reply, in which he gave to his correspondent a sketch of his life's experiences, much of which was drawn from the memoranda which have already been so copiously quoted. The Chancellor wrote in confidence, and with freedom and simplicity. Fortunately, a copy of this epistle has been preserved, and from it is drawn his own statement concerning his elevation to the Supreme Bench, and the effect of that event upon the judicial system.

"In February, 1798," wrote Chancellor Kent, "I was offered by Governor Jay, and accepted, the office of youngest judge of the Supreme Court. This was the summit of my ambition. My object was to retire back to Poughkeepsie and resume my studies and ride the circuits and inhale country air and enjoy *otium cum dignitate*. I never dreamed of volumes of reports and written opinions. Such things were not then thought of. I retired back to Poughkeepsie, in the spring of 1798, and in that summer rode all over the western wilderness and was delighted. I returned home and began my Greek, and Latin, and French, and English, and law classics as formerly, and made wonderful progress in books that year. In 1799 I was obliged to remove to Albany in order that I might not be too much from home, and there I remained stationary for twenty-four years.

"When I came to the Bench there were no reports or State precedents. The opinions from the Bench were delivered *ore tenus*. We had no law of our own, and nobody knew what it was. I first introduced a thorough examination of cases and written opinions. In January, 1799, the second case reported in first Johnson's cases, of Ludlow *v.* Dale, is a sample of the earliest. The judges, when we met, all assumed that foreign sentences were only good *prima facie*. I presented and read my written opinion that they were conclusive, and they all gave up to me, and so I read it in court as it stands. This was the commencement of a new plan, and then was laid the first stone in the subsequently erected temple of our jurisprudence.

"Between that time and 1804 I rode my share of circuits, attended all the terms, and was never absent, and was always ready in every case by the day. I read in that time Valin and Emerigon, and completely abridged the latter, and made copious digests of all the English law reports and treatises as they came out. I made much use of the *Corpus Juris*, and as the judges (Livingston excepted) knew nothing of French or civil law, I had immense advantage over them. I could generally put my brethren to rout and carry my point by my mysterious wand of French and civil law. The judges were Republicans and very kindly disposed to everything that was French, and this enabled me, without exciting any alarm or jealousy, to make free use of such authorities and thereby enrich our commercial law.

"I gradually acquired preponderating influence with my brethren, and the volumes in Johnson, after

I became Chief-Justice, in 1804, show it. The first practice was for each judge to give his portion of opinions, when we all agreed, but that gradually fell off, and, for the last two or three years before I left the Bench, I gave the most of them. I remember that in eighth Johnson all the opinions for one term are '*per curiam.*' The fact is I wrote them all and proposed that course to avoid exciting jealousy, and many a *per curiam* opinion was so inserted for that reason.

"Many of the cases decided during the sixteen years I was in the Supreme Court were labored by me most unmercifully, but it was necessary under the circumstances, in order to subdue opposition. We had but few American precedents. Our judges were democratic, and my brother Spencer particularly, of a bold, vigorous, dogmatic mind and overbearing manner. English authority did not stand very high in those early feverish times, and this led me a hundred times to attempt to bear down opposition, or shame it by exhaustive research and overwhelming authority. Our jurisprudence was, on the whole, improved by it. My mind certainly was roused, and was always kept ardent and inflamed by collision."

In 1798, as Chancellor Kent has recorded, he disposed of his house in New York and returned to his old home at Poughkeepsie. He had never been captivated by the pleasures of city life, and preferred rather the quiet of the country as conducive to study and reflection. It was therefore with pleasure that he embraced the opportunity of a change of residence, and returned to his former home and that of his wife at Poughkeepsie. He soon discovered, however, that his duties required him to be absent much of the time from his home, and that a residence at Albany would enable him to enjoy much more of the home life and association with his wife and family.   He therefore again removed, and to Albany.

The social life at Albany in which Mr. Kent moved, and of which in a measure he was the centre, as a judge and afterward as chancellor, was at that period particularly charming and pleasing to his tastes and character.   The enormous development which he had introduced in the systematic study of law, the care, precision, and learning which were brought to the elucidation of problems then new and not clearly understood, while with masterly pen he was striving to inject into the jurisprudence of his State the enlightened comprehension of the science of law and the principles of equity practice, had naturally drawn about the court the leading lawyers and thinkers of the day. Untrammelled by the introduction of statutory enactments, infringing upon and confusing the prerogatives of the court, limiting and hindering its expansion, the field was fair for individual opinion and ample and exhaustive study and research, which would enable the Chancellor to grasp the fundamental principle and upon that build up the unperishable fabric of the law as at present understood.   Cumbersome and intricate as the old practice of the Court of Chancery was, it still had the attribute of elasticity.

The Chancellor determined the practice, not the legislature, which could not foresee all contingencies, and substantial justice was done, without the intervention of codes and statutes.   There was also lacking the strict observance of formal practice, now so marked a characteristic of our courts.   The Chancellor always sat at any time, unless engaged in the duties of Council of Revision, and was ever ready to hear and determine what might require attention. The simple character of the times enabled the office of the Chancellor to be the Court of Chancery, and as his office was his study at his home, it came to be an established custom for the lawyers to collect in the afternoon or after dinner, then usually taken at five P. M.   As a natural sequence it was not surprising that the collection in Mr. Kent's parlor partook somewhat of the nature of a levee, the Chancellor holding court in his study, and the chancery lawyers and younger members of the bar drinking tea and chatting with the ladies.   Mrs. Kent frequently referred to this as perhaps the most interesting period of her life, much of which was due to her own attractive qualities, lively wit, elegance, and cultivation.

But this is a digression, in advance of the narrative.

At the end of six years of service as Associate Justice of the Supreme Court, Mr. Kent was in 1804 advanced to the position of Chief-Justice.   The vacancy was caused by the election to the office of Governor of the State, of Chief-Justice Morgan Lewis, who for many years had been in close and friendly relations with Judge Kent.   At this time party politics and partisan bias ran high.   Judge Lewis was an ardent Republican, or anti-Federalist, while Judge Kent, Judge Spencer, and others on the bench were strong Federalists.   Just on the eve of the election, when both parties had put forth their strength,

and when as yet the result of the election was doubtful, Judge Lewis, meeting Judge Kent at chambers,
and discussing the probabilities of the election,
said, —

"Judge Kent, if you will vote for me I will make
you Chief-Justice if I am elected."

The manner in which such a remark is made is the
interpretation of the meaning of the speaker. It can
hardly be thought possible that Judge Lewis had any
intention of even suggesting a bribe to his distinguished confrère, the remark being probably made
in the nature of a pleasantry, to see what reply the
suggestion would call forth. Judge Kent evidently
understood his friend's question in the manner intended; for, without hesitation, he replied, —

"No, sir. Personally, I admire and respect your
character and attainments; but I utterly detest your
political principles."

The fact that, at once upon entering upon office,
Governor Lewis advanced Judge Kent to the position
of Chief-Justice, is in itself a tribute to the high character of the chief-magistrate, and his thorough sense
of justice.

Judge Kent's duties as Chief-Justice did not materially differ from those of the lesser office, except
that he occupied a seat in the Council of Revision,
in which his struggles, as a Federalist, against the
rising tide of French influence, made his office at
times almost a burden.

But fragmentary memoranda are found among his
papers of his experiences during the sixteen years of
his occupancy of a seat upon the Bench of the Su-

preme Court. One of these memoranda is of his initial experience.

" It fell to my lot," he records, " to be selected to hold the October Term (1798) in the city of New York. The yellow fever had been so destructive in the city since the 25th of August, had excited such a vast proportion of the healthy inhabitants, and had propagated such universal alarm and anxiety, that it was the opinion of all the judges that no special business ought to be transacted, and the term was held and continued for the fortnight *pro forma* merely, and to prevent the total dissolution of suits. I held the court the first two days, on the 16th and 17th of October, at the Tavern, on the west end of Harlaem Bridge, and was attended by the sheriff and clerk and several lawyers. The rest of the term the court was held at the State Prison, in the suburbs of the city; and during the progress of the term the fever abated rapidly, so that by the 25th of October the citizens began to crowd into town and to resume business.

" During the leisure of this term I read at Robert Benson's, where I lodged, Sir George Stanton's account of the Embassy to China. It is very instructive and well written, and tends, upon the whole, to exalt greatly the opinion of our people of the population and manners of the people of China. I also visited frequently the State Prison, the new workshop, the prisoners, their work and victuals, the wall, the sewers, the solitary cells, the fireplaces (which are on Count Rumford's plan), etc., and I conclude it is the most finished and best conducted institution of the kind upon earth. Thomas Eddy, the principal promoter and superintendent of the thing, deserves great credit, and will probably acquire lasting fame by the success of the scheme. The Quakers are certainly the most spirited and active class of citizens in the community in promoting humane and benevolent undertakings."

Toward the close of this epoch of his life, he notes that he held his first court of Oyer and Terminer, June 5, 1798, at Oneida, and tried the case of Silvia Wood, who was convicted of murder, but died in prison of suicide before the day of execution. "Only eight convictions of murder before me," he again notes, "during the sixteen years."

"The Jewish judges rode the circuits," he reminds himself in another note. "'And Samuel judged Israel all the days of his life, and he went from year to year in circuit, to Bethel and Gilgal and Mizpeh, and judged Israel in all those places.' 1 Sam. ch. 7, ver. 15 & 16."

In another place is found his brief summary that in these sixteen years he held one hundred and forty courts, and tried seventeen hundred and fifty-five cases.

As illustrating the firmness of Judge Kent's character, and his willingness to accept all responsibility in carrying out the duties of his position and enforcing the proper observance of the law, may be cited the following. During the latter part of the war of 1812 General Brown had seized upon the persons of certain citizens of the State of New York, not under military authority, for violation of some military orders. A writ of habeas corpus was granted by Judge Kent, and the sheriff ordered to produce the prisoners.

General Brown refused to surrender them to the civil authorities. The sheriff made his return of the writ, and, upon his explaining the reason for not producing the prisoners, Judge Kent directed him to call out the posse comitatus of the county, to enforce the order of the court, together with the further direction, if the force was not sufficient, to call out the posse of the neighboring counties; and further intimated that he should order out the entire force of the State, if necessary, to enforce the decrees of the court. The situation was very precarious. The unpopular war had been dragging itself along upon the upper frontier of New York, and now what threatened to be a clash between the Federal and the State authority was a matter of great importance to the weak authority of the Federal Government. Judge Kent refused to recede from his position, maintaining, among other reasons, that, upon matters affecting the substantial rights of the citizens of the State of New York, the civil authority was supreme and must be obeyed, as the State was not in insurrection and martial law had not been proclaimed. Strong representations were made to General Brown by prominent gentlemen, and he finally permitted the prisoners to be handed over to the sheriff. They were brought before Judge Kent, an examination was held, and they were immediately remitted to the custody of General Brown, sufficient cause for their detention having been shown. The principle of the right of the people, under that great charter of Anglo-Saxon liberties, the " habeas corpus," had been vindicated, and the incident closed.

It was in December, 1805, that Judge Kent formed

a close professional connection with William Johnson, with whose name his own is inseparably connected. The two were personal friends previous to Mr. Johnson's appointment to the office of Reporter of Decisions of the Supreme Court, and, without doubt, it was largely through the influence of Judge Kent that the appointment was made. A letter addressed to Judge Kent by Mr. Johnson, bearing date of December 23, 1805, is a proof of the close and intimate friendship of the two men: —

William Johnson to Judge Kent.

NEW YORK, December 23, 1805.

DEAR SIR, — I received your letter inclosing the certificate; I feel obliged by your attention to my pecuniary interest in this appointment. Though of no small weight in this mercenary world, it was a consideration that least occupied my mind. One of the most pleasing incidents in the execution of the duties of my office will be its leading me into your society, which I have so little enjoyed since your removal from this city.

I feel no little anxiety about the first number of the reports, which must inevitably be too imperfect, and I fear incorrect, and the partiality of my friends has created expectations which will not be fulfilled. I have obtained from Mr. Caines [1] thirteen cases, which he mentioned were all that lay over for the judgment of the court in the next term. Mr. Hopkins has, however, furnished me with another since. Mr. C. offered me his notes of arguments, but I declined the acceptance of them, thinking it best to omit the arguments of counsel, and give only the facts and opinions of the court; relying on the candor of the Bar,

---

[1] Mr. Johnson's predecessor.

for this inattention, in the peculiar circumstances of the publication of the first number. I shall, before leaving town for Albany, abridge the cases in my possession, and be thus far prepared to commence publication. Mr. C. told me that he should publish the reports of the last term, which conclude the year. The cases of practice which may be thought important, and which he may omit, I expect your notes will enable me to publish. Indeed, I shall rely very much on your aid in the outset of the work, as I know I always may on your friendship and advice.

Ten years later, when Judge Kent had been advanced to the office of Chancellor, Mr. Johnson was transferred to the Court of Equity, as Reporter of Decisions in that tribunal. Some of the letters written by these two friends are preserved, and disclose, not only a complete understanding in matters professional, but a close personal friendship as well. In a letter transmitting a number of decisions recently made, to his Reporter, the Chancellor writes: " I am only afraid of reporting too much, and I shall stand in need of your judgment on that point, seeing I am alone in my court, and have no other aid; and I shall place more reliance on your judgment than my own."

Again, in enclosing an opinion to Mr. Johnson, the Chancellor gives him an account of a journey which he has recently taken, in company with Mrs. Kent, by stage-coach, through the region of the Green Mountains. " We had thus, by Saturday evening of the first week," he writes, " ridden two hundred and sixty miles in stages, in four days, and twice traversed the broad back of the Green Mountains, and seen all the glories of the upper Connecticut. The people were industrious and civil.   We saw no poverty nor rudeness, nor distress, but the country in the highest luxuriance.   I was chatty and courteous to stagemen and innkeepers, at bar-rooms and on piazzas, and was wonderfully pleased with the simplicity of the scene.   It was far superior in interest to the crowds of fashion on Broadway, and I suspect that few citizens or citizenesses of Broadway, of our age and character, would have committed themselves to such a tour, in such a mode, and with such daring and exciting rapidity.   I think Mrs. K. and I deserve to be enrolled among the actors in the heroic ages.   We found what we sought, health and pleasure."

In another letter to his Reporter, after despatching the business in hand, he chats of his general reading. "This moment," he says, " I have laid Virgil on my table, and I am determined to amuse myself in reading him forthwith.   I have nothing else to do.   I have just finished Ferrière's ' History of the Civil Law,' and I was charmed with it.   My three children are all with me, and I am of course brimful of happiness."

Many years later, when, upon the eve of Chancellor Kent's retirement, — he having reached the age of sixty years, — a new Reporter was given the position so long and so honorably held by Mr. Johnson, the Chancellor wrote to his friend: "You retire with my gratitude, love, and admiration, and if my name is to live in judicial annals, it will be in association with yours."   Two days before his retirement, in transmitting to Mr. Johnson his final opinions, and in severing a relation which had been so long continued, the Chancellor wrote thus: —

Chancellor Kent to William Johnson.

I cannot think of the dissolution of the official connection between you and me without a tender recollection of the endearments of our past friendship, nor without a hope that the intercourse and friendship between us may continue unimpaired. My respect, esteem, admiration, and attachment to you as a pure and accomplished character, is as deep-rooted as the principle of life, and you must never cease for one moment to look upon me as a friend affectionately devoted to your interest, your happiness, your fame, and the happiness of your wife and children.

For the twenty-five years during which Judge Kent occupied the Bench of either the Supreme Court or of the Court of Chancery, he made Albany his home. As Supreme Court Judge, his duties required him to take long journeys to every part of the State, in order to hold the Circuit Courts at the various county seats. In making these trips he notes that he visited almost every county seat in the State and held courts. These journeys were performed by stage, in the better settled portions of the country, but more usually on horseback, or in a " chair," as a buggy, or buckboard, was then called.

These trips, sometimes occupying three or four months, were upon the whole very irksome to him. He was deprived of the society of his wife and family and intimate friends, which was a constant source of regret. Also, in a great measure, he was cut off from the pleasures of literary pursuits, it being quite impracticable for him to carry his library with him. He was therefore reduced to the society of one or two favorite classics. Of law books he required none, as he usually decided all simple questions as they came before him, reserving his decisions only on the more complicated questions, until he could write his opinions. He frequently notes that he has brought home with him from his trip bundles of cases which will occupy him until the next term, to study and decide.

He kept a careful diary of these circuits which he held, for reference, allusion to which has been made; but he appears never to have met with any adventures of travel which were worthy of record. He informally records that the people whom he met were civil and obliging, although, at times, the journeying might be hard and the fare rough. Many letters to his wife have been preserved, which speak of such incidents, but the burden of them all is his intense regret at being separated from his family for such lengthy periods. These letters disclose a phase of his nature which those who knew him only in his judicial character might not discover.

Judge Kent to his Wife.

NEW YORK, Tuesday eve, April 10, 1804.

DEAR BETSY, — Perhaps this letter will not be worth 19 cts., but you must take it as you took me, and I will detail the little occurrences of the two last days. They are trifling to others and may be amusing to you. I dined this day with James. There were Mrs. Dorcas Bailey, Mr. and Mrs. Aspinwall, Mr. Morris, and Mr. H. Wyckoff, and the two Miss Linns. The chat among gentlemen, when left to themselves, is about those eternal themes, the Election and the Bank and Burr. I had rather hear dear little precious Will [1]

---

[1] The Chancellor's only son, Judge William Kent.

call for " Pa-pa " and " up-up," and cry " hah-hah," than
to hear the best composition in music that ever Handel
performed. I hope you let him go into the office and show
the books and Betsy's little trunk and my drawers and the
pipe, and let him go to the pump and the church and the
river as often as he wishes.

Last evening I called also at James', and there was a full
crowded room of ladies at tea and seven dozen candles and
a pair of lamps. Sister Caty seems to see a great deal of
company. . . . Robt. Benson dined with me at Boyd's yesterday, and the old gentleman is a great Burrite. I sleep in
a clean, snug, elegant, front bedroom, and enjoy myself as
well as was to be expected, separated from all I hold most
dear.

The courts were opened to-day and business was begun.
Woolsey is down, and I find I might have stayed at home till
yesterday. I shall expect you in May. The sail and visit
will be short, and can be made vastly agreeable. It will be
necessary to see you by that time, as I shall begin to forget
you amidst the numerous beauties that are constantly before
my eyes here. Susan and Mary Linn look very pretty, but
it is time the first is married. I am afraid her charms will
not be impressive long. I am very economical, and I shall
buy but very few books, and shall reserve my money for your
use and for your gratification ; and ought you not to love such
a husband?

Judge Kent to his Wife.

NEW YORK, Friday, April 20, 1804.

DEAR BETSY, — My days flow very uniformly here, and I
have nothing to tell you more interesting than that my
heart is warm and devoted to my wife and children. Very
dull indeed the court has hitherto been, and everybody
seems to be occupied with politics and engaging themselves
with the two polluted factions. I keep quite aloof and

mind my court and reading and walking. I am awakened every morning in my neat bedroom by carts and sweeps, or the milkman " screaming to the rattle of his pail of tin ; " and we breakfast at 8 precisely, on tea or coffee and buckwheat cakes. Then I walk for a mile and perhaps visit a bookseller and go into court at 10 and stay till near 4, and then at a dinner party. The evening affords a little leisure to visit and I employ it accordingly. Last evening I called and smoked a pipe with old Dr. Rodgers and his prim and venerable partner. The evening before I was at Mr. King's and there I saw a good many things worth mentioning. There were Mrs. Low, Mrs. Patrune, Mrs. Morton, of Boston, the authoress of " Beacon Hill," " Philenia," etc., etc., and a Mrs. King, who was dressed, as I thought, very gayly. Her husband is plain and dignified, and of very impressive manners. I have seen the widow Vanwyck, who has laid aside the gloom of last fall and is very smiling and affable and anxious to talk about the cities abroad ; and I have dined with Mrs. O'Kane. She is homely — quite so ; I am astonished she ever was admired : but she is very sprightly and genteel. Their furniture is splendid. I think it is overloaded with magnificence; and Mrs. King's parlor pleased me better, because the furniture was elegant and simple. Let me see — I propose that we get a mattress ; pair of plated lamps ; settee for drawing-room ; paper for room below.

You must give me advice on all these heads ; as I said before, I reserve all my money this spring for your gratification. I spend nothing here and have to receive at least $300. So you will perceive I have ample means and I shall wait for your instructions. I have most forgotten dear little Will. It always so happens that the mother monopolizes all my thoughts when I am absent. However, I promise to make it up for my children when I am with them. Only think, two weeks have fled, and in four from to-morrow I set my face homeward. During the three days of election next week, I shall have play spell, and shall devote it to studying my cases, for I have done very little at that as yet. To-morrow, after court, I go out with General Hamilton and I shall stay with him on Sunday and shall have an opportunity, if a good day, of wandering all over the Harlem hills. He is very much mortified at the conduct of the Federalists and is melancholy and presages all the dire events that any gloomy imagination can create.

Judge Kent to his Wife.

NEW YORK, Sunday, May 13, 1804.

MY DEAR BETSY, — After several days of chilly easterly winds, we have a beautiful day and my spirits are lively. This arises principally from the reflection that I am half through Term time, and that next Sunday I shall be sailing along the verdant, or the picturesque, banks of the Hudson. It is probable I shall leave this city on Saturday, and I am making every arrangement for that purpose. Little Bess is quite tired of New York and almost as homesick as I am.

We had yesterday a celebration of the acquisition of Louisiana; the military paraded and the guns fired, etc., but it was a paltry procession. Above half the churches refused to let their bells ring. The judges were all by letters invited to walk in procession, but we all kept in court at business. . . . We meet every evening at Judge Livingston's, and Brother Moss took little Bess all about to see museums and curiosities. He is worth a dozen of me, as I am so engaged with court and dinners and consultations. . . .

I dined yesterday at Moses Rogers'; he lives on the Battery, in Penfield's House. The Battery is now beautiful and enchanting. The verdure and the trees and the scenery are brilliant. It wants nothing but a mountain towering on

one side of the harbor to equal the Bay of Naples.   At
dinner was Mr. Wolcott, Mr. Tracey (who says he saw you
at the Springs and that you are a lively woman ; let me add,
by the bye, that you are enchantingly lovely), Colonel
Talmaise, of Litchfield, and a number of others, and ladies.
These vexatious dinners are to me worse than the courts.
But, thank God, they are most over for this season.   I am
in hopes to make some pleasant tours with you this fall
and to make you compensation for the loss of your New
York jaunt.   I am pretty resolute that I will do something
pretty clever for you in that way, and at least I can enjoy
these things in anticipation.

During a session of the court at Salem (Washington County, N. Y.), he longs for the companionship
of his wife and family, and for the delights of home.
"The anticipation of approaching nearer and nearer
to my beloved home," he writes, "will sweeten and
brighten the moments.   What is there besides wife
and children and the countless petty comforts of home
that is worth enjoying in this world?   I really think
nothing.   Deprived of these, I should be a poor ma-
niac, without heart to feel, or head to guide me.
Rest contented that your husband prizes you and his
daughter and son with as much fervency as can be
wished for or expected."

A letter from Judge Kent to his wife, during her
temporary absence from home, is equally full of regrets
at the separation : —

Judge Kent to his Wife.

ALBANY, August 25, 1806.

DEAR BETSY, — The winds became propitious to you after
the sharp lightning of Friday evening, and I trust you had a

quick and pleasant passage. I was uncommonly gloomy the evening after you left me, and on Saturday morning my most beloved brother took his departure. Little Will has had his eyes frequently suffused with tears at the recollection of his mother, but —

> "Gay hope is his by fancy fed,
> Less pleasing when possessed;
> The tear forgot as soon as shed
> The sunshine of the breast."

On Saturday in the afternoon I took him and Bess over to Bath for a little sail. Yesterday he went with me to church, and I heard Dr. Perkins. I dined with my next neighbor to-day. It is now 1 o'clock, and Will is playing and chirping before the door. I keep a basket filled with peaches and pears, and Bess behaves with the gravity of a matron. William Johnson and Bleecker have been most of the forenoon in the office, thumbing my books and whiling away the time in varied and elegant conversation. I have entered on my classical career, and have been going over the Georgics of Virgil, with Southey's elegant version, but the solitude of the house is too great for comfort and study. The evening especially is dismal, and I am obliged to confess that —

> "Though no disease my torpid veins invade,
> Yet melancholy's phantoms haunt my shade."

Johnson has returned from Lebanon, and he admires that vale exceedingly. It is one of the pleasantest inland valleys he ever saw. Yesterday he visited the Shakers, and was struck with the unparalleled neatness of their dwellings and with the mummy, or death-like, appearance of the women. Bleecker possesses rather more feeling toward the singular beauties of the country, and longs to visit Lake George and the inmost valleys of the Catskills.

Will has just come in from the street, and is now engaged

in rolling a watermelon over the carpet, in stretching himself on the floor, and singing songs. My dinner will soon be up. It is to be very frugal, a small pudding and a steak, that's all. My prayer is to be blessed with the company and happiness of my wife and children, with a continued strong and glowing relish for letters or science, in all its enchanting departments, — in short, that

> "Science and soft affection's blended rays
> May shine unclouded on my lengthened days."

Again, in the summer of 1807, Mrs. Kent paid a visit to her relatives at Poughkeepsie, leaving the Judge for a time to his own devices and the care of their two children. How well he performed his task, the following bright and affectionate epistle will show : —

Judge Kent to his Wife.

ALBANY, Tuesday, August 25, 1807.

DEAR BETSY, — I had the pleasure of learning your safe arrival at Poughkeepsie by a line from Mrs. Linn. Your journey during the two very hot days was very fortunately performed, and I was afraid you would have suffered great inconvenience. I have charming solitude at home, and have begun to read with great alacrity. I begin to think that single life is best for the student, and therefore you will be so good as to let me remain here alone as long as possible. There is not a soul in the house this afternoon. The cake boy has just been here, and I keep the basket stored with jumbles for my son, and with crackers for my daughter. I give toast and milk in the morning, and Will has full scope at the sugar cup ; and at noon I feed Bess with beefsteaks, and see that some good pieces are cut nicely for the son. So you perceive I do very well. When the news arrives, I pore over my maps and trace every step of the Conqueror of the Baltic.

Old Mrs. Seton called this afternoon to ask me how I did, and I met every courtesy with a bow, and followed her out to the very bottom of the steps. Miss Linn paid me a visit with Miss Bridges yesterday afternoon, and notwithstanding their excessive shyness I got them both seated in the office ; but I could not prevail upon them to honor me at the tea table, and they fled off soon, lest they might alarm your feelings and awaken your suspicion.

One more of these charming personal letters must be given, letters which so well display his love of home and family; the ease with which his mind turned to lighter themes from the contemplation of grave problems; and the vein of gentle humor with which he was gifted.   This letter was written during his absence at Hudson, in attendance at court in that town.   One of his coadjutors, Judge Van Ness, is holding court at Albany, and him he commends to the courtesies of Mrs. Kent.

Judge Kent to Mrs. Kent.

HUDSON, September 27, 1807.

DEAR BETSY, — I told Judge Van Ness that I should draw an order on my wife for every civil usage during his stay in Albany. He may want my sulky, and if he does you must see that Jack cleans it well for him.

I came down in five hours exactly, in the steamboat, and I was charmed with the — sail, I was going to say. I mean I was delighted with the paddling. We had thirty passengers. After dinner on Friday the Judge and the Adjutant General (who is here also with his wife) walked with me to the top of Windmill Hill, and a grander prospect I never saw. Yesterday I settled my business with the bank, and I found to my agreeable surprise that I had $850 lying there for me.

I made therefore all the payments I wished and have reserved $200 to carry home, so that I believe now the looking-glass must come this fall ; all this *entre nous.*

Yesterday in the afternoon the Judge and myself rode to Claverack and we spent the evening with a parcel of ladies at Judge Gilbert's, and his daughter Angelica charmed me by her singing and music and manners and elegance so that I shall not probably be able to think of you any more until I return home.

By the bye, a sublime spectacle is to be seen in the western sky, a little after dark. A comet has made its appearance and I beg of you to be out on the watch for some evenings to come. It has a grand sweeping tail and is a sight as majestic as any that ever hung out in the heavens to the astonishment and admiration of mortals.

Of Judge Van Ness a word, in passing, is proper. He was a pupil of Mr. Kent about the year 1793, and to the training thus received was doubtless largely due his subsequent eminence. Judge William Kent, the son of the Chancellor, about the year 1840, made a brief memorandum concerning Judge Van Ness, which has been preserved.

"Van Ness," wrote Judge Kent, "was then an enthusiastic Democrat. He attempted to convert, as he used to tell the story, Domine Gebhard, a venerable clergyman of his native village of Claverack, where for many years he preached orthodox doctrines in the Dutch tongue. Van Ness took to him Paine's 'Age of Reason,' which he presented with an eloquent harangue on the new era just commenced, and the departure of prejudices and superstitions and the downfall of kings, etc., etc. He used to say that he was something daunted, towards the close of his speech, by the cold, steady gaze of the clergyman, who listened in perfect silence. When the young republican had finished, he offered the book with a polite bow, to his clerical friend, who accepted it with equal grace and placed it immediately — behind the back log of his fire!

"There was no further attempt to convert the minister, and, on the contrary, for many long years afterwards, he had no more reverent attendant than Mr. Van Ness, in his little old brick church in Claverack-hill, which, within and without, in its quaint architecture and queer congregation, was such as Washington Irving loved to describe.

"Van Ness' democracy was somewhat shocked by the execution of Louis XVI., and it was converted into warm indignation at the French Revolution, when the horrid and unmanly murder of Marie Antoinette was perpetrated. He was not a man to pursue a cold medium in his feelings. He became an ardent Federalist, and remained one during the residue of his life."

VI

WITH the close of his third term in the Assembly of his State, Mr. Kent ended his active participation in political life. It can never with truth be said, however, that his ardor cooled, or that he did not follow to the last, with deep interest, the drift of political sentiment. His intense application, upon the lines of study which he had laid down for himself, and his active judicial work, left him scant leisure in which to engage in political discussion. Still, it was with marked interest that he watched the result of the presidential canvass in which Jefferson and Burr were the rival candidates during 1800–1.

As has been shown in his "Memoranda," he became, in early life, a Federalist by conviction, and a great admirer of the able writers of that party. Although Burr was the nominal Federal candidate, it was with feelings of concern that Mr. Kent watched the election, which might elevate him to the office of Chief Magistrate. In the electoral college, it will be remembered, Thomas Jefferson and Aaron Burr each received an equal number of votes, and the election, as a result, was thrown into the House of Representatives. The country at that time was not as now covered by a network of electric wires. Moreover, in many cases, presidential electors were not pledged to a particular party or candidate previous to their election. It therefore so came about that, in the middle of December, 1800, more than a month after the election of electors, the result was not definitely known. On the 17th of that month Judge Kent was addressed by Hon. Jonas Platt, a member of Congress from New York, as follows: —

Hon. Jonas Platt to James Kent.

December 17, 1800.

DEAR SIR, — Congress has as yet done so little as to afford no news for this manufactory. All the votes are known here except those of Kentucky and Tennessee ; in all the other states Jefferson and Burr have an equal number of votes, and but very little doubt exists but that they will come out even. The Jacos [Jacobins] tremble at this prospect and fear that the election may be altogether defeated, or what is much worse in their view, that little Aaron Burr will hold the reins over them. . . .

Upon the whole we are at this moment swallowing the last drop of the dregs of humiliation.

Hon. Jonas Platt to James Kent.

December 25, 1800.

Information is received which ascertains beyond all doubt that Jefferson and Burr have an equal number of votes. The Jacos are alarmed, and Federalists seem distracted with doubts. A great variety of projects are suggested by our friends, and the necessity of Federal unanimity is not fully estimated. I think I discover some symptoms of an ambition in two or three of our friends to be considered the leaders to whom the successful candidate is to owe his preferment.

There has yet been no caucus of the party generally ;

and some advise against it.   All seem to admit that the
choice between the two candidates rests with the Federal
party in the House.   Some suppose that stipulations ought
to be demanded before we declare our preference ; and
that agents should be appointed to manage the conference ;
others suppose such a measure dangerous and highly disgraceful to our party.   What think you of all this?

Mr. Platt, further writing in February, says : —

We have counted the votes and find them as was expected.[1]   The House of Representatives have balloted
seven times and the result has been invariably eight for
Jefferson, six for Burr, and two divided.   Our sitting is to
be perpetual till a choice.   Parties yet pretty temperate,
but obstinate.

Still later Mr. Platt writes : —

WASHINGTON, 11th February, 1801.
12 o'clock at night.

DEAR SIR, — We have just finished the 19th balloting
and the result still uniform.   Eight votes for Jefferson, six
for Burr, and two divided.   The suspense is awful, but the
conflict of passions not yet very violent.   We ballot regu-
larly at intervals of an hour.   Refreshments of every kind
are brought us, and how long the siege will last, or which
party will capitulate, is uncertain.

Two members are very sick abed in an adjoining room.
This scene would be ridiculous if it were not so important.
A stronger illustration of the absurdity of this part of the
Constitution could not possibly be given.   I presume it is
needless to tell you that New York divides six to four,
Maryland and Vermont equally divided.

[1] The statement of the votes, as enclosed in this letter, showed a
total of 276 electoral votes, of which Jefferson had 73; Burr, 73;
Adams, 65 ; C. C. Pinckney, 64; John Jay, 1.

Mr. Jefferson, as history records, was elected President on the thirty-sixth ballot. No written record exists by which it may be known what were Judge Kent's emotions in learning the final result of this long contest. As a Federalist, he regarded with abhorrence the political opinions of Jefferson, and the conduct of Burr in the Clinton affair, in 1792, had filled him with disgust. It is probable, therefore, that, although he was eager to learn the result at the earliest moment, he was not a very zealous partisan of either of the most prominent candidates.

In the spring of 1804 occurred that memorable gubernatorial canvass in New York, in which Burr was again a prominent candidate. It has already been shown[1] how, in all human probability, expressions of opinion as to Burr's fitness for the responsible position which he sought, which had passed between Alexander Hamilton and Judge Kent, were the cause of the memorable duel in which Hamilton lost his life, and Burr his reputation and the respect of mankind. Judge Kent's letter to his wife, written in the height of the contest, has an interest at this point:

Judge Kent to his Wife.

NEW YORK, April 26, 1804.

MY DEAR WIFE, — . . . The election is nearly over, and the Burrites are sanguine and appear flushed with the laurels of victory. They claim a decided majority in this city. The Federalists have been generally brought out. The cold reserve and indignant reproaches of Hamilton may have controlled a few, but they are but few. The passions of

---

[1] *Supra*, p. 33.

party have carried the generality of them along the turbu-
lent stream of the times.   Even Judge Benson has yielded
to the current, and with the generous fidelity of party spirit
has declared he will go with his party, and has voted for the
Burr ticket throughout.

I went out with General Hamilton on Saturday, the 21st,
and stayed till Sunday evening.   There was a furious and
dreadful storm on Saturday night.   It blew almost a hurri-
cane.   His house stands high and was very much exposed,
and I am certain that in the second story, where I slept, it
rocked like a cradle.   He never appeared before so friendly
and amiable.   I was alone, and he treated me with a minute
attention that I did not suppose he knew how to bestow.
His manners were also very delicate and chaste.   His
daughter, who is nineteen years old, has a very uncommon
simplicity and modesty of deportment, and he appeared in
his domestic state the plain, modest, and affectionate father
and husband.   Mr. Boyd came out and fetched me home,
and as I have adjourned business during the election, I have
kept pretty closely in Mr. Boyd's office studying my unfin-
ished cases.

I come back to my ruling passion, which is assuredly not
ambition or glory or avarice, but literary and elegant retirement and a glowing and vehement attachment to my wife
and children.

Despite his increased cares in his important judicial
office, Judge Kent not only did not abandon his habits
of systematic reading and study, but, on the contrary,
his position appeared to increase his ardor and thirst
for knowledge.   " It is only," he wrote to his brother
in 1799, " by becoming thoroughly master of Greek
and Roman learning, —

> ' Of all the ancient sages thought,
> The ancient bards sublimely taught,'—

and also a profound acquaintance with English classics and with the sages of the law, that a man can attain to distinction and dignity and impart to the mind all its energies and all its grandeur.   I am reading Tacitus and Erskine and Ferguson and the reviews, all in the course of the same day, and have made new and most fixed resolutions to pass thro' the vestibule and enter the venerable temple of learning."   For several years during this period, it was his habit to make, annually, a record of the works he had read during the year past.   These records always included extensive researches in the realm of jurisprudence, besides wide reading of Latin, French, and English authors.   In the year 1799, " after 1st of August," he notes that he read Tacitus and Juvenal, Mably's Le Droit Public de l'Europe, four volumes of Raynal, the New American Review for 1797, Gillies' View of the Reign of Frederick II. of Prussia, Pursuits of Literature, Robertson's Histories of North and South America, Ferguson's Roman Republic, Ulloa, nine volumes of European Magazine, beside several volumes of reviews.   In 1800 he read Horace in Latin, six volumes of Raynal and Voltaire's Peter the Great in French, and in English, twenty volumes European Magazine, Parker's Travels, Vaillant's Travels, the New American Review for 1798, the Asiatic Register for 1799, Lynne's Embassy, Bectron's Lippoa, four volumes Asiatic Researches, Bonaparte's Correspondence (in Egypt), Clymer's Narrative, Houta's Switzerland, Costera's Catherine II., and Coxe's Russia.

In 1801 his Latin and French reading was more extended.   He read Florus (Epitome de Gestis Romanorum), Sallust, Paterculus (Historiæ Romanæ), Juvenal, and Grotius' Mare Liberum. In the French he perused, according to his record, Vertot's Sculden, Bougeant's Westphalia, De Pauni's America, and two volumes Anacharsis (Barthélemy's Voyage du jeune Anacharsis en Grèce, 4 volumes, 1788). In English he read Coxe's Sweden, Swinburne, Mordaunt (Moore), The Nation, Roscoe's Lorenzo (William Roscoe, Life of Lorenzo de' Medici), Selden's Mare Clausum, Tooke's Russia, Garrick, by Murphy, and Clavigero's Mexico, besides a large number of volumes of magazines and reviews, and journals of Congress.

In 1802 he read Virgil, Eutropius, Lucian, and Juvenal. In French, parts of Gibbon (Mémoires Littéraires de la Grande Bretagne?), and the two remaining volumes of Anacharsis. In English, the record includes Hampton's Polybius, Melmoth's Pliny, Gibbon's Rome (twelve volumes), History of the Campaigns, McKenzie's Travels, Webster on Pestilence, Barrows' Travels, Billings' Voyages, Rennell's Memoir of the Geography of Africa, Gibbon's Miscellanies, Salmon's Rome, Gifford's Juvenal, and reviews and magazines innumerable.

"I have entered with indefatigable ardor," he writes to his brother in December, 1802, "on my course of studies, and am making great strides in the several books to which I am confined." And again, a year later: "I got home from New York much sooner than I expected, and I have brought home, as usual, a fresh supply of new books for my winter's amusement, and have entered on my studies with spirit and resolution." In 1804 he read Bacon,

Sparks' Washington, Shakespeare, and Boswell's Johnson, besides legal writings in French and English, and Horace, Cicero de Officiis, and Sallust. In 1805 he records among his readings Cicero de Legibus, Livy, and Juvenal again. In English, he read Stewart's Philosophy, Gillies' translation of Aristotle, Pinkerton's Geography, Elements of Criticism, and Drake's Literary Hour. In 1806 he took up Horace once more, and read the Georgics of Virgil; in English, Roscoe's Leo X., Cumberland's Life, The Secret History of St. Cloud, Jackson on Commerce, and several volumes of the Edinburgh Review.

In July of this year he refers to these readings in a letter to his brother: "I have got hold of and am reading some of the latest publications; as, Roscoe's Leo X., in four volumes, a present from Elisha Kane; Cumberland's Memoirs, Life of Lord Nelson, and Secret Anecdotes of the Court at St. Cloud."

During this period scarcely a letter out of the many written to his brother fails to contain some reference to his reading and studies. "I have laid out above $100 in books, and my library of course progresses in knowledge and value," he writes after his return from a stay in New York. And again: "I have just finished the fifth and last volume of Washington's Life, and it is worth all the rest. It is an excellent history of the government and parties in this country from 1783 to the death of the General. There are few other works which are new that I have purchased, except some law-books."

In August, 1807, during one of the brief periodical

absences of his wife from home, he writes to her one of those sparkling letters which must have been so welcome to the absent one : —

Judge Kent to his Wife.

On Wednesday I had two old bachelors to dine with me, Mr. Johnson and Captain Benson ; and my present situation is very much in the same gloomy and forlorn state, or partaking of the same aspect. We formed a plain and grave society. In the afternoon Graham took Will and me out in his carriage to Whitehall ; and there I found the young collection of Misses who had walked out at six in the morning and had a very romping day. We sat down, a large party, to a grand tea-table loaded with boiled corn. In the evening Judge Sedgwick smoked his segar here, and railed in company with me at modern degeneracy, and sighed over the ruins of ancient virtue. Yesterday morning was very rainy ; and while I had risen early and walked the room a little, and got just prepared for a fine intellectual feast on one of my new French books, who should knock but General North, who said he came to breakfast and to stay till the rain was over. Away went in an instant the brightness of the vision, and down I sat to stale chat, and with mortified resignation at the loss of a day. But fortunately, after breakfast the sun broke out, and I was left to pursue my career. My library has at present prodigious charms and incomprehensible interest. I pore over it all the day long, and enjoy the hard study and spare diet which many a wife has disliked as well as Milton's. This morning I also rose very early to seek for peaches for the children. Be assured I take excellent care of them. We go to bed early. The chamber is rather solitary. It wants the inspiring presence of my wife ; but still it is neat, clean, and quiet, and I enjoy the gentle slumbers of a temperate and honest student.

During the whole period of his life Mr. Kent made many, and for the time very extensive, tours throughout the Eastern States and Canada. These tours he usually made in the ordinary public conveyances of the day,— either coach or post-chaise,— and at times in his own wagon, or " chair." He was frequently accompanied by his wife, and, in later life, perhaps by one of his daughters. The record of each of these tours was faithfully kept, but they are for the most part dry, and devoid of those details which usually make the tales of a traveller such pleasant reading. He seems, unfortunately, to have neglected to note little incidents of the trip which cast their bright light on the ordinary details of life, and to have contented himself with the bold and practical description of the wood and fields and villages which he traversed; which has rendered these journals rather fitted for a descriptive geography than a miscellaneous biography.

Among Chancellor Kent's journals and memoranda is discovered a minute concerning his travels. " While I resided at Poughkeepsie," he records, " I began first to make my travelling excursions, which in after life contributed so largely to my health and delight. The first trip that I made with my wife was in August, 1788, to New York and to the fishing banks. We went from Poughkeepsie in a sloop, and together with General Bailey and General Hughes and their wives we went from New York to Sandy Hook in a sloop, and say ten miles at sea, and landed and wandered about the sands at the lighthouse, and then we returned and went from New York to Rockaway, and were highly delighted with the spectacle of the ocean.

In July, 1791, I went alone on horseback to Troy, and then, with my dear old father, we crossed over to Waterford, and kept up on the west side of the Mohawk to Schenectady, and on to Canajoharie, where we visited the Kanes and my brother. The next day they joined us, and we proceeded up the Mohawk to Whitestown and lodged. We swam our horses over the Mohawk at Utica, then called Old Fort Schuyler. There we saw Elias Kane and his new store, and Peter Smith, a young grocer, in a shanty, who turned out to be afterwards the very wealthy Peter Smith, father of Gerrit Smith, the great and fanatical abolitionist. The father was a plain and interesting young man. Jonas Platt had just settled with his young wife at Whitestown, and he went with us to Fort Stanwix, now Rome. The road was through the woods to the old fort, all then standing in naked desolation. We saw in the woods, at Oriskany, the vestiges of the battle in 1777, when General Herkimer was killed. The road on the Mohawk below the German Flatts, up to which the old settlements had reached, led through the Mohawk Flatts, covered with peas, oats, wheat, and corn, which seemed to me to be a perfect paradise. The Plains of Campagna Felice never surpassed them in luxuriance and beauty.

"The next journey was in September, 1792, with my wife, in a new gig and horse, — which I had made out, after two years' effort, to purchase, — up the Hudson to Albany, and up the Mohawk to Canajoharie, and then over the hills to, now, Sharon and Springfield, to my brother's store and ashery [potash works],

for he then had become a country merchant, and there
we lodged surrounded by the tall maples and beeches.
The next day we went to the head of Otsego Lake and
got rowed through it nine miles to infant Cooperstown,
where we lodged.   This was the *ne plus ultra* of our
tour.   No European jaunt could have charmed us
more, though it might infinitely have instructed us.
On this tour we stayed with T. V. W. Graham, Esq.,
of Albany, a cousin of Mrs. Kent, and a prosperous
young lawyer.   We went to Waterford and visited
the Cohoes with Mrs. Davies, the mother of Henry
Davies, the lawyer.   On our return to Albany we
visited Peter Van Schaack, at Kinderhook, and my
Federal essays and zeal in favor of Mr. Jay's election
procured me a warm reception and compliments.
I was become quite famous by my various little productions and political declamations in the village
print at Poughkeepsie; so much so that in one of
Fenno's Gazettes at Philadelphia, he extracted one,
and by preface said, 'An elegant writer in a Poughkeepsie Journal of the 2d inst., whose productions
we conjecture have before contributed to the entertainment of our readers,' etc., etc.   I have now in my
garret Fenno's Gazettes in several volumes, bound.
They were the 'National Intelligencer' of that day.

"Mr. Van Schaack entertained us at Kinderhook
most kindly, and we admired his charming Dutch
wife.   He was as full of Mr. Jay's election and the
abomination of the seven canvassers as I was, and
was besides delightful by his anecdotes, and classic
and poetical quotations, and keen and polished criticisms, and apposite allusions."

The first extended journey which Mr. Kent made
was to Fort Stanwix and Wood Creek. Upon the
manuscript record of this journey he made this memorandum: "My dear father accompanied me, and my
brother also, in part west of Canajoharie." Wood
Creek, he explains, is about one mile west of Fort
Stanwix, and Fort Stanwix one hundred and twelve
miles west of Albany, at the head of the navigation
of the Mohawk River. The journey was performed,
for the most part, by water up the Mohawk. At
times he would leave the river and take short journeys
into the country, observing the condition of the soil,
the luxuriance of the crops, and the habits and manners of the people.

In 1794 the journey was to New Utrecht, Long
Island. On this journey he was accompanied by Mrs.
Kent and two gentlemen. The interest was chiefly
centered on a newly erected bath-house, — or, as it
would be called in this day, club-house, — erected by a
company of subscribers, including some of the personal friends of the party. Here a stop was made for
a day, the party obtaining excellent accommodations
at reasonable rates. After a visit at Flatbush, the
return home was quickly made.

The next year a journey, which had long been
planned, was made to Lake Champlain. Ticonderoga
and Crown Point and the islands of the lake were visited; after which the journey was extended to Mon-
treal. Again, in 1797, Mr. Kent, accompanied by his
wife, made an extended tour through the Eastern
States. The route lay by packet to Newport, thence
to Providence and Boston, in both of which cities

short visits were made.   It is to be regretted that his
notes concerning these important Eastern cities are so
meagre.   His interest, however, would seem to have
been centered mainly upon the agricultural regions
of the East, and the people who inhabited them.
From Boston the journey was continued, much of the
way by post chaise or private conveyance, through
a portion of New Hampshire and the valley of the
Connecticut.   Visits were made at Springfield, North-
field, and Hadley, whence the course was taken south-
ward to Hartford and New Haven, and thence to New
York.

Two years later, with his wife, Judge Kent made a
brief trip to Newburgh, which he describes in his
memorandum as " enchantingly pleasant."   " The
sum of the happiness of human life," he notes, " as
Dr. Johnson has sagely remarked, is made up of petty
incidents and trifling circumstances."   A passage in
this memorandum is interesting, as illustrating Judge
Kent's powers of description.   " The river is here a
mile and a half wide," he writes.   " The water was
smooth, the radiance of the western sky mild and
beautiful; and shortly after we had entered on the
river the full moon just appeared, rising over the top
of the Fishkill Mountains and tingeing the feathered
clouds around her.   The evening had already cast
too deep and brown a shade for us to perceive objects distinctly at a distance; but the grandeur of
the river, the town of Newburgh on the western
bank, and the solemnity of the mountain view to
the south rendered the scene as interesting as it was
transient.   After landing at Newburgh we walked on

the new Windsor Road for a mile and a half to Mr.
Boyd's. It was a walk peculiarly impressive. The
moon shone clear, but the road and place of desti-
nation were to us new and unknown, and conspired
to give anxiety and interest to the walk. We descended down a long hill to Chamber's Creek. The
valley was deep and long, and covered with woods.
It rung with the serious music of the katydid, and it
left an avenue open to the east just sufficient for to
throw the eye on the Hudson. After having passed
the valley with spirit and intrepidity, and ascended the
opposite hill perfectly safe and sound from any as-
saults from dogs or fiercer men, or any startling spec-
ters of the night, or of the imagination, we found the
snug and happy dwelling of Mr. Boyd, and a cordial
and friendly reception. The landscape around him
was very fine. It was at once rural and rugged and
sublime. To the north you heard at a little distance
the murmur and falls of the Chamber's Creek deeply
sheltered from the view. To the west, at the distance
of a couple of miles, there arose a solitary and rocky
and bald-featured hill. To the east you had a glimpse
of the Hudson through the aperture of the hills we
had just traversed, and beyond the river to the east
and to the south the sight was bounded by the Highlands, a range of grand and lofty mountains.

"We were awakened in the morning of Saturday,
September 14, by the lightning and thunder of a cloud
in the west. It hung round the western horizon from
daybreak till 8 o'clock, and it then came over in a
most awful and majestic manner. A gloomy scud
rapidly preceded it and crossed the river to the east

and skirted the mountains. The effulgence of the eastern sky was suddenly darkened, the summit of the mountains appeared towering above the scud for a few minutes, and gave the scene inexpressible grandeur. I never saw anything to be compared to the awe and sublimity of the view. But the atmosphere was too soon filled by the tempest. The shower became furious and threatening, with the incessant flashes of lightning and roar of the thunder. It lasted about half an hour; and the lightning destroyed a barn full of wheat, on the eastern side of the river against Newburgh."

In the summer of 1802 it fell to Judge Kent's lot to ride the Great Western Circuit, which included a journey of some six hundred or seven hundred miles, to be performed in the roughest and most uncultivated portion of the State, and, as it was then thought to be, upon the limits of civilization. That this trip should have been performed without incident or unpleasant adventure argues well for the tranquillity of the country. Incidentally he made a trip to Niagara Falls, then but rarely visited from the Eastern States, which made a great impression on his imagination.

Judge Kent, in his memorandum made of this journey, thus describes the Falls and his emotions at beholding them: —

"The sheet was a deep green, due to the great thickness of the column. The spray, the cloud of vapor, the roar, the violent swiftness, foam, abrupt and broken waves, and terrible concussion and reverberation of the water below the abyss, overwhelmed us with astonishment mingled with terror. We proceeded to the edge of the falling column, and no far-

ther is it in the power of man to go.   The dark abyss
behind the column cannot be penetrated, and if it
could, the violence of the wind and tempest would
destroy all power of breathing.   I am satisfied it
never was or will be penetrated.   I stopped short of
the *ne plus ultra*, and terror at last overpowered in me
every other sensation.   I also almost trod on a rattlesnake, coiled up before me, which added mightily to
my apprehension of danger.   I passed under the
Table Rock, which projects over from the top of the
enormous precipice in a most threatening position.
I went on until I saw a little Table Rock and several
other large shelving rocks hanging in the air over my
head at an enormous height.   The large and broken
fragments of the falling rocks, which are almost daily
crumbling off, lay all around me with marks of very
recent fall.

" The rain beat vehemently on me, the sides of the
stony mountains where I stood were extremely slip-
pery, the thunder of the waters drowned every other
noise and almost overpowered the senses.   The un-
fathomable abyss into which the river precipitates,
and from which it rushes with convulsive foam and
impetuosity lay before me.   I felt no remaining impression but terror and awe, and I turned back to a
place of less danger, and where pleasure would revive.
I cannot compare the scene below the Falls to anything
in nature, nor do I believe such another scene exists.
How poor, feeble, and insignificant a creature is man,
placed at the foot of such sublime and terror-inspiring
scenes, such application of incalculable powers in
nature.   All other objects dwindle into comparative in-

significance.   The scene sets all comparison, all rivalship at defiance.   It is, in one word, the most awful
and sublime of the wonderful works of nature."

Under the date of October 2, 1807, is found a
memorandum which is of peculiar interest.   Heretofore the journeys made by Mr. Kent, by water, had
been made in packet vessels; but on this date he
records his first experience in travelling by means
of steam.   In August, 1807, the first steamboat
employed in regular service in this country, the
"Clermont," was put upon the route between New
York and Albany, on the Hudson River.   Two
months later than this event he writes from New
York to his brother: —

I went up as far as Hudson in the steamboat in precisely
five hours, and I was charmed with it.   It goes up and down
the river twice a week, and went off on Wednesday from here
with sixty passengers, and will bring up to-morrow a case of
fresh fish.   This boat is all the rage here.   The new market
is in operation in my street, and the old one is pulled down.
This makes it very lively, and we think very pleasant, before
our door.   The steamboat station is at the dock at the
bottom of my street.

VII

IN such a wise the life of James Kent passed, until in it a new era dawned.   It was in 1798 that he became a judge of the Supreme Court.   In the capacity, first of justice, and later of chief-justice, he passed sixteen years, and to him, happy years.   His ambition to reach a judicial position was amply gratified. His means, although not great, were ample for the comfortable support of his family and for the gratification of his desire for the accumulation of books.   The wife of his youth was the companion of his middle years, and his domestic life was to him a constant source of delight and satisfaction.   In February, 1814, he was transferred to the Court of Chancery, and appointed Chancellor.   His commission to this exalted office bears date of February 24, 1814, and the signature of Daniel D. Tompkins, Governor.   The circumstances attending his entrance upon this important position, and his method of conducting his office, are best told in his own words.   In his letter to Thomas Washington, written in 1828, from which epistle copious extracts have already been made, he says : —

"In 1814 I was appointed Chancellor.   The office I took with considerable reluctance.   It had no charms. The person who left it was stupid, and it is a curious fact that for the nine years I was in that office there was not a single decision, opinion, or dictum of either of my two predecessors (Ch. Livingston and Ch. Lansing), from 1777 to 1814, cited to me or even suggested. I took the court as if it had been a new institution, and never before known in the United States. I had nothing to guide me, and was left at liberty to assume all such English Chancery powers and jurisdiction as I thought applicable under our Constitution. This gave me grand scope, and I was checked only by the revision of the Senate, or Court of Errors. I opened the gates of the court immediately, and admitted, almost gratuitously, the first year, eighty-five counsellors, though I found there had not been thirteen admitted for thirteen years before. Business flowed in with a rapid tide. The result appears in the seven volumes of Johnson's Chancery Reports.

" My course of study in equity jurisprudence was very much confined to the topics elicited by the cases. I had previously, of course, the modern equity reports down to that time, and, of course, I read all the new ones as fast as I could procure them. I remember reading Peere Williams as early as 1792, and made a digest of the leading doctrines. The business of the Court of Chancery oppressed me very much, but I took my daily exercise and my delightful rides among the Catskill or the Vermont Mountains, with my wife, and kept up my health and spirits. I always took up the cases in their order, and never left one until I had finished it. This was only doing one thing at a time.

" My practice was, first, to make myself perfectly and accurately (mathematically accurately) master of

the facts.   It was done by abridging the bill, and then
the answers, and then the depositions, and by the time
I had done this slow and tedious process, I was master
of the cause and ready to decide it. I saw where
justice lay, and the moral sense decided the court
half the time; and I then sat down to search the
authorities until I had examined my books. I might
once in a while be embarrassed by a technical rule,
but I most always found principles suited to my
views of the case; my object was so to discuss a
point as never to be teased with it again, and to anticipate an angry and vexatious appeal to a popular
tribunal by disappointed counsel.

" During these years at Albany I read a great deal
of English literature, but not with the discipline of my
former division of time.   The avocations of business
would not permit it.   I had dropped the Greek, as it
hurt my eyes; I persevered in Latin, and used to read
Virgil, Horace, Juvenal, Lucian, Sallust, Tacitus, and
Cicero's Offices, and some of them annually.   I have
read Juvenal, Horace, and Virgil eight or ten times.
I read the Edinburgh and Quarterly Reviews and
American Registers *ab initio* and thoroughly, and
voyages and travels and the Waverley novels, etc., etc.,
as other folks do.   I have always been excessively
fond of voyages and travels."

It has been the intent, in the preparation of this
work, to display to the mind of the reader Kent the
man, rather than Kent the lawyer and judge. Of the
character of this man, in his professional capacity,
the volumes of his " Commentaries," and the voluminous Chancery Reports are, in themselves, an ample

exposition. Since, however, the personal intimacy
of Judge Kent with Alexander Hamilton has been so
fully shown forth, and the undoubted connection has
been disclosed which existed between certain utter-
ances of Judge Kent and the memorable duel on the
banks of the Hudson, in the summer of 1804, one of
the opinions rendered by Chancellor Kent is deserving
of notice in his biography.   In 1816, four years after
the death of Alexander Hamilton and probably inspired by that event, the Assembly of the State of
New York passed an act to suppress duelling.   By the
provisions of this act every person elected or appointed
to any public office in the State was obliged to incorporate in his official oath the engagement that he had
not taken part in a duel during the year just past, and
that he would not do so in the future.   The act came
up before the Council of Revision, that its constitu-
tionality might be passed upon by that tribunal.   The
Council at that time consisted of the Governor, Mr.
Chancellor Kent, Mr. Chief-Justice Thompson, Judges
Spencer, Van Ness, Yates, and Platt.   Although the
Chancellor did not succeed in bringing the majority
of the Council over to his views, the opinion is of
interest, since he unquestionably sacrificed his own
personal feelings and opinions, upon the question of
duelling in the abstract, to what he regarded as the
principle of constitutional liberty.   The opinion here
follows : —

"The Chancellor, to whom was committed the bill
entitled An Act to Suppress Duelling, reports that
the bill is inconsistent with the spirit of the Constitu-

tion and the public good, and ought not to become a law : — Because,

" By the second section of the bill every person to be elected a member of the Senate or Assembly, or to be elected or appointed to any office, civil or military, except town officers, and every person to be admitted a counsellor, attorney, or solicitor of any court, shall in addition to the oaths now prescribed by law, take an oath or affirmation that he has not been engaged or concerned in a duel since the first day of July, now last past or next hereafter, as the construction may be, nor will be so concerned during the continuance of the act and while an inhabitant of this State.

" This provision establishes a test, or qualification for office, unknown to the Constitution, dangerous as a precedent, and inconsistent with the principles of liberty.

" It cannot be necessary for the Council to declare that they solemnly bear testimony against the practice of duelling, as being cruel and wicked and equally condemned by the law of the land and by the just and benevolent precepts of Christianity. To take life in this way is murder by the common law, whether he that gave or he that accepted the challenge falls. And if conviction and punishment have not duly followed the crime, it has not been the fault of the law, nor of the judges by whom it was pronounced.

" But to whatever cause we may impute the feeble execution (as the bill evidently supposes) of the existing laws on this subject, there is no occasion that will warrant the introduction of unsound principles of legislation.

" Test oaths as a qualification for public trusts, other than the oath of allegiance and the usual oath of office, are inconsistent with the letter and spirit of American institutions. In some instances there is an express declaration against them. The requisition in the present case is not founded on any religious test, but is equally tyrannical; for it requires every man, before he can enjoy or receive any public trust, to acquit himself upon oath of a particular crime, without being legally accused of it, and when he stands innocent under the intendment of the law. The bill in this respect reverses the maxim of the common law and presumes every man guilty.

"With equal right, if not with equal reason, he might be compelled to clear himself of every other crime, without being put to answer by indictment or presentment, and without the privilege of an appeal to his peers. It is dangerous to admit a principle so destructive of civil liberty into the code of our statute law. A most terrible inquisition might thus be created over the consciences of men.

" The penalty of refusal to answer is not indeed in this case the rack, or the stake, but it is extremely severe, being no less than a disqualification to hold any place of honor, profit, or trust, or even to exercise one of the learned professions.

" Duelling does not appear to be so grievous a public evil, nor does it usually denote such a depravity of moral principle, as other examples of murder, and as arson, rape, forgery, and various kinds of larceny, swindling, and fraud. It often proceeds from a lofty and scrupulous, but misguided, sense of reputation. Why may not, then, other offences, and all other immoral acts, be brought to the same test and checked by the same means?

" Times may hereafter arise when an undue zeal for reform, or a fierce and intolerant fanaticism, might be easily led to proceed from crime to crime, and from one misdemeanor to another, with the same potent remedy, until every man is obliged to renounce his civil privilege or swear to the purity of his whole life.

" The bill extends this oath to attorneys-at-law, before they can be permitted to practice; but it is not extended to candidates for the other learned professions, though the same reason would seem to apply, and though the admission of physicians and surgeons is equally the subject of legislative regulation. The bill, therefore, is not impartial in the imposition which it creates. If the principle be just, it ought to have a general and equal application. It ought to be extended not only to candidates for office, but to every man who offers himself to vote, and especially to jurors, who are concerned in the administration of justice.

" The latter part of the oath is equally new and repugnant to sound principles of government. The oath hitherto imposed upon a person entering into a public trust is the ordinary oath of office, importing that they will execute their trust faithfully, and importing nothing more; and when the trust ceases, the obligation of the oath also expires. But the oath in this case is that they will refrain from a particular crime, having no special relation to their office, not only while in office, but during the continuance of the act, and while inhabitants of this State.

"This is binding by a religious solemnity, and
for life, one class of citizens, to the exclusion of the
rest, and in their private as well as public capacity,
to obey a law equally applicable to all the community.
There is no reason why the oath should apply to them
when they become private citizens any more than to
the rest of the people. It is also very questionable
whether it be wise or expedient to bind private citizens by oath to obey any particular law that is of
public and permanent concern.

"The impression of an oath is apt to be weakened
in proportion as it is less special in its object and less
immediate in its application. The civil obligation to
obey the law is the same without as with the oath;
and to call in the aid of religion, to the support of a
single case in the penal code, may impair the force
and sense of obligation to general obedience.

"This extraordinary sanction may as well be applied to every as to any public law; and the effect of
such a provision upon the efficiency of oaths and the
consciences of those who take them would, as we
fear, be exceedingly injurious. It is no doubt the
duty of the law-giver to provide suitable penalties for
the violation of every law; but we apprehend that
there is no instance to be met with in the ordinary
course of civil government in which the citizens were
called on to bind themselves by oath to the perpetual
observance of any public law.

"All that is precious and valuable in society depends upon the credit of testimony upon oath, and
every measure that diminishes the reverence or im-
pairs the confidence due to that great sanction to
truth is most deeply to be deplored."

The objections being read and considered, the bill passed notwithstanding; the Governor, Ch. J. Thompson, Judges Van Ness and Yates voting for it, and Chancellor Kent, Judges Spencer and Platt against it.

The Chancellor's reverence for the great principle of constitutional liberty is further illustrated by an anecdote which has been handed down in family tradition. It is currently reported in the family history that when waited upon by a temperance committee and urged to give his authority and sanction to the principles and aims of a mass meeting by adding his name to the list of those who had pledged themselves not to use intoxicating liquor, being unduly pressed after his first polite negative, he made the following reply, declining the request: " Gentlemen, I refuse to sign any pledge. I never have been drunk, and, by the blessing of God, I never will get drunk, but I have a constitutional privilege to get drunk, and that privilege I will not sign away."

Judge Kent was fifty-one years of age when he took his seat as Chancellor. As has been detailed in his " Memoranda," he was extremely reluctant to accept the office. This reluctance arose from two sources: first, because the seat on the Chancery Bench appeared anything but attractive on account of the little influence which the former chancellors had wielded, and the moribund condition of the court; but principally because he had found Albany the seat of intense party strife. The surge of " Jacobinism " which had swept over the country, and under the leadership of Madison had plunged the United States into war with England, had made him weary of judicial life. There is no mistaking Judge Kent's views on this subject, for as early as April 28, 1809, he writes to his brother: —

James Kent to Moss Kent.

April 28, 1809.

The pacification with England is a very propitious event for the United States and for England, and I think that both Governments have come off with honor, and that England has seized the occasion with address and placed us with regard to France just where she wants us.

Few and brief are the allusions which he makes to the war.

In a letter to his brother, November 10, 1812, he says: —

I am not very anxious about the election of Clinton, though upon the whole I wish it, but more out of detestation of Madison's war conduct than confidence in Clinton's wish for peace. It is the election for the next House of Representatives on which I repose my most anxious hopes.

In July, 1813, he again writes to his brother, then a congressman at Washington: —

Judge Kent to Moss Kent.

July 14, 1813.

Our military operations on the Canadian quarter go on very much to my mind. Mr. Gaston's speech is admirable in every respect, and the argument of the Federalists on Webster's resolution is most triumphant and unanswerable. Be assured I sympathize completely in all the feelings that are excited against the abominable war of Madison, and which will more and more fail in its object, for it grows daily more and more unpopular and feeble. It is as contemptible as it is wicked.

Again, the same year, he writes to the same correspondent : —

Judge Kent to Moss Kent.

December 24, 1813.

The prospect of our affairs is chilling. I see no ground for hope, for we never can expect peace so long as the men reign over us who have such deadly malice towards England. May God in his infinite mercy grant speedy and rapid and decisive success to the arms of the allies in every direction. If Bonaparte is down, our government will relax into moderation and justice, but not before.

Again, in April, 1814, he writes to his brother-in-law, Hon. Theodorus Bailey : —

Albany was never so extravagantly expensive to live in, nor never so thronged with people as it has been this winter, and probably never will be again for many years. I have no doubt we shall have peace this summer. Not a bill has passed, in any shape whatever, not a paragraph in any law, that looks like aid or approbation of the war.

That Chancellor Kent's views upon the war were not shared by many of his intimate friends cannot be doubted. Perhaps it may be that Judge Van Ness, knowing the Chancellor's opinions, took some enjoyment in bringing before his eyes the action of the contending armies, as appears in the following letter : —

Judge Van Ness to Judge Kent.

CLAVERACK, December 8, 1813.

DEAR SIR, — I congratulate you on the glorious achievements of our armies in nether Canada. We have not been quite as successful as could be wished, to be sure, but our Joshua has been as far as the Jordan and looked upon the land flowing with milk and honey. You and I must pray that like old Joshua, he may not be doomed never to eat it. So far, so good. Another year and things may work better still! Madison and his brethren have only ordered a " curia ad vult ; " they will make John Bull hop next year.

The cursed allies, too, had the impudence not to suffer the great champion for the liberties of the sea to advance an inch; nay, it is said they even had the insolence to chastise some of his soldiers who have quartered upon his territory. Indeed, some accounts in the newspapers go so far as to say that several French generals have actually been taken by these barbarous allies. This, though merely said in the newspapers, of course is but a humbug. That perfect cannibal of an Englishman, one Wellington, too, has been so outrageously uncivil as to drive the French out of Spain. When Bony catches him, what an awful hiding he will give this Wellington !

An anecdote is recorded of Chancellor Kent, which strikingly illustrates the abomination in which he held those statesmen who, in his estimation, had plunged this country into an unholy war with England. It was upon the occasion of the passage of the Erie Canal Bill, by the New York Senate, in 1817. Although the bill had passed that body, it was yet to pass the ordeal of criticism by the Council of Revision. Of this council Lieutenant-Governor Taylor

was president, an earnest and formidable opponent
of the measure.   There were present, besides President Taylor and the Chancellor, Chief-Justice Smith
Thompson, Judge Jonas Platt, and Judge Joseph C.
Yates, afterward Governor of New York.   The bill
was solemnly discussed in all its bearings, and its fate
hung trembling in the balance.   Indeed, it seemed
already lost, for the members of the Council
present were equally divided in opinion upon the
measure.   The Chief-Justice held that the bill gave
arbitrary rights and powers to the commissioners,
transcending private rights, without sufficient provisions and guards.   The Chancellor, always conservative toward what seems to him innovations upon
long established custom, felt that it was a gigantic
project which was proposed, and one which would
require the wealth of the whole United States to ac-
complish.   He thought it inexpedient to commit the
State to so great an undertaking, until public opinion
should be more fully crystallized.   Judges Platt and
Yates were favorable to the bill; the casting vote was
thus in the hands of Taylor, and he was awaiting
with the greatest eagerness the moment when he
might exercise it, to the destruction of the measure.
At the critical moment Vice-President Tompkins
entered the Council Chamber, and, seating himself,
began to discuss the bill.   It was at once evident that
he was opposed to its final passage.   " The late peace
with Great Britain," he said, " was a mere truce, and
the credit and resources of the State should be employed, not in great civil works like this, but in preparing for war."

Chancellor Kent was instantly interested and alert. "Do you think so?" he demanded, earnestly.

"I certainly do," was the reply. "England never forgave us our victories, and, my word for it, we shall have another war within two years."

The Chancellor was instantly ablaze. Springing to his feet he exclaimed, with the utmost vigor and animation, —

"Then if we must have a war, or have a canal, I am in favor of the canal! I vote for the bill!"

The die was cast. The man who was so earnestly desirous of defeating the bill had over-reached himself and, by the means designed to defeat it, had furnished the one argument needed for its passage; and the bill for the building of the Erie Canal became a law.

As has been outlined, Judge Kent watched with eager attention the political convulsions which had been devastating Europe, and prostrating the nations of the world at the feet of the French conqueror. The best attainable maps of Europe were bought and still form a part of his library. Over these, pen in hand, he pored with close attention, tracing out the march of the armies and indicating the position of troops engaged in the great battles, with untiring interest and wonderful accuracy. Many manuscript volumes, still preserved, show the care and attention with which he studied the scanty news of the day. News from Europe traveled very slowly, — painfully slowly, it would seem to us at this time. The news by packet was never less than sixty days and frequently many months old, this delay being caused by the irregularity of the methods of communication. Nothing of importance escaped his eye, even at a time when he was immersed in business and striving to plant his foot firmly upon the first round of the judicial ladder.

As early as September, 1790, when he had first entered upon political life as Assembly-man from Dutchess County, he wrote to his brother, on the receipt of an unusually interesting mass of European intelligence : —

James Kent to Moss Kent.

September 23, 1790.

. . . We have been attentive here of late to the interesting intelligence from Europe. Events and revolutions proceed there with such rapid succession that we have hardly leisure to contemplate one before we are called to another. A few years ago the American world was convulsed, and Europe was gazing on with anxiety and surprise. The scene is reversed, and, thank God, we are safely sheltered under a fabric from whence we may securely listen to the storm at a distance. The flight of the French king you have fully understood. What the French will do with Royalty is a problem we have not as yet the light sufficient to solve. The new Constitution of Poland is published, and exhibits symmetry and wisdom. I suppose you have not seen it. It is published in the New York papers and in Fenno. It is an immense work, considering the previous slavery and wretchedness of Poland, and their king has the deserved reputation of a sage and a patriot. Our last news is of the British mobs, which has not yet reached you. A mob of Birmingham has made great destruction, and behaved, as all mobs do, with ferocity and cruelty. . . .

Two years later he again displays his deep interest in the Polish situation and affairs in France.

Judge Kent to Moss Kent.

October 15, 1792.

. . . The total prostration of the new Constitution of Poland by the imperious hand of Catherine, and the violent breach in that of the French by their Jacobin Clubs and frantic populace, are events in the world of European news which must excite alternate alarm, sympathy, and indignation in the hearts of American republicans. The miserable Poles have fallen without the least disgraceful imputation, but the French have to answer to the world and their posterity for many a seditious debate and many a sanguinary council. The Marquis Fayette was ordered to be arrested, and was taken by the Austrians in attempting to escape (as it is supposed) to England or America. Our politicians generally conclude the king will be murdered now he is dethroned, and that the Duke of Brunswick will make his way to Paris; but if he does he must make his way through slaughter and desolation. What will become of that unhappy people, it is the province alone of awful futurity to unfold. How much ought we to prize and cling fast to the pillars of our free and excellent national government at home. These considerations make me reprobate so much Jeffersonian politics, and make me also averse to innovations on the form, even, of our State Constitution to correct the abuses of its administration. If we have not resignation enough to preserve our government amid the present shocks of party, how can our republics uphold themselves for a series of ages?

Mr. Kent's comments upon the conduct of affairs abroad, and especially upon Bonaparte's attempted conquest of Europe, are exceedingly vivid and valuable, as the thoughts of an onlooker in one of the great historic periods of the world.

Judge Kent to Moss Kent.

September 25, 1793.

The President's proclamation has received the decided sanction of the Union, and the Jacobin intrigues of the French minister have been generally resented. But I believe the feelings of this country are, as they ought to be, strongly in favor of the French. Russia, Prussia, Austria, Holland, England, Spain, and Portugal are all in league against one single power, and most of them avowedly because France has established a popular government. So powerful a league is without example. The French have made and published their new Constitution; its ratification is referred to the primary Assemblies, and the 10th of August fixed for the final decision. I have no doubt it is adopted. It will have a tendency to unite the French. It will be a standard to rally around, and I hope will dissipate their shameful factions. The Constitution is a departure from what we deem in this country sacred axioms of good government. There is no permanency in their judicial, or unity in their executive, no check or division in their legislature. Be it as it may, if it unites them it will be most useful. Hereafter they can ameliorate and correct it. Condé in French Flanders has taken Valenciennes; a most formidable garrison still holds out, and I conclude will not be taken this campaign. . . .

Judge Kent to Moss Kent.

NEW YORK, August 3, 1795.

. . . The news this day circulated in the prints is that Luxembourg is taken by the French with 10,000 prisoners, that the Dauphin, or son of Louis XVI. is dead, and that the great city of Copenhagen, containing, as Cox says, 80,000 souls, is almost in ashes by means of a dreadful fire. Every vessel brings a tale of woe from Europe and from the West Indies. We are happy if demagogues do not blind the public judgment and dupe the public passion about Mr. Jay's treaty, and throw us into confusion. It is strange we have no authentic account whether or no the President has ratified it.

Judge Kent to Moss Kent.

September 19, 1796.

. . . The foreign news is very interesting. The rapid progress of the French arms, their obstinate battles, and the terrible havoc on both sides, in the armies on the Rhine, are enough to arouse the attention of all mankind. Europe is now more seriously threatened with universal conquest and domination than any time before since the date of the Roman Empire. The French Republic has become a military one, and their mighty hordes of veteran and enthusiastic troops, under the guidance of consummate generals and resolute, imperious, and ambitious councils, threaten to lay prostrate all the nations around them. You will see by the last paper the commanding attitudes they are in, and their insults to Switzerland, Tuscany, Genoa, and other neutral nations. They seem determined to crush Great Britain under the weight of all Europe. The British Navy seems, however, to present an insurmountable barrier to their ambitious projects. God grant that French armies and British fleets may communicate so much awe and moderation to each other as to check all undue pre-eminence of either, and save other nations from the exactions and insolence of both.

Judge Kent to Moss Kent.

POUGHKEEPSIE, May 11, 1799.

You may prepare yourself to be amused (if scenes of devastation and revolution can indeed amuse), during the summer, with hard-fought battles and rapid conquests in Germany; for I perceive the French have begun an active campaign, and I fear they will revolutionize, which is the same thing as prostrating, Austria, Turkey, Spain, and Portugal, before they terminate the campaign. I forebode dreadful ill to Europe, and dreadful successes to the barbarians of France.

Judge Kent to Moss Kent.

July 16, 1799.

We seem this day to have pretty authentic news that the Brest fleet has joined the Spanish, and gone into the Mediterranean, and surely fierce Bellona will crimson the sea with rivers of human blood.   Earl St. Vincent has passed Gibraltar after them, Nelson is there already, Lord Bridport will soon follow; and here will be far above 100 sail of the line, the Russian and Turkish squadrons included, the proudest fleet that inland sea ever bore, even if we revert back to the squadrons at Lepanto, at Actium, at Salamis, or at any other memorable epoch in Greek or Roman story.

Some years later, in writing to his wife, he says: —

April 26, 1804.

There is no decided news from Europe.   Private letters from high and well informed characters assert that Bonaparte was certainly serious in invasion, because his preparations have been immense and beyond all precedent and calculation.   On the other hand, the means of resistance by Great Britain have multiplied equally, and their fleets have rode out the winter storms, and kept up a strict blockade of the French coast during all the rigors of the season. It is believed that Bonaparte must see the success of the invasion impracticable, and it is concluded he will attempt it soon, or he will (which is more probable) discharge his mighty forces like a torrent on the North of Europe, and carry conquest and desolation over Denmark, Sweden, and Prussia. No doubt some event of mighty impression and awful results is impending. However, we shall be safe, and I regard Albany as desirable a retreat as any part of the world.

As the time approached for the termination of the "age of battle," he wrote to his brother, in October, 1807: —

. . . The present unsettled state of our concerns abroad must undoubtedly render every kind of investment a little precarious. But we must take our chances with the rest of the world. The state of Europe is awful, both as it respects the degraded and debased condition of the countries under the despotism of France, and as it respects the safety and existence of the only independent power left. I think more of European operations than of Burr's trial and such stuff at home. If it be really true that the grand English fleet and army are to take the Island of Zealand and the Danish fleet, there will be a stupendous series of events very shortly for our amusement.

Six years later, to his brother at Washington he writes: —

Judge Kent to Moss Kent.

July 14, 1813.

The details of the bloody battle near Leipsig, on the 2d May, have just been received, and I am not without much anxiety for the campaign in Germany; but I feel confident for the ultimate success of the struggle for national independence carried on by Russia, Prussia, Spain, and England.

A few months later, his interest in European affairs being still maintained, he again writes: —

Chancellor Kent to Moss Kent.

ALBANY, March 31, 1814.

. . . The astonishing events in France excite all my attention. I think of them when I rise and I think of them when I lie down. I am afraid the Allies will make peace without prostrating the dynasty of the Scourge and Nuisance of Europe. I shall not be satisfied until Napoleon is dead and buried, or at least immured for life in the castle of Schlüsselburg.

And later he sounds a joyful note of relief upon the fall of Napoleon, whose career had been to him so long an object of eager interest, and fraught with such serious consequences to Europe.

Chancellor Kent to Moss Kent.

January, 1816.

. . . I believe that the mode of administering the [our] government is rotten to the core. But Bonaparte is a prisoner and the French Empire prostrate, and the terrors of Walsh's and the distresses of Burke's pen are dissipated; and that is a great panacea for a thousand ills.

In August, 1821, a State convention was called for the purpose of framing a new constitution for New York. Of this body Chancellor Kent was a member, and he may be fairly said to have represented the op-

position in the convention.   His efforts were ably
seconded by his life-long friends, Ambrose Spencer,
Stephen Van Rensselaer, Abraham Van Vechten, William W. Van Ness, Jonas Platt, and a few others, who
represented the crumbling remains of the Federal
party.   The thoughts, habits, and political affiliations
of a lifetime were centered in this final effort to stem
the tide of Democratic innovation, which, rising more
and more, seemed to threaten to overwhelm the entire
system of jurisprudence in all its departments, and to
sweep away those institutions which, derived from
ancient Anglo-Saxon source, were closely interwoven
in the fabric of the government, its customs, and its
laws.

It is not to be wondered at that, actuated by these
views, Chancellor Kent should have manfully battled
for the remains of those institutions, their perquisites,
emoluments, and dignities, rather than by submitting
to the outward form of change in an organization
which undoubtedly required reorganization, follow the
tide of public opinion in the establishment of new
forms and methods of government, legislative and
judicial.

Mr. Kent's life had been spent in combating the
growing desire for change, and inculcating into the
jurisprudence of his State the grand principles of
law upon the sound basis of strict scientific deduction derived from the English authorities.   His labors
had borne fruit, had systematized, enlarged, enriched,
and established the entire fabric of jurisprudence, but
could not hold together the system, of which he was
the head, upon the lines laid down by the old Consti-

tution.   The State had outgrown the methods which
existed under that Constitution, but it is doubtful if
the innovations suggested were of such a character as
to be much of an improvement upon the existing
methods.

The constitution of the various committees was
markedly indicative of the drift of public opinion;
with the exception of Mr. Tallmadge, a doubtful
Clintonian, all the chairmen were Republicans, — then
the name of the present Democratic party, — and
the entire convention was in the hands of that party,
which had declared itself in favor of change and
innovation.   As might have been expected, the reports of the various committees were in favor of the
new order, and the chief points may briefly be stated
as follows : —

The Committee on the Council of Revision reported
in favor of abolishing that Council and vesting the
veto power in the Governor.   This report was adopted
after much discussion upon many amendments.

The Committee of the Executive Department reported upon the advisability of reducing the term of
the Governor to two years.   Upon this point Chancellor Kent and the other members of the ultra Federal
party took strong grounds against the ultra Democrats, who advocated a one-year term; and after a
prolonged discussion and considerable voting taken
on amendments, the recommendation of the committee was adopted, the Federalists voting with the
moderate Democrats.

The recommendation of the Committee on Suffrage,
abolishing a property qualification and extending the

suffrage to all white citizens over the age of twenty-one, was one of the prime questions of the hour; against its adoption the Chancellor and the entire Federal party vainly strove, endeavoring to retain a property qualification, and at the same time exclude the negro from the right of suffrage.

In the efforts of the Democrats to reconstruct the Judiciary, the Chancellor and his associates took no very active part, further than to express their opinion upon the advisability of the measures, and, throughout the discussion, he and the remainder of the Judges held a position of dignified reserve in regard to the final disposition of their official positions. The official character of Chancellor Kent and Judge Spencer, and the conduct of the courts under their management were fully vindicated and extolled, even by the opposition members of the convention, who were opposed to the overturning of the Courts of Chancery and the Supreme Court; and this position was maintained by Governor Tompkins and Messrs. Van Buren, Paulding, Wheaton, King, and others of the Democratic party.

The term of office of Mr. Kent, as Chancellor, was drawing to a close. He had fought, during his whole career, against change and innovation, — for the rights of the individual as distinguished from the rights of the people, upon what he considered the true principles of individual and constitutional liberty; but although he had done, within his sphere of duties, all that one man could do, it required more than the enunciation of principles, no matter how deeply rooted, to create respect for established usage.

His last appearance before the public, and the final overthrow of these usages which he considered so essential to the welfare of the government, was a bitter disappointment to him as a man, but it eventually proved itself to be that crowning mark of discipline which Providence seems to have thought fit to bestow upon this singularly gifted man. It deeply impressed upon him the lesson that principle lies deeper than form, that established usage should not be venerated for that cause alone, and that change of form, no matter how radical, cannot shake the fundamental principles of law and justice.

By embittering the final days of his office as Chancellor, and throwing him out upon the world, after treating him with contempt by first reducing an already exceedingly small salary, and creating no fund from which a pension might have been given to a man who had passed his entire life in the performance of such distinguished service to his country, the Legislature of his State not only emphasized the habitual ingratitude of republican assemblies and the spleen of party rancor, but they unwittingly did a service to their country at large, the result of which has proved to have been of inestimable benefit to the whole of these United States.

That the attitude of Chancellor Kent in the convention was approved by his friends of years, although he was overwhelmed by the popular tide, is shown by a letter from Hon. Jonas Platt: —

Jonas Platt to Chancellor Kent.

October 29, 1821.

MY DEAR SIR, — I thank you cordially for your kindness in keeping us well advised from day to day of the proceedings of the convention. Although this daily repast did not always gratify the taste of us "judicial delegates," yet I assure you, we felt very grateful to the cook, who, with all his skill, could not give a good relish from such materials. Pardon this low-lived metaphor, which illy comports with the dignity of a Lord Chancellor.

I now tender you my thanks for something worthy of yourself. I mean, for the able, patriotic, and dignified stand which you have maintained in resisting the torrent from the volcano. I rejoice on your own account as well as for the honor of the State, that you have been stationed in the straits of Thermopylæ. You have erected there a noble monument, my dear friend; and even our ungrateful republic will one day do justice to your merits and character. You have never before been exposed to the buffeting of Jacobin factions. "Gaudet tentamine virtus." "Indignante invidia florebat justus." "Post nubilis, Phoebus."

During the period embraced by the term of Mr. Kent's office as Chancellor, from 1814 to 1823, are found but few letters or memoranda from which to quote. His brother Moss, who up to this time had been his life-long correspondent, and to whose interest and care is due the preservation of many of the letters which have formed the material of this memoir, was now a resident of Albany, and the register of the Court of Chancery. Except for a few letters to William Johnson, the Reporter, the history of that

period is to be found only in Johnson's Chancery
Reports, in themselves a lasting monument to the
Chancellor's tireless industry and vast legal erudition.

As the Chancellor progressed in life, and as he
neared the close of his official career, he became more
and more absorbed in his duties.   When hearing an
argument, he became completely wrapped up in the
discussion, listened with close attention, took few
notes and those usually only on the facts, and if the
discussion was of more than usual interest, kept up a
running commentary upon the points of the argument,
at times to the confusion of the counsel addressing
him.   All attempts at sophistry or of distortion of
facts were quickly detected and rapidly rebuked with
a quick, impatient " Your facts do not bear out
your contention, sir," or " Pooh ! pooh ! that 's no
law," as marks of disapproval, or " Yes, that 's good
law," or " That point is well taken," as the argument
met with his approval.

His manner to the inexperienced practitioner was
kind and gentle, and every member of the Bar who
came before him, no matter who he might be, was
sure of careful and courteous attention.   Simple and
direct in his methods, he very much disliked anything
which savored of discourtesy, or sharp practice, between the members of the Bar who practiced in his
court, and was particularly opposed to that class of
practice which has grown up since the introduction
of the Code, whereby the sharp practitioner may
harass and annoy his less wary opponent and obtain
costs upon trivial motions.   Such actions when taken
before him were invariably defeated, and in many

instances the mover was only too glad to retire, precipitately if not gracefully.

One instance of the tact with which he at times met and disposed of such questions has been noted by an eye-witness. When sitting as Chancellor, a very important case was argued before him, in which many eminent counsel were engaged, and among them one of the most famous of New Jersey's chancery lawyers. As he arose to address the court, an objection was made by one of the lesser lights among his opponents, that the gentleman from New Jersey, not having been admitted to practice in the Chancery Court of New York State, could not with propriety be heard. The Chancellor was manifestly very much annoyed at this breach of professional courtesy, even if, technically, the objection was good, and in passing upon the point said: "I admit the point, although I do not think that at this stage of the proceedings it should be raised. Although the learned counsel has not been admitted to this court, I am not informed of any valid reason why he should not be; and, further, as it is customary to inquire into the qualifications of all candidates for admission to practice, if my learned brother is willing, I will proceed with his examination at once; and I appoint the mover of this motion a committee to make the requisite examination before me now, before we proceed with the argument."

It is needless to add that the junior counselor was quite unprepared to make an exhibition of his legal attainments before the Chancellor and such a distinguished gathering of the Bar, and was only too glad to withdraw his motion and substitute one for the admission of the New Jersey lawyer, which was immediately granted, and the case proceeded without further delay.

It is related that upon another occasion a certain counselor, much given to lengthy statement and argument upon trivial points, excepted to an item in a Master's report. After making his point he was proceeding to elaborate it at considerable length. The Chancellor became impatient and soon interrupted the lawyer with the query, —

" Mr. Riggs, what is the amount of the item in dispute? "

" One dollar and seventy-five cents, your honor," was the reply.

" I won't hear it! I won't hear it! " exclaimed the Chancellor, with energy. " I would rather pay it myself."

Toward the close of his term as Chancellor, the friction between the various branches of the judiciary became pronounced, and the Court of Errors was by some believed to be somewhat swayed by political considerations in reviewing the opinions of the Chancellor. How far this may have been true it is not necessary to inquire, but it is evident that Chancellor Kent was deeply wounded, for, in April, 1820, he wrote to William Johnson: —

I return you my thanks for the three volumes of the canon law. I have cursorily turned them over, and I think their very curious learning relates more to the doctrines of the Roman Catholic priest than of the Protestant civilian. But I have no doubt I might find them occasionally useful, if I had any courage left to pursue curious and erudite researches.   But, to tell you the truth, I am discouraged and heart-broken.   The judges have prevailed on the Court of Errors to reverse all my best decisions.   They have reversed Frost *v.* Beekman, the Methodist Episcopal Church *v.* Jacques, Anderson *v.* Boyd, and others.   After such devastation, what courage ought I to have to study and write elaborate opinions?   There are but two sides to every case, and I am so unfortunate as always to take the wrong side.   I never felt more disgusted with the judges in all my life, and I expressed myself to Judge Platt in a way to mortify and offend him.   According to my present feelings and sentiments, I will never consent to publish another opinion, and I have taken and removed out of sight and out of my office into another room my three volumes of Chancery Reports.   They were too fearful when standing before my eyes.

"In 1823," wrote Chancellor Kent, in continuing his epistle to Thomas Washington,[1] " a solemn era in my life had arrived.   I retired from the office at the age of sixty, and then immediately, with my son, visited the Eastern States.   On my return the solitude of my private office and the new dynasty did not please me. I, besides, would want income to live as I had been accustomed.   My eldest daughter[2] was prosperously settled in New York, and I resolved to move away from Albany, and ventured to come down to New York and be chamber counsel.   The trustees of Columbia College immediately tendered me again my old office of Professor, which had lain dormant from 1795.   I undertook (but exceedingly against my

---

[1] *Supra*, p. 157.
[2] Then Mrs. Isaac S. Hone.

inclination) to write and deliver law lectures.   In the
two characters of chamber counsel and college lecturer, I succeeded, by steady perseverance, beyond
my most sanguine expectations, and upon the whole,
the five years I have lived here in this city since 1823
have been happy and prosperous.   I have introduced
my son into good business, and I live near my
daughter, and I take excursions every summer with
my wife and daughters all over the country.   I have
been twice with her to Canada, and we go in every
direction.   I never had better health.   I walk the
Battery uniformly before breakfast.   I give a great
many written opinions, and having got heartily tired
of lecturing I abandoned it, and it was my son who
pressed me to prepare a volume of the lectures for
the press.   I had no idea of publishing them when I
delivered them.   I wrote anew one volume and published it, as you know.   This led me to remodel and
enlarge, and now the third volume will be out in a few
days, and I am obliged to write a fourth to complete
my plan.

"My reading now is, as you may well suppose,
quite desultory, but still I read with as much zeal and
pleasure as ever.   I was never more engaged in my
life than during the last summer.   I accepted the
trust of receiver to the Franklin (insolvent) Bank,
and it has occupied and perplexed and vexed me
daily; and I had to write part of the third volume
and search books a good deal for that very object,
and I have revised the proof sheets.

"On reviewing what I have written, I had thoughts
of burning it.   I speak of myself so entirely, and it is

entirely against my habit or taste, but I see no other way fairly to meet your desires."

On the reverse of his copy of the letter, which has been so freely quoted, and which has served to reveal so much of the Chancellor's inner life and character, is found this minute, in his own neat handwriting : —

The within is the copy of a letter I wrote to a gentleman at the South in 1828. It was fairly pressed out of me.

VIII

ON the 31st day of July, 1823, Chancellor Kent reached the age of sixty years, and the period of retirement from official position.   The Constitutional Convention, in which he himself had borne a part in 1821, had fixed this age limit to the Chancellor's term of office.   It is to the advantage of posterity that he was thus forced from public life. The sixty years which he had lived were but preparatory to the great work that rendered his name immortal.   "As a judge and as Chancellor, he had done enough for his own fame and for the interests and honor of his own State.   It was to the whole Union that his services were now due, and were soon to be rendered."[1]

On his retirement from official life, addresses were presented to him by the Bar of the city of New York, of Albany, and of the entire State, expressive of their veneration, regard, and gratitude toward him, and their sense of the value of his judicial labors during the twenty-five years in which he had occupied seats upon the Bench.   Although during this period he had earned a comfortable support for himself and his family, he had not acquired sufficient property to enable him to live wholly at his ease.   The home in

[1] Duer.

the country, where he might enjoy elegant leisure for study and literary pursuits, was still a dream of the future. He must still work, and, that he might do so to the best advantage, he again removed, with his family, — now consisting of his wife, a son, and two daughters, — to the city of New York. Here he established an office for chamber practice, and almost immediately he was re-elected to his former chair of law in Columbia College, which had remained unoccupied during all the years since his resignation.

At a dinner given in his honor, in 1889, by the New York Bar, on the sixtieth anniversary of his admission, Mr. Benjamin D. Silliman, in speaking of old New York lawyers, thus recalled Chancellor Kent in whose office he had been a student at law : —

When he left the Bench (and indeed to the end of his life) he was in the fullness of mental vigor and strength and wisdom, and of the goodness and gladness of his guileless heart. His serene cheerfulness and kindness delighted all who had intercourse with him. He was " in wit a man, in simplicity a child." His personal qualities secured to him the love, as his learning, dignity, and purity did the reverence, of all. I have never known any other man whose reading and study were so universal as his. It could not be said of him, as it was said of a distinguished English lawyer, that " he knew a little about everything, and not much about anything," for the Chancellor knew all about everything he had ever studied, and he had studied almost everything. In connection with his universal reading was his absolutely phenomenal memory. He literally forgot nothing. A mind so stored, and with its treasures so secured, could know no solitude. It found within itself abundant and choice companionship.

He began the work of preparing his law lectures with great zeal, but he was much in demand as a diner-out, and these social demands — which he seems to have endured, rather than to have courted — were a serious interference with his work. In January, 1824, he wrote to his brother: —

Chancellor Kent to Moss Kent.

January 4, 1824.

I am involved in a great deal of company, and we have been overwhelmed with calls and visits. In spite of what I can do I am obliged to dine out a good deal. I have for two or three weeks engaged with great zeal in preparing law lectures. I have written out several, and mean to make a beginning the first of February. I am in hopes of being able to give a broken and imperfect course, and make a good experiment. I shall do all I can to deserve success. I walk a good deal morning and evening, and live pretty well, though not without occasional gloom and anxiety. I sigh for a plainer, simpler society than the one I am in, but I don't know that I should be better contented anywhere else.

If I can indemnify myself by my business and lectures, it is all I want. I choose not to impair my little capital, and I trust I shall not. If in eighteen months I find it to be otherwise, I shall then retire to some quiet and cheap country place, but *spero meliori*.

A few days later he again writes: —

Chancellor Kent to Moss Kent.

January 16, 1824.

We are in a whirlwind of company and are oppressed with calls and invitations. I dine out half my time and it distresses me very much, as it is such a great impediment to my studies and the preparation of my law lectures.   But I keep my health well and take a great deal of exercise. Monday I dined with Mr. Davis (who is in town from Boston), with my son-in-law on Tuesday, and that evening Uncle Phil [Philip Hone] had a splendid party and dance and music, and I was obliged to go.   To-night I must go to the Post-office, where an entertainment is getting up.   I dined yesterday with Mr. Bayard, to-day I dine with Colonel Varick, and to-morrow with Governor Lewis, and so I go on.

I have got eight or ten lectures written out and mean to begin the first of February, and shall probably deliver but two formal lectures a week, with one more private for the matriculated students only.   By this means I can keep up two lectures a week until June, and that shall be the extent of my first imperfect and broken course.   It is an experiment, and I shall do my best to make it successful. . . .

By the coming of autumn of this year, the Chancellor was in the full tide of delivery of his law lectures, but it may be that the memory of the failure of the plan, years before, had produced in him a feeling of pessimism, for, in November, 1824, he again writes to his brother: —

Chancellor Kent to Moss Kent.

November 9, 1824.

I have commenced my lectures and they give me a good deal of trouble and anxiety.   I am compelled to study and write all the time, as if I was under the whip and spur. But I take early and regular and habitual exercise, and am very temperate, and on the whole am very healthy.   I have no reason to complain, but on the contrary have the most persuasive motives of gratitude to God for his continuous goodness.

It was on the completion of this series of law lectures, in the spring of 1826, that the idea was first suggested to him of allowing them to appear in printed form. This course was strongly urged by his son, Judge William Kent, who clearly appreciated the great value which such a work would have, if his father could be induced to present to the public the vast store of historical and legal learning that he had accumulated in his professional career. It was, therefore, at the age of sixty-three that Chancellor Kent set himself the task of reducing to writing the voluminous mass of the Common Law of his country, which he had been so diligent in expounding throughout his official career. Using his lectures as a basis, he amplified them somewhat and began their publication under his own supervision, and at his own expense.

The cost of bringing out this first volume in sheets, he notes to have been $1076.27, which was a very considerable venture considering his limited means, — and it is extremely doubtful if he would have continued the publication of the remaining volumes, if the first had not met with a warm reception.

" Having retired from public office in the summer of 1823," he wrote in the preface to the first volume, " I had the honor to receive the appointment of Professor of Law in Columbia College. The trustees of that institution have repeatedly given me the most liberal and encouraging proofs of their respect and confidence, of which I shall ever retain a grateful recollection. A similar appointment was received from them in the year 1793; and this renewed mark of their approbation determined me to employ the entire leisure in which I found myself in further endeavors to discharge the debt which, according to Lord Bacon, every man owes to his profession. I was strongly induced to accept the trust from want of occupation; being apprehensive that the sudden cessation of my habitual employment, and the contrast between the discussions of the forum and the solitude of retirement might be unpropitious to my health and spirits, and cast a premature shade over the happiness of declining years.

" The following Lectures are the fruit of the acceptance of that trust; and, in the performance of my collegiate duty, I had the satisfaction to meet a collection of interesting young gentlemen, of fine talents and pure character, who placed themselves under my instruction, and in whose future welfare a deep interest is felt. Having been encouraged to suppose that the publication of the Lectures might render them more extensively useful, I have been induced to submit the present volume to the notice of students, and of the junior members of the profession, for whose use they were originally compiled. Another volume is wanting to embrace all the material parts of the Lectures which have been composed. It will treat, at large, and in an elementary manner, of the law of property and of personal rights and commercial contracts; and will be prepared for the press in the course of the ensuing year, unless in the mean time there should be reason to apprehend that another volume would be trespassing too far upon the patience and indulgence of the public."

The sale of the book, however, exceeded his highest expectation, and he was encouraged to continue the work. From this time forward all his spare time was occupied in correcting proof and in preparing for the press the succeeding volumes, which now began to appear in rapid succession. The second volume was printed in December, 1827, and the third volume in October, 1828. Such was his diligence that a fourth was added in April, 1830.

When the Chancellor published his first volume of Commentaries it was contemplated to complete the work in two volumes. But he speedily discovered that greater breadth was required, and it was expanded into a third and yet into a fourth volume. " I am printing a third volume of Commentaries," he wrote to his brother in September, 1828, " and correcting a proof of eight pages daily. I have near two hundred pages already printed, and I shall be obliged to print a fourth volume. I cannot crowd what I have into the third volume, including a large index."

Again, two months later, he was able to write: " We attend to business diligently, and I shall shortly commence writing my fourth volume of Commentaries." But such were the difficulties of the subjects treated that his progress was not as great as he could have wished. January 2, 1830, he again wrote to his brother: "I am busy, very busy with my fourth volume, but the subjects are very abstruse and perplexing, and I move very slowly and warily through the mazes of contingent remainders, executory devises, uses, trusts, and powers, and the modifications

which they have received by our Revised Statutes."
It was early in this year, however, that the work was
completed and the final volume given to the public.
It met with instant and enthusiastic success. The
commendations which it called forth from men of
the highest eminence, on the Bench and at the Bar,
were sufficient to ensure the perpetuity of the work.
Chief-Justice Savage wrote : —

Chief-Justice Savage to Chancellor Kent.

May 6, 1830.

DEAR SIR, — A few days before I left home I had the
honor of receiving from you by the hands of Mr. Foot the
fourth volume of your Commentaries.   Having heretofore
received from you the three previous volumes, I embrace
this occasion to present you my grateful acknowledgments
for so valuable a donation.   I hope I may be permitted to
say that from your elevated standing both as a judge of the
Supreme Court and as Chancellor much was expected from
your labors after your retirement from the Bench, and that
public expectation has not been disappointed.   Your Commentaries will remain a living testimonial of your learning
and industry to future generations.   Your labors have contributed more than those of any other individual to elevate
the American judicial character.

May you long live to enjoy the respect and esteem which
your character and talents have acquired.

In acknowledgment of a copy of the Commentaries, sent with the author's compliments, Chief-Justice
Prentiss, of Vermont, wrote : —

Chief-Justice Prentiss to Chancellor Kent.

DEAR SIR, — On my return home a few days since, after
an absence of several weeks, I found your obliging letter of
the 13th ult., with an order upon your bookseller, directing
him to deliver to me the third and the fourth volumes of
your Commentaries. I beg you to accept my thanks for
this instance of your kindness and civility, and be assured
that I shall avail myself of the first opportunity to forward
the order and obtain the books.   Coming from any one
they would be esteemed a valuable present, but more
especially so when presented by the learned author himself.
Before the work was announced to the public I had become
familiar with your reported opinions in the Courts of
Equity and Common Law, and entertained a decided conviction that no opinions, either in the English or American
reports were more learned, luminous, and sound, or expressed in a purer and more classical style.   They were
entirely sufficient in my estimation to entitle you to the
highest rank among the lawyers and jurists of the age, and
it may with truth be said that to your judicial labors and
those of Parsons and Marshall, we are principally indebted
for the elevated character which the jurisprudence of this
country at present sustains.   The learning and ability
evinced in your opinions, contained in Johnson's Reports,
very naturally led me to form high expectations of the
merits of the work on which you have been recently engaged : and it is but justice to say that so far as I have
had opportunity to examine the work, it has answered every
expectation and amply sustained your high reputation.   In
devoting your time and talents to the accomplishment of a
work of so much utility, you have rendered an acceptable
service to the profession, not only in your own State, but

throughout the Union.   You will excuse me for saying thus much on the merits of your labors, since the occasion seemed to authorize me to say something, and truth and sincerity would not allow me to say less.

Letters similar in their tenor were received by Chancellor Kent from Chief-Justice Prentiss Mellen, of Maine; from Governor J. C. Smith; from Chief-Justice Shaw, of Massachusetts; from Professor Silliman, of Yale College; from Judge Platt; from William Wills, an eminent English writer upon jurisprudence; from Judge Porter, of Louisiana; from Judge Henry Baldwin, of Washington, D. C.; and from many others equally eminent and learned.   The first edition was rapidly exhausted, and so early as September, 1830, we find Chancellor Kent writing to his brother: "I must waive all anxieties for the future and betake myself to the new and various reading that daily arises, and prepare my Commentaries for a new edition."   A few weeks later he again writes: —

Chancellor Kent to Moss Kent.

December 22, 1830.

I have just completed the sale of all the entire sets of my Commentaries, though I have a good many odd volumes of the first, third, and fourth volumes.   The first is separately wanted for academies, and the third and fourth to supply defective sets in the hands of former purchasers.   I shall probably, before the end of the next year, prepare myself for printing a new and corrected, and somewhat enlarged edition.   This I shall not do until the booksellers have had sufficient opportunity to sell what is on hand, nor do I declare any such intentions.   I only mean to show that I am doing very well with the work and that it promises to be a source of moderate but permanent income.

A comparison of the first and second editions will show what an enormous advance was made in the preparation of the new work, in which the form of a series of lectures is retained, but the entire context broadened out into almost its present comprehensive shape.   In August, 1832, he writes to his brother: —

"I have now just about finished my index and put the finishing stroke to the second edition of my Commentaries. I shall send the last edition to the printer in a day or so."

Chancellor Kent never allowed his Commentaries to be stereotyped, but up to the very last moment kept pace with the newly reported decisions, and corrected and annotated the proofs, as they came from the press.

He was by no means in favor of the methods of the modern schools whereby law is "made easy." He had reached the exalted position which he had held, by dint of persistent work and untiring study, and he realized what was the true duty of those who followed the profession to which he had devoted his life.

It is related that, being questioned by one of his proof-readers, while preparing one of the editions of the Commentaries, as to why it would not be to the advantage of both lawyer and client if all Latin and intricate technical phrases were reduced to plain English, so that every man might read and understand the law, he is said to have replied: —

"It's all right; we don't want every man to be his

own lawyer, and he could not be, even if all the Latin was in the plainest possible English. What kind of legal protection would you have if every man could be a lawyer? All things are changing, it is true, but when you find law made easy to the meanest comprehension, look out for countless volunteers in our noble profession, to whom good Latin and correct English are alike inaccessible."

The second edition of the Commentaries appeared in due time, and this, too, met with ready sale, for in the autumn of 1835 still a third edition was demanded. "I am quite busy," he wrote to his brother, October 20, 1835, "as the printers began yesterday to print the third edition of my Commentaries and the examination of the pages, before they go, and the correction of the proof sheets will keep me occupied considerably every day for months to come. I shall have to correct the whole, when in the course of printing and to make an index. This is quite a laborious job. There are a great many books of reports and treatises that must be examined, and notes to my Commentaries added, as they go successively to the press."

It was not until the completion of the fourth edition, which appeared in 1841, that Chancellor Kent's life work ended. That he considered this to be his final effort seems probable from a note in his Ledger in which he says : —

"The printing bill for the fourth edition was unduly large, but it is to be considered that this edition was much larger, and a great many more pages, and a great many more small notes, and the addition of a table of cases. This rendered the fourth edition much more heavy to print, and took more labor and time."

It was then, at last, that he rested from his labors, for he does not appear to have contemplated another edition until just before his death. As late as March, 1847, he wrote to his son : —

Chancellor Kent to Judge William Kent.

NEW YORK, March 22, 1847.

MY DEAR SON, — I have got quite startled about the decreasing numbers of my Commentaries. In reckoning up the number of sets left, I find that I have but 499 sets out of the original number of 3000 left, and of that 499 there are 150 less of Vol. I., so that, in fact, I have left unsold but 349 entire sets. I must begin a new edition next autumn. I hope I shall have strength, health, and resolution enough to go through with it without calling on you.

You need not be at all uneasy about me. For our great age, Ma and I are wonderful folks ; we are cheerful, spirited, active, social, capable of all our relative duties, and withal extremely tender, affectionate, and not querulous.

It is hard to over-value the civilizing influence of Kent's Commentaries on American Law. It was a work emphatically demanded by the requirements of the time, and, furthermore, the age was ripe for the beginning of the development of this country. It was at once so comprehensive in its character, so accurate in its deductions and reasoning, so highly scientific in the true acceptation of the term, so clear and simple in its statements and design, that it at once found its way into the hands of the general practitioner, and with him it went out to all parts of the American world.   In the Justice Courts, in the terms held at county towns, and in the high courts of the States, it was the highest authority upon the fundamental principles of the law; ever broadening its sphere, particularly throughout the ever widening West, until the whole country, from ocean to ocean, was permeated by the same principles, the same deductions, and practically the same laws, based, for the most part, upon the life work of New York's greatest lawyer.

Considered in the light of a law book its range has been extraordinary.   It has run through fourteen editions, the latest having been issued during the year 1896, and the demand and sale for it is steady from all parts of the country.   It is the first book placed in the hand of the law student, it stands on the shelf of every practicing lawyer, and whenever an intricate case is presented for consideration, many a careful lawyer will turn to it to refresh his mind on the principles of the question before him, before proceeding further with his investigation.   This is Chancellor Kent's true monument; in it breathe the principles of truth, law, and equity, and, like Blackstone's Commentaries on English Law, the revered masterpiece of British jurisprudence, Kent's Commentaries will stand enshrined in the hearts of hundreds of thousands of American lawyers, the great Bar of the United States.

In leaving the subject of the monumental work of Chancellor Kent, completion must be sought by the presentation of two letters, found among his papers.

The first of these is of peculiar interest, as having been written by Mr. Sumner, while he was yet a Reporter of Decisions, and before his name became enrolled among the greatest of American statesmen.

Charles Sumner to Chancellor Kent.

BOSTON, April 5, 1836.

DEAR SIR, — I have the honor to ask your acceptance of the accompanying copy of the first volume of my Reports of the judgments of Mr. Justice Story on the first circuit. Your well known friendship for the learned Judge (upon which he has so often dwelt within my hearing), and your enthusiasm for the law make me indulge the expectation that the present volume, containing many thorough and luminous opinions on various and almost opposite branches of the law, so strikingly illustrative of the wide and comprehensive learning and ability of their author, will not be without its interest to you.

I feel happy in the opportunity afforded by this letter of expressing to you my lively sense of the deep debt which every American lawyer owes to you, and no one feels it more than myself, for the light which you have cast over the dark and rugged paths of legal study : first, by the large and splendid series of judicial opinions, in which justice was so nobly administered and the law so steadfastly advanced ; and second, by your admirable Commentaries, which have now become the manual of the practitioner, as they have since their first publication been the institute of the students. Not a day passes without reminding me of the value of your labors, and without strengthening in me those feelings of attachment as towards a cherished instructor.

Edward Everett to Chancellor Kent.

BOSTON, 31 October, 1845.

MY DEAR SIR, — I have intended ever since my return home last month to recall myself to your friendly recollection, for the purpose of expressing to you the great satisfaction with which, during my residence in England, I witnessed the extent to which your professional character and labors are known and appreciated there. It is certainly no injustice to others, nor flattery to you to say, that your name and that of the great man whose loss we have lately been called to deplore,[1] were oftener mentioned by the jurists of England with whom I had the honor to be acquainted than those of any of our countrymen. I was led to think that an estimate of the weight of your authority and of his had been formed in the House of Lords and in Westminster Hall, which might be called generous if it were not so entirely just.

For myself, I owe you a great debt of personal obligation. I was constantly inquired of as to points of American Law, in reference to which the little general reading I have on the subject often left me at a loss for an answer. In such cases your Commentaries were my unvarying resort, and I seldom failed to find what I needed.

Although closely engaged in the preparation of the Commentaries for their successive editions, Chancellor Kent still found time to carry on a large and interesting correspondence with many men of note. From all parts of the country poured in upon him numerous requests for opinions upon every conceivable point of law, abstruse or intricate. These applications came at times from England, which was now beginning to seek

[1] Judge Story.

investment for its surplus wealth in the stock enter-
prises and bonds of the newly built and projected
railroads in our country.

Adhering closely to the plan of a division of time
which he had adopted in his youth, he set aside a
certain portion of his day to each of his various avocations, the preparation of his Commentaries, counsel
practice, and correspondence.   He also steadily kept
pace with the rising flood of legal reports and decisions, of which he may be said to have been the father
in this country.   Although his correspondence was
so large that, at times, he complained of the burden
it imposed, he cheerfully continued to meet all its
requirements.   He carefully answered all letters, not
only those of a private character, but at times answering inquiries upon matters of great public importance.

In the later years of his life the Chancellor formed
an intimate personal acquaintance and friendship with
Daniel Webster.   That the great Expounder of the
Constitution did not scruple to draw, upon occasion,
upon the fund of wisdom accumulated during an
experience of many years by his friend; and that
they were politically in accord, the following correspondence is ample proof: —

Chancellor Kent to Daniel Webster.

NEW YORK, January 21, 1830.

DEAR SIR, — I ought to have replied earlier to your letter
of the 15th instant, but I have been diverted by a number
of perplexing avocations, each of them, singly, petty in its
nature, but conjointly such things make up the sum of the
life of ordinary minds; and now to the purpose.   I beg

leave to decline any opinion on the question you state;
first, I have not time to do it justice, and render anything I
would say worthy of you; second, I am not going to undertake to instruct a senatorial statesman, who has thought on
the subject infinitely more than I have, for it comes officially
before him.

Hamilton, in the Federalist, No. 77, was of the opinion
that the President could not remove without the consent of
the Senate.   I heard the question debated in the summer
of 1789, and Madison, Benson, Lawrance, etc., were in
favor of the right of removal by the President, and such has
been the opinion ever since and the practice.   I thought
they were right, for I then thought this side uniformly right.
Mr. White of Virginia was strenuously opposed to that construction.   You will find the discussion in Fenno's U. S.
Gazetteer for July or August or September, 1789.   Mr.
Madison reasons technically like a lawyer.   Now when I
come to think on the subject, with my confirmed wary views
of things, I pause and doubt of the construction on account
of the word "advice."   That word is pregnant with meaning, and means something beyond consent to nominations,
or it would not have been inserted.   The "consent" (so it
might be argued) applies to the individual named.   The
"advice" is the measure itself which draws to it the whole
ground of the interference.   Again, it is a great, a general
principle in all jurisprudence that where there is no positive
provision in the case regulating the principle, the power
that appoints is the power to determine the pleasure of
the appointment and the limitation.   It is the power to
re-appoint; and the power to appoint and re-appoint, when
all else is silent, is the power to remove.   I begin to have a
strong suspicion that Hamilton was right, as he always was
on public questions.

On the other hand, it is too late to call the President's
power in question, after a declaratory act of Congress and

an acquiescence of half a century. We should hurt the reputation of our Government with the world, and we are accused already of the republican tendency of reducing all executive power into the legislative, and making Congress a national convention. That the President [Andrew Jackson] grossly abuses the power of removal is manifest, but it is the evil genius of democracy to be the sport of factions. Hamilton said in the Federalist, in his speeches, and a hundred times to me, that factions would ruin us, and our Government had not sufficient energy and balance to resist the propensity to them, and to control their tyranny and their profligacy. All theories of government that suppose the mass of the people virtuous, and able and willing to act virtuously, are plainly utopian, and will remain so until the Saturnian age.

Daniel Webster to Chancellor Kent.

WASHINGTON, April 27, 1830.

MY DEAR SIR, — I thank you much for both your letters. They have helped me. I can hardly find a just and reasonable man, who can speak what he thinks, who does not admit that my amendment is right in principle. Yet party envy, hatred, and malice are most likely eventually to defeat it. We are fallen on evil times, as times are when public men seek low objects, and when the tone of public morals and public feeling is depressed and debased. I hope our children may see a better state of things, — a state of things in which that part of our prosperity and greatness which depends on ourselves may bear some little proportion to the many favors with which Providence has distinguished our country.

Daniel Webster to Chancellor Kent.

[PRIVATE AND CONFIDENTIAL.]

BOSTON, October 29, 1832.

MY DEAR SIR, — Mr. Calhoun, as you are doubtless aware, has published a labored defence of nullification, in the form of a letter to Governor Hamilton. It is far the ablest and most plausible, and therefore the most dangerous, vindication of that particular form of revolution which has yet appeared. In the silence of abler pens, and seeing, as I think I do, that the affairs of this government are fast approaching a crisis, I have felt it to be my duty to answer Mr. Calhoun. And as he adopted the form of a letter in which to put forth his opinions, I think of giving my answer a similar form. The object of this is to ask your permission to address my letter to you. I propose to feign that I have read a letter from you, calling my attention to Mr. Calhoun's publication, and then, in answer to your supposed letter, to proceed to review his able argument at some length, not in the style of a speech, but in that of cool constitutional and legal discussion. If you feel no repugnance to be thus written to, I shall be obliged to you for your assent; on the other hand, if any reasons suggest themselves to your mind against such a form of publication, another can be readily adopted. I cannot complete the paper before election, as I am at present a good deal pressed with professional affairs; but I hope to bring it into light in the course of next month.

I have little to say to you, my dear sir, upon political subjects. The whole ground is open to you. I trust you will be one of those who will have votes to give, and I devoutly pray that you may yet see some way of uniting the well-disposed to rescue us from our peril.

Chancellor Kent to Daniel Webster.

NEW YORK, October 31, 1832.

DEAR SIR, — I have no objection that you should address, in the form of a letter or letters to me, your remarks on the Vice-President's scheme of nullification, and that you should assume it to be in answer to a letter from me relative to that subject. I shall deem it an honor to be addressed by you while engaged in the investigation of such an interesting subject. The Vice-President enclosed one of his pamphlets to me, and I read it attentively. It is ingeniously written, but such a construction of the Constitution and such principles as he deduces are visionary and most unsound and sophistical. His repugnance to all solid constitutional principles would fix a deadly power of destruction in the very vitals of the government. The crisis is indeed portentous and frightful. We are threatened with destruction all around us, and we seem to be fast losing our original good sense and virtue. The democracy require all their candidates for Congress in this city to give another pledge to support all the measures of the administration. Can anything be more degrading and monstrous? Is the proud House of Representatives and the grand inquest of the nation to be composed of such materials?

We are in hopes of carrying the electoral ticket, in which I am included, but the struggle will be tremendous. It will be the great battle of Armageddon between the Genius of Liberty, and the Spirits of Darkness; and suppose we should succeed, what then? Pennsylvania and Vermont, if they succeed, will certainly vote for Wirt, and then, at all events, the case goes to the House of Representatives, where Jackson will get thirteen States. New York would vote, I presume, either for Clay or Wirt as would best insure success, but Massachusetts, Jersey, etc., and especially the former, will be tenacious and hold out for Clay. I foresee difficulties. If Pennsylvania and New York succeed with their electoral tickets, there is no chance for success but for every electoral college opposed to Jackson to unite on their candidate, and I see no probability of such a union but upon Wirt.

If we succeed in our election I shall take the liberty of writing you again, to ask for a free communication of sentiments; if we fail, then indeed we may hang our harps upon the willows, or the witch-elm that shades Saint Fillan's Spring.

Your speech at Worcester was admirable for its logic as well as for its fervor and force. If we are to be saved we shall be largely indebted to you. Si pergama dextra, etc.

Again, as late as 1846, Daniel Webster is found submitting a question, which he undoubtedly designed to argue, to the consideration of his friend, Chancellor Kent. The Chancellor replied: —

Chancellor Kent to Daniel Webster.

NEW YORK, March 20, 1846.

MY DEAR SIR, — I have some difficulty in answering the grave question you submit to me. I have not had the benefit of any discussion, and I learn of no precedent to guide me. My diffidence in regard to the point is sincere and embarrassing. Under circumstances, it appears to me that it does not belong to the Executive department of our government to determine on the expediency of the notice and to give it. It is an item in the progress of executive negotiation. The President, in his message of December, is not of a very conciliatory spirit in respect to the Oregon question, but he seems to deem it still open to negotiation though the notice could be given and the joint occupation terminated. Further negotiation may still be had consistently with the convention of 1818.   The notice would leave the parties where they were prior to that convention, that is, in a pacific state under a pending negotiation. Congress has nothing to do with diplomatic matters.   The Senate is in many respects a branch of the executive power but the House of Representatives has nothing to do with negotiation.   They cannot interfere with notice, with sending or withdrawing ministers, or sending them away, or with negotiations or communications with foreign governments. They can vote for war, and there is the limit of the exercise of their power.

If any branch of the Legislature is to advise notice on any step in international matters, it is the Senate.   Upon the whole, my impression is that Congress has nothing to do with a giving notice or any advice concerning it.   These are my earliest impressions.

The appointment of Chancellor Kent as one of the presidential electors of his State was a last expiring effort to perpetuate a system in the election of the Chief Magistrate, which has, of late years, entirely disappeared.   Under the Constitution it was the intention, undoubtedly, in providing for an electoral college, that the representative men, who held the position of electors, should enter upon the discharge of their duties untrammeled by the pledge of party obligation, or the bias of partisanship.   Thus freed from all restraint, these electors, should deposit their votes for the man who, in their collective judgment, most fully met the requirements of the situation. That Chancellor Kent still held to the ancient traditions of the office, the following correspondence and the indorsement of the letter to Judge Spencer will clearly indicate.

Chief-Justice Spencer to Chancellor Kent.

NEW ALBANY, September 21, 1832.

MY DEAR FRIEND, — I returned two or three days since from a visit to my sons in the West, and it affords me great pleasure to be enabled to say to you that our prospects of electing Granger and Stevens and the electoral ticket nominated at Utica, with your name at its head, are most cheering; it is the universal belief of all well-informed men (our friends of course) that we shall succeed. Appearances are very flattering in this and the adjoining counties, and I am of opinion that, independently of the vast changes in the West, there will be changes in the river counties alone, should we hold good the vote of 1830 in the western counties, to elect our ticket.

As I had anticipated, attempts have been made to misrepresent you to the public and to induce a belief that you had freely given your opinion on the Presidential candidates. This I am persuaded you have not done and will not until the proper period. A writer in the "Argus" thought to win you by his blandishments to decline being an elector; this writer I take to be the notorious Sam Young, who loves you with a bitter hatred. The fact is that your character, your pure disinterestedness, and your patriotism, caused the Jackson leaders a panic, when they perceived your name on both tickets, for they well know the universal respect which that name had earned, by talent and service, which will be better appreciated by posterity than the present generation.

I am glad to perceive that you remain unmoved by all they say to you or of you. I recommend a perseverance in that course, and that you neither admit nor deny anything. Perfect silence only is required, and let those poisoned, degraded papers say what they please, your friends will defend you. My feelings have never before been so acute as they now are when I contemplate the calamities which await the nation if that barbarian Jackson shall be elected.

Again upon the same subject Judge Spencer writes to the Chancellor, in October, 1832: —

[PROFOUNDLY CONFIDENTIAL.]

I understand that some time since you received a letter from one David Miller of Genesee County, requesting your opinion, or rather asking for whom you intended to vote as Vice-President and President in case you were elected; that you answered this letter saying that you should vote for Wirt and Ellmaker, and it was actually put into the post office, but afterwards taken out. These facts are only known to a few and can do no hurt.

My son has just informed me that this same Miller, who has made such a noise as an anti-Mason, is about coming out denouncing you as adverse to Wirt and anti-Masonry, and our friends apprehend that it will do a serious injury to your election unless it can be counteracted. Before I state the precise object of this letter, let me say to you that, although a friend to Mr. Clay and anxious for his election, I see no hope of effecting it. We can never elect him with Pennsylvania and Vermont against him, and the electors in these States are bound by solemn pledges to vote for Wirt and Ellmaker.

My opinion is that all the anti-Jackson strength must be concentrated on one candidate, and that we must defeat Jackson in the college, or he will surely be our next President. There is not the least hope that the House of Representatives will elect Clay or Wirt; most assuredly there will be thirteen States for Jackson. Under these circumstances I shall advise our electors to vote for Wirt and Ellmaker. Were I an elector in your place I should indeed vote for Mr. Clay, if my vote would defeat Jackson and elect Clay, and then I would, if necessary, retire from the world, in the consciousness that I had saved my country; but no such case of self-immolation presents itself, and, as the matter stands, I think it would be advisable, on the score of patriotism and expediency, to vote for Wirt. I should say much, but you will anticipate all I have said.

Now to the point. If you intend to vote for W. and E. if you are elected, I advise that you forthwith write a letter to John C. Spencer at Canandaigua (he leaves here on Tuesday morning next), stating Mr. Miller's letter to you, and that you have not answered him, not personally knowing him, but that you have no objection to stating candidly to a co-candidate on the electoral ticket your views and determination, should you be elected, then giving those views without any injunction to secrecy. My son will then see that this letter be circulated only where it will do good and prevent the mischiefs threatened. He will take his own time to give publicity to it.

Van Buren has been into Genesee, and my son told me several days ago that his confidants had boasted of a measure that would greatly change the vote of that county. This is the stratagem; Miller has been bribed, and the course I indicate is the only one which can counteract what I fear is a deep laid plan and which may extend far beyond Genesee. You know I would advise nothing dishonorable or injurious to you. I need not say to you that we must defeat Jackson by all honorable means, or our country is ruined.

If you think fit to say one word of what I have written, with a view to advice, for God's sake let it be to one person only, and let him be a discreet man, say David B. Ogden. Write me what you have done. Perhaps you had better enclose the letter for my son to me; it is best, and he shall stay here until after the boat arrives on Tuesday.

Endorsement on foregoing letter : —

I answered this letter immediately. I declined writing to J. C. S. and to disclose how I should vote, in order to have it shown, as it might have the appearance of electioneering and would be inconsistent with the dignified reserve I had hitherto been advised to keep and had kept. Alderman Stevens, my son, S. A. Foote, and David B. Ogden advised the course I took with this letter.

That Judge Spencer finally approved of the Chancellor's course is evident from the following : —

Judge Spencer to Chancellor Kent.

ALBANY, October 31, 1832.

MY DEAR SIR, — I am glad you did not comply with my request, and I see by the Genesee paper that Miller's treachery has done no harm and can do none ; had you written as I requested no use would have been made of your letter. If you read or see the "Albany Evening Journal," you will perceive the abortion of Van Buren's scheme to change Genesee County from its present position by operating on Miller, the journalist of Morgan. I can only say to you that in this region our prospects were never better. Our zeal and unremitted exertions cannot be surpassed, even in your city. God prosper the holy cause.

Equally interested in the Presidential election then approaching was Edward Everett of Massachusetts, who, in September, 1832, wrote to Chancellor Kent to ascertain, if possible, his judgment as to the political probabilities of the State of New York.

Edward Everett to Chancellor Kent.

CHARLESTOWN, MASS., Sept. 15, 1832.

MY DEAR SIR, — I take the liberty to trouble you with the inquiry, what, in your judgment, is the prospect of the approaching Presidential election in your State? Is the union between Mr. Clay's friends and the anti-Masons so general as to ensure the election of the list of electors, at the head of which your name is placed? If that list is chosen, to whom will its votes be given, in whole or in part? I am aware, dear sir, of the uncertainty that must attend these points, and of the delicacy of the last question, as addressed to you. My motives for making the inquiry, beyond that of a natural curiosity, are to be found in the circumstance that I am one of the delegates for this town to the National Republican Convention of this State, which meets at Worcester on the 11th of October, at which it will be highly expedient that accurate information from all quarters should be collected. You may depend upon a discreet and confidential use, and none other, being made of any communication with which you may favor me on this subject.

Chief-Justice Daggett of Connecticut, too, shared with Kent and Everett and Webster their apprehensions. The Worcester convention, which was at hand when Everett wrote the characteristic letter just quoted, — cool, calm, insinuating, and non-committal, — had been held, and Webster from the floor had delivered one of those impassioned speeches which raised him to the highest rank among the orators of his day. His speech had been published, and had been read by thousands. Upon laying it down after perusal,

Chief-Justice Daggett wrote these words of glowing eulogium and of fearful pessimism: —

Chief-Justice Daggett to Chancellor Kent.

NEW HAVEN, Oct. 29, 1832.

I thank you, my dear sir, for the four volumes of your Commentaries which you sent me. This work I cherish with more affection than any other except the Bible and Shakespeare. With a distinguished judge of the Supreme Court of the United States, I esteem it the best general treatise on law now extant.

Have you read Webster's speech at the Worcester convention? I know you have. Is it not most logical and eloquent? Can such an appeal to the good sense, the justice, and the patriotism of our fellow-citizens fail to affect the approaching election? Or will the people refuse to hear Moses and the prophets, or one from the dead?

I declare to you, my friend, though I witnessed the shutting of the port of Boston in 1774, the battles of Lexington and Bunker Hill in 1775, the rebellion of 1787–8 in Massachusetts, and the portentous period of 1789, I never felt such fearful forebodings as I now feel. "The Lord reigneth" is one consolation. This nation is too young, though corrupt enough, for destruction. May Heaven defend us!

The downfall of Federalism and the triumph of Jacobinism, or the Republican (now the Democratic) party, was a serious blow to Chancellor Kent. As he denounced Jefferson, so, too, he denounced with equal vigor the man of the hour, Andrew Jackson, and the political principles which he represented. In April, 1835, he wrote to his brother: —

Chancellor Kent to Moss Kent.

April 3, 1835.

Chief-Justice Spencer called on me this morning, and is as vigorous, vehement, and bold and dogmatic as ever. We cordially sympathize together in abhorrence of Jacksonism. He dines with me to-morrow. Daniel Webster is in town. I was at dinner with him and a large, select company at the house of James G. King, who is sensible, pure, generous, patriotic. Webster was the oracle ; and wisdom, if not truths divine, came mended from his tongue.

The last of this month I move to one of the houses across the street. I think I improve my situation and house. The raising of my rent drove me away. My studies of all kinds are pursued with my ancient ardor. I read all the new law books, reports, reviews, literary, political, and theological.

You will see by the New York papers of the 1st and 2d inst. that my son was secretary at a meeting at Tammany Hall. It was called by a very respectable committee from both parties, in order to declare and protect the chartered rights of the city from being transferred to the Albany Regency. The committee sent him a letter requesting him to be one of the secretaries, and the radical mob produced a row and broke up the meeting. There never was such misrule. Our Tory rich men are becoming startled and alarmed at our downhill course. My opinion is that the admission of universal suffrage and a licentious press are incompatible with government and security to property, and that the government and character of this country are going to ruin. This suffrage is too great an excitement for any political machine. It racks it to pieces, and morals go with it. It is probable England is going the same way. We are becoming selfish, profligate, crazy.

Our religionists are fanatics, and our temperance societies are pushing to disgusting excess and becoming intemperate

in temperance. E. Delevan is crazy, and so are all four
and five and six day meeting and revival folks. Such, *entre
nous*, are my sentiments. Give me the writings of Addison
and Locke, and the Presbyterianism of Dr. Ripley, Dr.
Styles, and old Dr. Rodgers.

The sentiments of Chancellor Kent toward Thomas
Jefferson and his principles are, perhaps, well shown
forth by a letter addressed to the Chancellor by
Theodore Dwight, in August, 1837. It is unfortunate
that no copy of his reply to this letter is preserved,
but from the circumstance that Mr. Dwight desired to
submit the plan of his work for his criticism, it cannot
be doubted that that gentleman was confident of the
sentiments of the man whom he was addressing.

Theodore Dwight to Chancellor Kent.

HARTFORD, August 3, 1837.

MY DEAR SIR, — Before I left New York, I had, during
my confinement to the house by rheumatism, spent some
time on a work that I had projected, on the principles and
character of Thomas Jefferson. It was my object to show
by evidence drawn from his own works, that all the objections which the Federalists had to him as a public man were
true. For the want of something better to do, since I have
been here, I have been engaged in the prosecution of the
plan, and have, to a considerable degree, completed it.
Not having opportunity to consult with old Federalists, for
the greater part of them are gone, and young ones are not
often to be found from whom I might derive any benefit, I
hope you will pardon me for troubling you with this letter,
in which I propose to give you a general sketch of my plan,
for the purpose of asking you whether I have omitted any
important item in the list of charges against him, and if so

what they are? The following are the heads of the catalogue of political and moral defects in his character. The Federalists believed : —

1. That he was opposed to the Constitution.

2. That he had an undue attachment to France.

3. That he would make use of the patronage of the Government to promote his own and his party's ends.

4. That he was hostile to an independent judiciary.

5. That he entertained dangerous opinions respecting the principles of the Constitution, particularly that the courts could not bind the executive.

6. That one generation of men or of societies cannot make laws or constitutions to bind their successors.

7. That he was a mere partisan in politics.

8. That he disregarded the Constitution when it stood in his way — the treaty-making power.

9. Insidious attacks upon Washington.

10. That he was no statesman — abstract of his messages.

11. That he was an enemy to Washington.

12. That he charged the Federalists with being monarchists.

13. Opposition to the Alien and Sedition laws.

14. Destitute of veracity.

15. Attacks upon Hamilton.

16. Habitually insincere and hypocritical.

17. That he would adopt the lowest arts of a demagogue.

18. Correspondence with Washington about dissensions in the cabinet.

19. Was not a Christian.

I hope you will think the list is long enough in all conscience ; but I should be sorry to do him injustice by omitting even a single bright trait of his character. My purpose is to make him the trumpeter of his own fame, by drawing from his own works the proofs of specific virtues ; and it is my wish to make the catalogue as complete as possible.

Will you have the goodness, after having read the foregoing bill of parcels, at some moment, to let me know if
any material article is omitted. You can consult your leisure ; and if you have any idea of making an excursion in the
summer in this region, I would much rather take the answer
to my inquiries from your own mouth ; as I might have the
opportunity, perhaps, to consult with you a little about the
manner of the execution of my work.

check

The plan I believe to be a good one. I only wish it had
been taken up by some abler hand. But seeing no prospect
of that, and feeling satisfied that if it ever is done, it must
be before the generation of Federalists has passed entirely
away, I undertook it.   In my judgment justice to a party of
as virtuous patriots and enlightened statesmen as ever lived
requires that the slanders and reproaches of one of the
worst of men should not be suffered to go down to future
ages uncontradicted and unexplained.

That Chancellor Kent was thoroughly in accord
with Mr. Dwight in his conception of the character
of Jefferson is fairly shown by his notes pencilled in
the first volume of George Tucker's " Life of Thomas
Jefferson," published in 1837, which illustrate not only
his method of making such memoranda, but reveal his
sentiments on reaching that portion of the narrative
which dealt with that period of Jefferson's political
career with which he himself was the most familiar.

Notes in Tucker's " Life of Jefferson."

"Very sage remarks on the illusions that mingle
in the recollections of the past, p. 95."

"Very sensible remarks on codification, pp. 104,
105."

"Mr. Jefferson insisted that the whites and the race of free blacks could not live together equally free in the same government. He was for the process of deportation and emancipation, p. 112."

"Mr. Jefferson's great hospitality to the English and German prisoners located near Charlotteville; he pleads beautifully for their comfort, pp. 121, 124."

"Jefferson's eulogy on French manners, temperance, architecture, painting, and music, p. 190."

"Striking reflection on Mr. Jefferson's plan of a Rural Club in Virginia; of him, Madison, Monroe, and Short, p. 221."

"What a deceptive vision! Three of these were Presidents of the United States."

"Mr. Jefferson, in 1787, showed himself an ultra Democrat. He preferred the Indians without any government, to the governments of continental Europe, p. 231."

"He was in favor of an occasional rebellion, p. 232."

"His eulogy on the Confederation as the best government that ever existed. He thought it very easy and safe for Congress to coerce the States, p. 242."

"His hostility to religion and the study of moral philosophy, p. 243."

"He thinks the Massachusetts rebellion a good thing; the tree of liberty must be refreshed from time to time with blood, p. 254."

"The danger and the actual apprehensions in Democracies is the tyranny of majorities, p. 278."

"Temperate and able discussion of Mr. Jefferson, and project that no law, or constitution, or contract binding after nineteen years, p. 291."

"The historian justifies Mr. Jefferson's minuting down and disclosing Mr. Hamilton's conversation with him on the British Monarchy, p. 250."

"After the historian brings the story down to 1790, when Mr. Jefferson assumed the office of Secretary of State, he becomes a devoted partisan of Jefferson's politics, and sides with him in all his illiberal and malignant attacks on Hamilton and the Federalists, and apologizes for all of Jefferson's radicalism and libels. The volume hitherto had been well, and quite fair, and impartially written, but I afterwards quit reading the volume with perfect disgust."

A glance at the political condition of the South at this period is useful at this point, and this is gained by a perusal of the letters of Chancellor de Saussure, of South Carolina, written to Chancellor Kent. The first of these letters is dated November 4, 1830. After transmitting to his legal brother some numbers of a law journal, recently established at Columbia, and discussing one or two points of law, the Southern Chancellor continues: —

Chancellor de Saussure to Chancellor Kent.

I have no doubt that you take great interest in what is passing in the South, as you know and appreciate the inestimable value of the Union. The whole South is deeply discontented with the measures of the general government in relation to the tariff for protection of manufactures and the prodigal expenditures of the public money on internal improvements, which furnishes the pretense for keeping up the tariff. South Carolina feels and resents these abuses more than any other Southern State, but they all sympathize with her and will act with her when all hope of redress shall be extinguished. South Carolina is wonderfully unanimous as to the evil, and the necessity of persevering and ceaseless resistance to the oppression and injustice.

There is, however, a great difference of opinion as to the proper method of resistance, and how long we should forbear before we proceed to extremities. All this produces great uneasiness among our wisest and best men. You may be assured, however, that it is a gross mistake to suppose that any of the eminent men who take the lead have any desire to dissolve the Union. They are excellent men of high principle, who value the Union at a very high rate, but who cannot consent to the exercise of unconstitutional and oppressive powers, which would soon transform this confederacy into a government of unlimited powers. To that we shall never yield. My days of action are over and I may not live to see the conclusion of this dispute. I pray God to preserve our country, free, united and happy.

One year later he again writes : —

Chancellor de Saussure to Chancellor Kent.

COLUMBIA, S. C., August 4, 1831.

MY DEAR SIR, — . . . We are still as ardent in our politics as ever. Indeed, party politics have become more violent than ever I knew them, except once, at the time of Jefferson's election to the Presidency. What is to be the result cannot be foreseen. The South is exceedingly unanimous in the dislike, and even abhorrence, of a tariff for protection for manufacturers beyond what would result incidentally from a real revenue tariff. Many ascribe the depression of the price of our produce, and consequently the depreciation of all our property, wholly to the tariff, by its direct and indirect action. Others ascribe the evil partly to that cause, and partly to over production; men take their sides according to their temperament.

Some consider the evils intolerable and have no hope of a remedy and are prepared for a secession from the Union, great as that evil would be, rather than to submit to a continuance of the present injustice. Another portion of the people are so anxious to preserve the Union that they will not yet give up the hope of relief from the Government. When the debt is paid there will be no pretense for continuing a tariff, producing ten millions beyond the mere revenue wants of the Government, and our moderates expect relief at or before that time. If it be not then obtained I believe South Carolina and probably the Southern States will secede. This would be a great calamity to America and would renew the rivalries, the struggles, and the wars of the Grecian republics of ancient time and of the Italian in the middle ages. I pray God in his mercy to save us from these calamities. This prayer is for our children and for our country, for at the age of 68 years, you and I have, I presume, nearly run our course in this world and are preparing for a better. May the remainder of your days be spent in ease and repose, and may you and your great services be honored and remembered as they deserve to be.

Chancellor de Saussure to Chancellor Kent.

COLUMBIA, November 17, 1831.

MY DEAR SIR, — . . . I hope you enjoy your health and spirits, and continue to possess the *mens sana in corpore sano* which you have heretofore enjoyed, and have therefore been enabled to instruct and delight your contemporaries. We are both of us approaching three score and ten, the usual term of even robust and temperate men, when we must look for the gradual wearing out of the machine. I hope it may be gently, and that we may be prepared for the great change when we have to render an account of our stewardship.

The times seem to be out of joint both in Europe and in this country. The fermentation in the public mind in Europe is very great. It is really the struggle of opposing principles, of liberalism against despotism. What is to be the issue, God only, in his infinite wisdom, can foresee. I am inclined to believe that the liberal spirit, which is that of the age, will prevail; but the transition may be through disorder and blood. And there is a good deal of ferment alive in the minds of our citizens in the Southern and some of the Southwestern States. They will never be reconciled to a tariff for protection. And though the moderation of many of our citizens restrains the violence of the great mass for the present, that restraint cannot be enforced if the redress sought be not obtained in a reasonable time. At all events, if the tariff be not reduced to a liberal revenue standard, when the national debt is paid, the violent men will prevail; and I fear for the safety of the Union. The dissolution of that holy ark of our safety would be the signal for all sorts of calamities, foreign or domestic, which God in his mercy avert! Do not believe that it is a mere faction, working to destroy the Union for personal aggrandizement. Many of our ablest men are of opinion that a tariff for protection is oppressive, unequal, and unjust, and contrary to the spirit of the Constitution, and not to be endured if the remedy be not applied by Congress. Many of us (for I am of that number) continue to hope for redress, and deprecate extreme measures till all hope is extinguished.

IX

A S Judge Kent himself notes, he did not possess
forensic talent, nor was he ever distinguished
in contentions at the Bar. He spoke through his pen,
and, upon the few occasions on which he made public
addresses, he spoke entirely from his notes. He was a
graceful, eloquent, and interesting speaker. At a meeting of the New York Historical Society, on December 6, 1828, of which society he was the president, he
made the annual address. His memory at that time
went back to a former generation, and his characterizations of some of the men of the past were of deep
interest to his auditors. On Alexander Hamilton he
pronounced a magnificent eulogium. Of him he said :
" His transcendent services to the nation are sufficient
to render his name immortal." So greatly did he admire Hamilton living, and so deeply did he revere his
memory for years after his death, that it would seem
that language failed to express the depth of his inner
feeling. When, in 1832, the widow of General Hamilton, who was also the daughter of General Schuyler,
applied to the Chancellor for some of his reminiscences and impressions of her husband, he replied in
a lengthy monograph, which might almost be called
a biography in itself. This historical sketch of Alexander Hamilton was divided into three parts. In the

first he related his first personal knowledge of the subject, and brought the narrative down to the call for the Constitutional Convention in 1787. The second discussed Hamilton's services in relation to the origin and adoption of the Federal Constitution. The third considered in considerable detail his subsequent life.

"I knew General Hamilton's character well," he says in closing this discourse. "His life and actions for the course of twenty-two years had engaged and fixed my attention. They were often passing under my eye and observation. For the last six years of his life he was arguing causes before me. I have been sensibly struck, in a thousand instances, with his habitual reverence for truth, his candor, his ardent attachment to civil liberty, his indignation at oppression of every kind, his abhorrence of every semblance of fraud, his reverence for justice, his sound legal principles, drawn by a clear and logical deduction from the purest Christian ethics and from the very foundations of all rational and practical jurisprudence. He was blessed with a very amiable, generous, tender, and charitable disposition, and he had the most artless simplicity of any man I ever knew. It was impossible not to love as well as respect and admire him. He was perfectly disinterested. The selfish principle, that infirmity too often of great as well as of little minds, seemed never to have reached him. It was entirely incompatible with the purity of his taste and the grandeur of his ambition. Everything appeared to be at once extinguished when it came in competition with his devotion to his country's welfare and glory. He was a most faithful friend to the cause of civil liberty throughout the world, but he was a still greater friend to truth and justice."[1]

Upon the fiftieth anniversary of his graduation Chancellor Kent was invited to deliver the annual address before the Phi Beta Kappa Society of Yale College, with Edward Everett as his alternate. This invitation was accepted, and the address was delivered September 13, 1831. Of the manner in which this address impressed his contemporaries one may judge from the letter which follows from the pen of Chief-Justice Story of Massachusetts, with whom Chancellor Kent maintained a friendship of years.

Chief-Justice Story to Chancellor Kent.

CAMBRIDGE, Oct. 25, 1831.

DEAR SIR, — I should have long since thanked you for the present of your excellent Φ B K address if my absence on my circuit duties and my continued labors since my return here, had not interrupted my purpose. I have read your discourse with the highest relish, and partake of the enthusiasm with which your mind kindles at the reminiscences of former times. I know not how it is, but you carry me a voluntary captive in all your labors, whether in law, or in literature. You throw over everything which you touch a fresh and mellow coloring, which elevates while it warms, and convinces us that the picture is truth and the artist a master. I should dare to say this to few persons, lest they should suspect that I placed little value on my words. But you know that to repress this tribute would be to suppress a praise to which you have an unquestioned and an unquestionable title.

A passage from this address, in which Chancellor Kent extolled the study of the classics, is of especial

[1] *Vide* Appendix.

interest, as bearing testimony to the inestimable benefit which he believed that their study had been to
him in his struggle for success in his chosen profession.   After eulogizing the literature of the ancients,
as "eminent for sound judgment and severe simplicity," he continued : —

"During the time spent in the acquisition of the
learned languages, the attention of the student is directed to the purest classical writers ; and, while he is
becoming master of the tongue, he is, at the same
time, receiving his best and most lasting impressions
of the general literature and beautiful productions of
the ancients."

On the twenty-first day of May, 1832, Washington
Irving, after an extended residence abroad, arrived at
New York on his homeward journey.   He was cordially welcomed by his friends and admirers, who
tendered to him a public dinner.   This was given,
two days later, at City Hotel, New York, Chancellor
Kent presiding.   Mr. Irving was exceedingly nervous
throughout the evening.   "I look forward to it with
awe," he had written to his brother Peter, "and shall
be heartily glad when it is over."   His apprehensions,
however, were groundless, although three hundred
were present.   "The occasion," says Irving's bio-
grapher,[1] "was rare, the homage spontaneous, the
hilarity inspiring."   At the removal of the cloth the
toastmaster offered the first toast of the evening :
"Literature, Commerce, and the Fine Arts, their

[1] *Life and Letters of Washington Irving*, by Pierre M. Irving,
Kinderhook ed., ii. 225.

union, the glory of our parent land, soon destined to adorn our own." To this toast Chancellor Kent responded in these words: —

" We have met to express to a distinguished fellow-citizen, our gratitude for the exalted rank to which he has raised the literary reputation of this country; to testify our admiration of his genius, and to show that we cordially partake of the kindly and generous sympathies which pervade, and have been diffused by, his works. The mention of this subject calls up a crowd of associations and recollections, which even adequately to refer to would carry me far beyond the limits of the time and the occasion, but on which my feelings compel me for a few moments to linger. When the gentleman alluded to commenced his brilliant career (which we trust is far from its termination) by a display of the wit and humor, the keen satire and sprightly portraits which distinguished his earliest productions (and in which it is understood he was assisted by a kindred genius),[1] we had scarcely any literary character as a nation, though we are entitled to claim the exhibition of a due share of national energy and enterprise. Our taste and manners were greatly in need of improvement. The admirable work to which I refer partook largely of a dramatic character, and, being armed with wit and power of the highest, it undertook to chastise folly, correct faults of taste, reform bad manners, and mend the heart. The effort was well received, and the public judgment had no reason in any wise to be offended.

[1] " Geoffrey Crayon, Gent."

No composition of the kind was ever more distinctly stamped with the impression of sterling morals and invariable good feeling, or more free from envy, hatred, malice, and all uncharitableness. The work even abounded with touches of sentiment and pathos, and with fictitious scenes calculated to awaken the deepest sympathy.

"The legend of the first colonization of this city and of the adjacent shores must, at this moment, be vivid in the memories of us all, — such a mock heroic history, written in the finest strain of burlesque gravity, and of witty and ludicrous description, and of playful, but pointed, satire and ridicule. It has rarely, perhaps never, been surpassed, not even by Rabelais or Swift, in its power, spirit, and effect. It was at the same time, written with so much good temper and humanity that there is nothing in it justly chargeable with a tendency to make one worthy man its foe.

"The materials of both those satirical productions were of native growth. They partook of no transatlantic flavor. They were original and inimitable creations of American genius, in all its freshness, fullness, and strength, and solely exerted upon American topics. But the mind produced powers of thought and invention amidst the beautiful scenes of English rural life and the magnificent remains of Gothic grandeur. In the sketches and essays of Geoffrey Crayon, we have a series of liberal, moral, and pathetic reflections, interwoven with legendary tales of fascinating interest, and adorned with the utmost purity of taste and elegance of style. Many of the stories possess the charm of the finest fictions in the English

classics. The liberality, the gentleness, the philan-
thropy, the taste, the sound judgment and varied accomplishments of the writer, seemed at once to have
surprised and delighted the English reader. Those
sketches were attended with magical effects. Arro-
gance stood rebuked and ashamed, and prejudice was
subdued, and succeeded by admiration and love.

"We rejoiced to behold one of our own native sons
rival, on English ground, the grace and elegance, the
pathos and lofty morals of Addison, Goldsmith, and
McKenzie; we shared equally with our transatlantic
brethren in the pleasures afforded by his graphic descriptions, and hung with an equal intensity over the
description of some of his matchless English scenes
and incidents. But we are free to admit that we took
a far deeper interest in those enchanting visions which
brought us back to the borders of the romantic Hudson; 'to the blue hills of our own country, which we
love so dearly;' to the 'deep mountain glens' of the
Kaattskills, and to the 'twilight superstitions' of the
Sleepy Hollow.

"Through all the writings of our distinguished
countryman, even in his earlier and sprightlier productions, we meet with occasional sentiments of high
and grave import, the genuine growth of ardent feeling which go directly to the heart. Nothing can be
more soothing and gratifying to meditative minds than
such pensive, chaste, and mellowed reflections, arising
from views of autumnal scenery, the ruins of ancient
art, and the monuments of departed greatness.

"The gentleman who favored the world with these
productions, not content with enjoying the admi-

ration of the republic of letters to a very eminent degree, was in the meantime busy in earning for himself a title to a still higher niche in the temple of fame. Having access to original and fresh documents relating to the life of Christopher Columbus, he was encouraged and enabled to undertake and execute a great historical work, and on a subject the most rich in details, and the most magnificent in its results, of any that ever employed the pen of the historian. He brought to the task all his great and diversified powers. His materials were selected with judgment, studied with diligence, arranged with skill, exhibited with fidelity, polished with taste and recommended by finished specimens of a graceful, flowing, and dignified composition. The discovery of America was essentially a domestic theme. Though the enterprise was begun in Europe, it was consummated on this side of the Atlantic. The settlement of this New World seems to be a theme peculiarly appropriate to the pen of an American writer, who would naturally feel and appreciate, most deeply and justly, the inestimable value of the discovery, and the mighty consequences of the establishment of great nations on this continent, with their language and institutions, their freedom and religion, their arts and sciences spreading themselves over its surface. The choice was most propitious, and the 'History of the Life and Voyages of Columbus' will probably become the standard work on that subject through all succeeding ages. It equals the most distinguished historical compositions, not only in the dignity of the subject, but in the judgment, skill, spirit, and felicity of its execution.

"This eminent historian, honored and beloved abroad, now returns with joy to the home of his youth, and to the beloved companions and scenes of his earliest glory.

"Let us drink to — Our Illustrious Guest; thrice welcome to his native land!"

The Chancellor was, beyond doubt, gratified at receiving, a few days later, a word of commendation from his friend Daniel Webster: —

Daniel Webster to Chancellor Kent.

WASHINGTON, June 5, 1832.

MY DEAR SIR, — I have just opened the newspaper and read the account of Mr. Irving's dinner, and your speech thereat; and I resolved forthwith to write you one line, for the purpose of saying that the speech is a delightful little thing, just, sweet, affectionate. When I read the paragraph in which you prefer what relates to the blue hills and mountain glens of our own country to sketches of foreign scenes and foreign countries, I wanted to seize your hand and give it a hearty shake of sympathy. Heaven bless this goodly land of our fathers! Its rulers and its people may commit a thousand follies, yet Heaven bless it! Next to the friends beloved of my heart, those same hills and glens, and native woods and native streams, will have my last earthly recollections! *Dulce et decorum est*, etc.

In an address delivered before the Law Association of the city of New York, October 21, 1836, Chancellor Kent spoke in an impressive manner of the responsibilities and duties of the legal profession. "The responsibilities attached to the profession and practice of the law," he said, "are of the most momen-

tous character. Its members, by their vocation,
ought to be fitted for the great duties of public life,
and they may be said to be *ex officio* natural guardians
of the laws, and to stand sentinels over the constitutions and liberties of the country. I know of no
duty, next to the worship and obedience which we
owe to Our Father which Art in Heaven, that is more
imperative in its requisitions, and more delightful in
the performance, than that which the municipal law
of the land requires of its various professors. . . .
The cultivation and practice of the law is, and ought
to be, a sure road to personal prosperity and to
political eminence and fame, provided the members
of the Bar render themselves worthy of public confidence, by their skill and industry, their knowledge,
integrity, and honor, their public spirit and manly
deportment, their purity, moderation, and wisdom."

Charles Sumner to Chancellor Kent.

January 1, 1837.

MY DEAR SIR, — I gladly seize the opportunity of Judge
Story's transit through New York to thank you for the
present of your beautiful and instructive address delivered
before the Law Association. I have read it with the greatest
interest, and feel indebted to you for the elevated views
which you have given of the study of the law, and the
sketches of some of its expired lights in your own State.
No lawyer or law student could quit it without feeling
prouder than he was before of his chosen pursuit, and
being stimulated to new labors, in short, without attaching
himself with new zeal to the single talisman of success,
study.

When I think of the good which you have done, in promoting the study of jurisprudence, by the publication of your Commentaries and of this address, and by your high example, — I say nothing of the sweet influence of your social character and the important bearings of your long judicial life, — I cannot but envy you the feeling which you must enjoy. The mighty tribute of gratitude is silently offered to you from every student of the law in our whole country. There is not one who has found his toilsome way cheered and delighted by the companionship of your labors, who would not speak as I do, if he had the privilege of addressing you.

The interest which Mr. Kent took in all kinds of literary work was surprising, and the care with which he read, abstracted, and noted in each volume the points which most interested him, or which caught his attention, is indicative of his studious temperament and indomitable persistent industry. In almost every work of his library the blank leaves at the beginning and end of each volume are filled with notes, extracts, and references to other works. He literally read with a pen in his hand, and every interesting or disputed point was made the occasion for very full references and citation. The zeal with which he read and studied his books is likewise shown forth, as already suggested, in almost every one of the many letters which, throughout the passage of the years, he wrote to his brother, Moss Kent. As early as August, 1790, he wrote : —

James Kent to Moss Kent.

I have finished, within a few pages, Tully De Oratore. I consider that as a great achievement for this summer, especially as I have had no translation. I suppose him harder than Livy, as one is only narration and the other a didactic work. I master him so easily that I read six pages every morning and also one hundred lines in Homer. I am in the fifth Book of the Iliad, where Diomed makes such a brilliant figure, but what takes away from all his credit is that he is assisted by Minerva. . . . I have been reading the works of Macchiavelli, his " History of Florence." His " Prince " and his political discourses on the first decade of Livy are the chief works by which his fame has been celebrated with such various colors. His History is an excellent thing and his style nervous and simple. His " Prince " is a most singular performance and, taken literally (and we have no evidence that he was ironical), contains the most wicked and abominable maxims. His discourses are profoundly written, and his precepts illustrated by facts drawn from Livy and from the Florentine annals, so that, tho' I don't know what to make of " The Prince," I view him as one of the greatest political reasoners on facts and one of the greatest philosophers of modern times, if not of any times.

Upon the fly-leaf of one of his volumes of " Oeuvres de L'Abbé de Malby " (Paris, 1792) he notes : —

"The Abbé Malby appears to have drunk of the whole cup of modern French Philosophy and Democracy, and to be as intoxicated as any of their writers. The same eternal declamation against government and distinctions, the same puerile panegyric on equality and the rights of man, pervade alike all the French philosophers for the last fifty years, and have, no doubt, essentially fostered and incited the dreadful and devouring tempest of the French Revolution. The Abbé in this work, in the study of history, appears

to be a wild and contemptible philosopher.   He dares
not indulge his wishes for full equality, but is at all
events for the sumptuary and agrarian laws."

In the Chancellor's copy of Mary Wollstonecraft's
"Vindication of the Rights of Woman" (1792),
he penciled quite an extended biographical note, to
which he appended this criticism of the book, which
he had evidently perused with great care: —

"The fundamental principle on which the whole
argument of this work is founded is that, except in
affairs of love, sexual distinctions ought to be disregarded, and women considered in the light of rational
creatures.   The author discovers great energy of
mind, vigor of fancy, and command of language, but
several of her opinions are fanciful, and some of her
projects romantic.   Mr. Holcroft, in his 'Anna St.
Ives' (who in her leading features is a mere child of
the imagination), has the same doctrine, that 'mind
has no sex;' that woman is not inferior to man;
that, in a perfect state of society, no domestic appro-
priation of separate property can subsist, but all
would combine, in one universal effort of mind, to
dispel error and propagate Truth.   This is the genuine Godwinian philosophy."

"I think you took up Stuart's 'View of Society,'"
he wrote to his brother, in January, 1795.   "It has
been of great use to me in my researches into the
genius of the feudal policy.   If I am not greatly mistaken he has not only investigated deeply the pages of
Tacitus, but caught his fire and energy.   He is, in my

judgment, one of the most acute, spirited, and elegant writers that has ever adorned the temple of fame. I therefore wish you to set yourself immediately to read him and inform me shortly of the success of every part of your various literary and other pursuits."

Again, in September, 1796, he writes: —

Chancellor Kent to Moss Kent.

Novels are pleasing to me in my leisure hours. I have purchased since you have been gone, Fielding's "Joseph Andrews," Smollett's "Roderick Random," "Peregrine Pickle," "Count Faltham," and "Lancelot Graves," Defoe's "Robinson Crusoe," and Brook's "Fool of Quality." These are works of the first impression for wit, humor, the pathetic, and knowledge of man. They are classical productions of the kind. No writer that ever lived was superior to Fielding. He was a man of wonderful talents and inimitable humor. I now own all his works, and have just entered on the eighth volume of Richardson's "Clarissa." You will see just characters of Fielding and Richardson in the N. A. Review for 1781, in the introduction, page 25, I think, and where you will find the most elegant and critically just reviews of English literature under Anne and George that I ever met with.

In November, 1804, having been obliged to leave home for a time, for a session of court at New York, he writes to his wife, at the conclusion of the voyage:

"This morning we found ourselves safely and happily at the dock. I read on the voyage 'The Italian,' and melted at the tender and awful scenes of her soul-inspiring and sublime pen. Mrs. Radcliffe's [1] writings,

[1] Mrs. Ann Radcliffe, novelist, born in London, July 9, 1764, died February 7, 1823. "The Italian" was published in 1797.

no less than the keen observations and the remarks of my wife, make me bow to the equal talents and genius of female minds."

On the fly-leaf of an old edition of Shakespeare it is noted : —

"In 1804 I read Shakespeare. The Tempest is inimitable; Two Gentlemen of Verona is interesting; Merry Wives of Windsor attractive from the wit and numerous disasters of Falstaff; Twelfth Night, very indifferent; Measure for Measure, and Much Ado about Nothing abound in characters well drawn, and in interesting incident. The second is the best and has most of the comic humor; Midsummer-Night's Dream, and Love's Labor Lost are to me not worth reading; Merchant of Venice has an exquisitely drawn miser in Shylock the Jew; As you Like it is admirable; it is serious, pathetic, elegant, and sprightly. The character of Jaques is drawn with the finest touches of genius; All's Well that Ends Well is not worth the reading; but in The Taming of the Shrew the characters of Petruchio and Kate are highly and humorously drawn; Winter's Tale is extravagant; it embraces a whole generation, say twenty years, and introduces time to annihilate it. It runs from Bohemia to Sicily, and violates all the laws of probability. It restores a marble statue to life, and yet it is, on the whole, pleasing, interesting, and pathetic.

"In King John, the grief of Constantia, the generosity and bravery of the Bastard, the dialogues between Hubert and the King and Hubert and Arthur

16

show the master hand of Shakespeare; Macbeth is matchless; The Comedy of Errors is, I think, below Shakespeare's genius. The whole harmony and invention consist of four persons looking alike, and consequently mistaking each other and acting at cross purposes. Richard the Second is indifferent, — much bustle, but little dignity of sentiment or control of the heart. Henry the Fourth, the first and second are admirable, the first part by far the best, and will be ever interesting for those great and admirably drawn characters, Prince of Wales, Hotspur, and Falstaff. Henry the Fifth is a distinguished picture of action, bustle, and battle. Henry the Sixth, the three parts degenerate into dull narration, and it is doubted if Shakespeare wrote it. Richard the Third has some tender scenes and some noble description, but it is too unnatural and horrible in many parts. Henry the Eighth is a distinguished tragedy for the pathetic, and tender, and excellent character of Katharine, and the awful fall of Wolsey. Troilus and Cressida is very indifferent. Timon of Athens is a good picture of faithless and ungrateful flatterers. Coriolanus has much bustle and old Roman obstinacy and pride, but it does not strike me much. Julius Cæsar is highly interesting, from the grandeur of the story, and the impressive speeches of the principal actors. It is a play of the closet, and not of the stage. Antony and Cleopatra, I think nothing of."

In conclusion he notes, quoting from Drake: "It may be justly affirmed that many of Shakespeare's plays are barely tolerable, out of deference to the excellences of his happier productions."

Among the books of Chancellor Kent are found several volumes of " American Annals," by Abiel Holmes, the father of the late Dr. Oliver Wendell Holmes (Cambridge, 1805). In one of these volumes the Chancellor noted : —

" Dr. Holmes, the author of these volumes, died at Cambridge, Mass., June 4, 1837, aged 73. I was acquainted with him at college. He married the youngest daughter of President Stiles. I was at his house in August, 1823. He was an excellent man and I loved him much when we were at college, from June, 1779, to 1781. He was pastor of a church in Georgia from 1785 to 1791. In 1792 he was a settled minister at Cambridge, where he resided the residue of his life. As annals of the United States this book displays great industry and research, and is exceedingly valuable; but as American annals at large, it is meager and miserably imperfect. Few of the Spanish writers have been consulted, those few only in translations, and Herrera, the most important of all, in a very mutilated one. The author's collection of French authorities is also equally incomplete, and of the many important works that the ex-Jesuits have bequeathed to the world, not one appears in the catalogue. He ought to have begun his history with the first voyage of Cabot, and not with Columbus, whose history is as well known as that of Noah."

On a fly-leaf of the Chancellor's copy of William Gifford's translation of the Satire of Decimus Junius Juvenalis (Philadelphia, 1803) are these notes : —

" In 1807, Mr. Hodgson's translation of Juvenal
appeared.   No single classic has been more frequently
translated.   The Edinburgh Review (vol. xii., p. 501)
lowers a good deal the high character generally
given to the Roman satirist.   They say he writes
like a reformed rake, and like one who has lost the
delicacy of moral taste.   They admit he is a fit study
for the antiquary and the philosopher, but he ought
to be a sealed book to all but profound scholars.
On the other hand, the Monthly Review (vol. lv.)
speaks thus of Juvenal: ' His masculine genius, his
high-toned morality, his noble contempt for meanness,
and his irresistible indignation against vice, place him
in the fore rank of writers formed for the improvement and correction of man.'

" There is great truth in most of the remarks of
the Edinburgh Review and the gross obscenity and
disgusting filth do undoubtedly disgrace the pages of
Juvenal and denote a perverseness of taste.   But I
think that his masterly delineation and deep and
tragic intonation renders his moral most solemn and
impressive.   The peculiar characteristics of Juvenal,
his dignity, his vehemence, his profound horror of
vice, his bursts of uncontrollable indignation, are
happily and almost uniformly preserved in the translation of Mr. Gifford.   It unites, in no common
degree, fidelity with spirit, and is, with a few excep-
tions, the best version of a classic in our language.
They say that all the translations of the tenth Satire
are thrown in the background by Johnson's imitation,
and that management can reconcile them to the de-
testable grossness of the sixth.

"The Baviad of Mr. Gifford, an imitation of the first Satire of Persius, first detected and exposed the absurdities and effeminate conceits of the Della Crusca school. Merry and Mrs. Robinson, under the names of Lorenzo and Laura Maria, bade fair to banish Shakespeare, Dryden, and Otway, when Gifford laid them open to universal contempt and ridicule, with a grave severity of sarcasm that reminds the reader of the classical ages. The same attack is vigorously repeated in the Moviad, and these two short works may carry their author's name down to succeeding ages. Their conciseness is favorable to their continuance; for there is much truth in Fréron's *bon mot*, applied to the variety of volumes of which Voltaire's works are composed. 'This luggage is too cumbersome to travel to posterity.'"

In his copy of the Memoirs of Frederick and Margaret Klopstock (Philadelphia, 1810), Mr. Kent notes: —

"Klopstock, Schiller, and Goethe are a triumvirate which no country except England can equal. Klopstock had no knowledge of mankind, and could not describe those evil passions to which his own breast was happily a stranger. He could paint, indeed, with exquisite, perhaps matchless beauty, the characters of tenderness or religious hope, or the agonies of despairing penitence; but not the horrible workings of jealousy, ambition, hatred, and pride. His evil characters in the 'Messiah' are all meager sketches, but the 'Messiah' is still a noble work. There runs through the whole a persevering spirit of piety and poetry, which amply compensate for occasional mysticism; and there are some descriptions, and still more effusions of eloquent feeling, which the admirers of Milton will find it hard to parallel. The genius of Klopstock was influenced by the perusal of Milton and Young. Madame de Staël translated his ode on the rivalship of the Muse of Germany with the Muse of Albion."

The wide range of the Chancellor's reading is illustrated in a letter to Professor Silliman, of Yale College, the eminent mineralogist.

Chancellor Kent to Professor Silliman.

ALBANY, August 7, 1819.

DEAR SIR, — I am obliged to interrupt your studies for a moment to thank you for the pleasure and instruction you have given me in another work of yours which has lately been presented by you and to which I have become a subscriber. I have read attentively such parts as were most interesting to me of the four numbers in first volume of your "Journal of Science," and you have communicated such charm and luster to the science of mineralogy and the other kindred branches that I have been led to regret my exclusive attention hitherto to the more dull and dry science of jurisprudence. If I were young in life I have no doubt I should enter with zeal into your favorite study, and endeavor to match some of your generous enthusiasm in the pursuit.

The science you are engaged in offers new views of the wonders of creation, and affords new and striking traces of the wisdom and benevolence of the Deity. The parts of the volume that most pleased me were your review of Professor Cleveland's "Mineralogy," of Cuvier's "Theory of the Earth," on an anticipated visit to the North Pole, on the just and spirited vindication of Trumbull's painting, and the fine eulogy on the character of the Abbé Barry, etc. The journal of Mr. Cornelius on the features of the Southern States was very pleasing; in short, all the articles that I could well understand were read with great interest and satisfaction.

The following sketch of William Pinkney is found in manuscript on the fly-leaf of a volume entitled "Some Account of the Writings and Speeches of William Pinkney," by H. Wheaton (New York, 1826):

"Mr. Pinkney is a free-spoken man; he is plain and bold, and a little inclined to sarcasm and airs of insulting superiority. His style has the free flowing and elegant simplicity and the chaste beauties of the judicial opinions of Sir William Scott.[1] He handles the opinions and decrees of Sir James Marriott without much reverence. Mr. Pinkney shows himself by this paper ('Memorial against the Rule of 1756, and the Attacks by the British, down to 1806, on Neutral Commerce') to be a publicist of great knowledge and ardent feelings, and of bold, dogmatic, arrogant, sarcastic, denunciatory, vehement, and masterly powers of declamation and argument. No man went greater lengths than he did in support of and devotion to the administrations of Jefferson and Madison, and implacable hostility to England. No man was more devoted to the administrations of Jefferson and Madison, in all their acts and policies with England and France, and he and Madison agreed well in them. His speech in the case of the 'Nereide' is a splendid

[1] Baron Stowell.

specimen of forensic eloquence and classical illustration and ingenious and powerful argument and accurate and profound knowledge of public law. His speech on the treaty power is admirable and finished. It ranks with the best of Cicero's speeches. May 16, 1826, Wheaton called on me, and spoke much concerning William Pinkney. He said his talents were splendid, but his moral character was bad; he was wrapped up in himself and deemed himself great, without an equal. He cared for nothing but what contributed to his individual vanity and self-gratification. He modeled himself upon Cicero, and had his polished style, his art, his ambition as an actor, and his same vanity. He was a perfect dandy in his dress, and devoted much time to his dear person. He was brave, and not vindictive, and upon the whole would make a sacrifice to gratify his love of self and of fame. He was destitute of the noblest moral qualifications, simplicity, modesty, generosity, purity, disinterestedness, and, in short, he was one of the ' brightest and meanest of mankind.' "

Almost immediately after its publication, the Chancellor, as noted upon a previous page, procured and eagerly perused Sparks' " Life of Washington " (Boston, 1804).[1] In his personal copy of the work are found these comments : —

" The letters of Washington are deeply interesting. They are written with admirable good sense and exalted patriotism. His prudence and discretion are above all praise. The free and frank manner in which

[1] *Supra*, p. 146.

he corresponds with Congress shows his unbounded influence and integrity and candor. His style is clear and forcible, and not destitute of elegance. He was truly the great master spirit that sustained the American Revolution. General Washington strongly remonstrated, in 1778, against the military appointments lavished on foreign officers, French and German. They were vain, presumptuous, clamorous applicants, and created great disgust in the American officers. General Washington regretted that ever a commission was granted to a foreign officer, even to Baron Steuben, — the Marquis Fayette always excepted, whom he tenderly loved. The patriotism, firmness, wisdom, prudence, enterprise, and matchless simplicity, integrity, and industry of General Washington, as displayed in these volumes, are beyond all precedent. The United States is indebted for its independence to him, more than to all Congress united. His letters are admirable, and display the great statesman no less than the discreet and daring soldier."

In these memoranda and notes, made, doubtless, for his own eye and mind alone, the Chancellor was exceedingly free and untrammeled, especially in his comments upon contemporaries. Even to his latest days, he ceased not in his detestation of the political principles advocated by Thomas Jefferson. Ardent partisan as he was, however, and fully recognizing what he regarded as well-nigh moral obliquity in his political opponents, he was still able to characterize with fairness the personal qualities of such opponents, and the literary value of their writings. In illustration

of this characteristic of Chancellor Kent, is reproduced a note inscribed, in the year 1836, upon a fly-
leaf of a volume of " Letters on Silesia," by John
Quincy Adams (London, 1804) : —

"John Quincy Adams, Senator in Congress from
Massachusetts, was, in June, 1806, installed in Cambridge, as Professor of Rhetoric.   In June, 1808, he
resigned his seat in the Senate of the United States in
disgust, because the Massachusetts Legislature had just
elected Mr. Lloyd as his successor, and condemned with
marked disapprobation the measure of the Embargo,
which he had advocated.   In the summer of 1809, he
was sent as minister from the United States to Russia.
He turned, in 1808 and 1809, to be an apostate like
his father, and became a malignant libeler of the
Federalists, and a base and unprincipled tool of the
Jeffersonian administration.   In 1813 he was appointed a Judge of the Supreme Court of the United
States; this he declined.   In 1813, being still resident
minister at St. Petersburg, he was, in conjunction with
Mr. Gallatin and Mr. Bayard, appointed to negotiate
a peace with Great Britain, under the mediation of
Russia.   He was one of the Commissioners that nego-
tiated the Treaty of Peace at Ghent, in 1814, with
Great Britain.   In February, 1825, he was elected
President of the United States.   In February, 1829, he
lost his re-election by a large majority, and Andrew
Jackson succeeded him as President.   He retired from
office with the detestation of the Boston and New Eng-
land Federalists, for his recent malignant calumnies.
In 1835, John Q. Adams was a candidate for the Senate

of the United States and was defeated. G. Davis, of
Boston, was preferred Mr. Adams then relapsed
into malignant and unprincipled anti-Federalism, and
abused the Federalists and the Hartford Convention
party (that was his plea) in unmeasured terms; and in
January, 1836, as a member of the House of Representatives, he abused the Senate and Daniel Webster,
and became a warm partisan of Jackson's administration and doctrines.

"On November 5, 1831, J. Q. Adams spent the
evening at my house. He was in good health, and
read with poetical enthusiasm some verses of his own,
on the house in which he was born, and the scenery
around it. They were highly poetical, pathetic, and
beautiful. He read a good deal In the plays of
Hamlet, Romeo and Juliet, and Othello, and criticised
ably on the design of the plays. Hamlet, he thinks
the greatest character in all Shakespeare. He was
profoundly meditative, and of the loftiest and finest
moral sensibility. He touches on the verge of madness all along, by reason of his keen feeling."

Chancellor Kent's opinion of Napoleon and his
career, while yet that brilliant, masterful genius was
storming through Europe, has already been recorded.[1]
A line in retrospect, written twenty-five years later,
cannot fail to be of interest. In his copy of " Napoleon and his Times," by Caulaincourt, Duke of Vicenza
(Philadelphia, 1838), is found this minute: —

"I read these two volumes in October, 1838, and
I found them very interesting. They are admirably

[1] *Supra*, 177.

written, and give fine, and I think very true graphic sketches of Napoleon's character. The great historical events in 1812 and 1813, 1814 and 1815, are truly stated, though very briefly, and the consolations, views, feelings, and distress of Napoleon, and especially in the closing scenes of 1814 and 1815, are deeply striking and pathetic. No human being ever paid more bitterly for the pangs his ambition and armies had inflicted on the rest of Europe. He considered himself betrayed by the friends he had elevated to greatness, such as Fouché, Davoust, Talleyrand, etc., and his humiliations and agonies were extreme in June, 1815. The whole portrait is drawn with a master hand. Napoleon was devoted to his army. His whole genius and soul were military."

His note in Thomas Carlyle's "French Revolution" (Boston, 1839), is brief and pungent: —

"In his 'Sartor Resartus' and his critical essays, Carlyle is a disciple of the Platonic School of Philosophy, beyond the reach of man's understanding."

In his copy of Prescott's "Ferdinand and Isabella" (Boston, 1838), Chancellor Kent penned this brief note: —

"The author of these volumes called on me at my house, in company with Mr. Charles Sumner, April 7, 1842. He looked fresh and hearty, and in middle life. He says he spent last evening with Washington Irving."

A few years later, Hon. William Kent, the Chancellor's only son, then a professor of law in Harvard

College, had the pleasure of dining with the historian Prescott, at his home in Boston.   This experience he thus described to his father:

I dined yesterday with William Prescott, the historian. He is a very charming person, bearing his faculties so meekly, and being so witty and genial in his conversation and manners, as to win all hearts.   We had at dinner Mr. Choate, who is a striking person indeed, something like Webster in appearance, with hair as black and complexion as sallow, and eyes as large and melancholy.   He is interesting in conversation, and seems to be a very critical scholar.   Then we had Ticknor, Sparks, and Sumner, and Dr. Frothingham the clergyman, and Mr. Gardener from the Kennebeck in Maine, and Dr. Bigelow the physician, and Mr. Bowen, editor of the North American Review. We were all, you see, very literary and grave people. Prescott lives in elegant style ; he inherited a large fortune, and his books alone would make him rich.   His house is furnished as beseems the historian of Spain.   In his drawing-room are portraits of Ferdinand and Isabella, sent him from Spain.   He has in his hall a full-length portrait of Cortez.   Isabella is beautiful on canvas ; has a face to adore for its angelic sweetness and beauty.

The library is the finest private library I have seen. Over the mantel-piece is a fine head of the great Captain Gonzalvo de Cordova, who looks the princely and noble creature that he was.   In this beautiful room we took coffee, and here he received his visitors ; and when he wishes to be private, a book-case revolves and discloses secret stairs, which lead to a retired room in the third story, where the window lights are adapted to Prescott's weak eyes, and where he manufactures his histories. Here was the place I passed last evening, and then, consequently, walked through a slight snow-storm all the way to Cambridge, when it was as dark as pitch, and near eleven o'clock.

But few of the many notes with which the books of his library are besprinkled have been quoted in this chapter. It is to be deeply regretted that the copious notes which he is known to have made throughout his set of the Waverley Novels cannot, at least in part, be reproduced. He read all these with avidity as they appeared, and was enthusiastic in their praise. Each volume, after perusing, he enriched with a fund of manuscript notes and comment, which were both a study and a pleasure to read. Unfortunately, this quantity of manuscript filled so many pages of each volume that the firm to which the rebinding of the old edition was intrusted determined to make a separate volume of the notes, and collected them together to be bound in uniform shape with the other volumes. This book, while in the hands of the binder, disappeared, probably being taken by some one whose honesty was not proof against the desire to possess a work so unusual in character. The loss is deeply to be deplored, as it leaves a void in his library which cannot be replaced.

In August, 1840, Chancellor Kent was addressed by Augustus E. Silliman, the President of the Mercantile Library Association of New York, with a request that he would prepare a list of books for the guidance of the members of the association in supplementing what had been, in many cases, a meager

education. The Chancellor replied at length, giving
a list of books which he recommended, adding, in
many instances, some words of criticism. An examination of the list discloses a preponderance of
works of travel and history. The list is, however,
interesting as displaying the condition of literature
at that period, and showing what were regarded by
the highest authority as standard works in each of
the leading departments of learning. The department of American history is especially interesting,
quoting, as it does, some authorities now obsolete.
Among these forgotten or incomplete works are
Burke's European Settlements in America, two volumes, 1760, which, he notes, is "much esteemed;"
Bancroft's History, in two volumes only, of which Mr.
Kent says, "There is much to admire in the research
and style of this work;" Grahame's History of the
United States, "a European production, written with
great gravity and dignity, moderation and justice;"
and Pitkin's History of the United States, 1763–1797,
"an accurate and trustworthy production."

In the department of poetry, Chancellor Kent
recommends the perusal of Shakespeare, Milton, —
especially his Paradise Lost, — Dryden, Butler's Hu-
dibras, Parnell's The Hermit, Addison, Tickell, —
Elegy addressed to the Earl of Warwick, — Pope,
Thomson's The Seasons, Collins' Odes and Pastorals;
Tasso and Ariosto, translated by Hoole and Rose;
Young's Night Thoughts, Gray, Goldsmith, Johnson,
Beattie, Cowper, Burns, Campbell, Rogers, Crabbe,
Southey, Scott, Wordsworth, and Byron. Of Ameri-
can poets, he dares not attempt to decide, but limits

himself to the recommendation of the works of two only, " townsmen of our own ": F.-G. Halleck and W. C. Bryant. "The lyrical pieces and *jeux d'esprit* of the first," he says, " are distinguished for their beautiful imagery, piquant wit, and polished diction." Of Bryant he says: " His poetry, pure and elegant in language, and pervaded with an intense sympathy, with all the varied beauties of inanimate nature, sinks into the heart of the reader."

In fiction, the Chancellor recommends the perusal of Don Quixote, Gil Blas, Telemachus, Richardson's Clarissa, and Sir Charles Grandison, Fielding, and Smollett, Johnson's Rasselas, Goldsmith's Vicar of Wakefield, Mackenzie's Man of Feeling, Moore's Zelucco, and Mordaunt, Mrs. Radcliffe's Mysteries of Udolpho, and The Italian, Crabbe's Tales, Godwin's Caleb Williams, Brown's Wieland, and Ormond (" American productions of great energy, but of grave character "), Scott's novels (" Every volume, every page, to be read. What novel, or what dialogue, is there in Scott, over which the reader may not pause and admire? "), Irving's Tales and Romances, Cooper's novels, novels by Dickens under the name of Boz, Bulwer's Rienzi, Pompeii, Athens (" He is celebrated for his genius, enthusiasm, and power of description, but he is deficient in practical good sense and simple delineation of the characters and sympathies that belong to actual life ").

X

THROUGHOUT the long and busy life of Chancellor Kent there was one unchanging undercurrent of feeling which appears in all his correspondence, — his strong and ardent love for his home, his wife, his family, and the pursuit of learning, of which he never wearied. His highest anticipation was that, at some time, he might retire from the "busy haunts of men," and, gathering about him his family and belongings on some sunny hillside, pass the rest of his days in ideal repose. It was the early cultivation of these peaceful pleasures and pursuits which brought such tranquil happiness to his declining years. In his address before the Law Association to which reference has been made,[1] he pointed out the dangers, not only of professional, but of modern life, in words which have their vivid application at the present day.

"We live in a period of uncommon excitement. The spirit of the age is restless, presumptuous, and revolutionary. The rapidly increasing appetite for wealth; the inordinate taste for luxury which it engenders; the vehement spirit of speculation, and the selfish emulation which it creates; the contempt for slow and moderate gains; the ardent thirst for pleasure and amusement; the diminishing reverence for

[1] *Supra*, p. 30.

17

the wisdom of the past; the disregard of the lessons of experience, the authority of magistrates, and the venerable institutions of ancestral policy, — are so many bad symptoms of the diseased state of the public mind. It requires a most determined perseverance and firmness of purpose, and a most devoted zeal in the rising members of the Bar, to resist the contagion, and pursue triumphantly the rewards and honor of professional reputation."

That he faithfully followed, in his walk through life, the practice of those virtues which were calculated to develop and broaden his higher spiritual and mental character, was known to all, and the spontaneous applause which followed him at every turn was the willing tribute of honor which the world pays to recognized ability and virtue.

It was not until late in life that the summit of his desire was reached. He did not profess to keep a diary, but in his later years he would from time to time make brief memoranda and notes of matters of interest to him. On the 31st of July, 1839, he recorded: —

" I am this day 76 years of age, and in unimpaired health. My dear wife is well, and I owe the deepest gratitude to the great Father of Mercies for our protracted and pleasant and healthy and delightful married life for 54 years and upwards. I am in a charming country seat at my Summit Lodge, surrounded with every blessing, and blessed with ample competence. My wife and all my children (and all are with me) enjoy the place with great interest and sensibility."

And so the Sabine Farm was at last attained, and here he passed the evening of his days in unalloyed peace and happiness.   At his house in New York the winters were passed amid his beloved books, and in social intercourse and pleasures.   Now he notes having dined with a party of friends, of whom Washington • Irving was one.   Now he records his attendance at a wedding, and now a carriage drive, with his wife and daughter, to pay an afternoon visit.   Again he makes minute that " Mr. Sumner, of Boston, drank tea and spent the evening with us."   Still again, he notes that he "visited in the evening Judge Thompson and his young wife, and then went to the old Club at Dr. MacVickar's, where I saw, among others, Judge Botsford, of New Brunswick, N. S., who graduated at Yale College in 1792, and was classmate and roommate with my cousin, Robert Grant."   On December 14, 1836, he notes that " A. B. Durand finished my portrait for the Cambridge Law School."

Although he was mindful of his lengthening days, he did in no wise relax his cheerfulness.   At 74 he was still young enough to meet with a party of friends, and pass a social evening.   In 1837 he notes: " The Kent Club met at my house this evening (May 13)." After giving a list of those present, among whom were numbered Charles O'Conor and Captain Marryat, the novelist, he notes: " We had a pleasant supper, ice cream, stewed oysters; and they drank a dozen of champagne and stayed till near twelve o'clock, a very respectable and gratified party."

Still later, in January, 1839, when he was nearly 76 years of age, he records the passing of an evening

in congenial company at a public house. " I went
down in the evening with Mr. Blatchford," he writes,
" and called on Mr. Webster at the Astor House.   I
found him at a private dinner table, eating grapes
and nuts, and drinking wine, with his son (the youngest, now a Sophomore in Dartmouth College), Mr.
Prescott Hall, Mr. M. Grinnell (congressman elect),
Mr. Draper, and others, and we had a charming
table chat until nine P. M.   Mr. Webster looks care-
worn, and thin, and a constitution impaired, and evidently in despair of the good and wise government of
his country.   He talked a good deal about the two
Adamses, and told anecdotes of them and of General
Stark, and Indian stories of the war of 1756, and we
eulogized Washington and Hamilton.   He thought
that Washington showed the various heroic and
statesman's powers of Marlborough and Wellington,
and he exalted greatly Hamilton, on the vindication
of the National Bank."

In August, 1839, he records : —

" I remained all day quietly in my house, reading
and writing in delightful solitude.   Ellen came to wait
upon me.   It was a chilly day, with northeast wind,
and showery ; the afternoon towards sundown there
was a most gorgeous landscape and black and bright
clouds and blue sky.   I enjoyed it in my loneliness
and thought much and tenderly of my precious wife.
I did not stir out of the front door, or see any person
but my two colored servants (Ruth and Ellen), from
1 o'clock P. M. on Saturday until after breakfast on
Monday.   It was quite a novel and interesting situa-

tion, and gave me an opportunity to indulge in promiscuous reading and examine my finances and write letters to my heart's content."

On the 5th of March, 1840, he makes this record: —

"Mr. Charles Sumner dined with me, and spent the evening with my son. He returned yesterday from Europe, having been absent two years from last December. He talked incessantly; is inflated with exaggerated egotism; has been familiar with Bench and Bar of Westminster; has ridden an English Circuit, and been familiar with the gentry and nobility; has seen the best literary characters in France and Germany, Vienna, Berlin, Brussels, Heidelberg, and Italy. Mr. Sumner showed me one of the original exchequer tallies, he also gave me the address of M. Mittermaier."

In May of the same year he records: "Mrs. Butler, formerly Miss Fanny Kemble,[1] niece of Mrs. Siddons, called at our house with her husband; she is an interesting little brunette, with fine, glowing, sharp black eyes."

In August, 1840, he makes an interesting minute:

"August 22. Daniel Webster dined with me on his own invitation. He was on his way to Morristown and to Sussex County to meet a gathering of the Whigs. Dr. Condit, of Morristown, dined with me.

[1] Frances Anne Kemble, born in London November 27, 1809; made her début on the stage 1829; went to America 1832; married Pierce Butler 1834; died January 15, 1893.

Mr. Collins dined here. It was a very interesting party, and Mr. Webster charmed the party. He is 57 years old, and looks worn and furrowed; his belly becomes protuberant, and his eyes deep in his head. I sympathize with his condition. He has been too free a liver. He ate but little, and drank wine freely."

In August, 1841, Chancellor Kent experienced the inexpressible pleasure of seeing his son a judge of the Supreme Court of New York, in the seat which he himself had occupied many years before. He makes record of the appointment on the 19th of that month: "My son was, on the 16th instant, appointed Circuit Judge of the First Circuit, in room of Ogden Edwards, whose office expired at his age of 60. The news of his appointment was announced in the evening papers. (Coincidence — On the last of August, 1798, I held the Circuit Court and Court of Oyer and Terminer in and for Kings Co. On the last of August, 1841, my son (unborn in 1798) is to hold the Circuit Court of Oyer and Terminer for Kings Co.) This is a species of hereditary succession honorable to both parties."

On the 25th of October he records: " Mr. Bacon, of Litchfield in Connecticut, called on me. He is well, strong, and prosperous, has two sons, and is aged 70. I went with him to the Circuit Court, and saw my son on the Bench. The visit to the court was impressive. To see my son sitting modestly and solitary on the Bench of the Circuit Court, trying a case on the same spot where I was trying civil cases in December, 1813, as Chief-Justice, was affecting."

On the 3d of April, 1842, the Chancellor made a beautiful and touching minute in his diary. "This day (it was also a Sunday)," he writes, "57 years ago, I was married at Colonel Bailey's, at his little farm-house, in the commons out of Poughkeepsie. Mrs. Kent and I have lived in uniform general health, and in very great domestic happiness down to this day. An enchantment seems to me to be always thrown around my own home and my own fireside and office, and the attractions of my beloved wife."

In the autumn of this year an event occurred which was of great interest to Chancellor Kent, and which furnished for him a fund of pleasure. It was at this time that the Croton water was first brought into New York, and in a letter to Daniel Webster he gives a minute description of its introduction, together with a description of the manner in which he was passing the evening of his life.

Chancellor Kent to Daniel Webster.

. . . I thank you for the kind feelings you have done me the honor to express, in respect to my health and condition. I am indeed in my 80th year, but, thank God, I am wonderfully well and active, and my ardor for reading and my susceptibilities, I think, are as alive as ever to the charms of nature, of literature, and of society. I keep aloof from all fashionable parties except when my daughter (Mrs. H.) has some small ones at my house, at which Ma and I are obliged to be present, and I chat and flatter as much as ever with pretty ladies. My reading is regular and constant, — all the reports of law decisions as fast as I procure them, all the periodicals, foreign and domestic, and old literature and new books are steadily turned over. I have been reading, a day or two past, at intervals, Dr. Arnold's History of Rome. His criticisms are doubtless true and just, but dull. I relieve myself by going from some of his allusions to one of the muses, or the books of Herodotus, or Livy; and they amuse my old age like enchanting historical novels. I don't like altogether bald, naked, sterile facts. I like a little of the poetry of history, as well as of life itself, in all its modifications. I deal sufficiently with dry and stern facts when I study law cases. I turned to one of Gibbon's chapters on the irruption of the Northern nations into the Roman provinces, and with what delight and what admiration! He has truth, forcibly stated, but adorned with taste, style, wisdom, and surpassing energy and eloquence of language.

I partly ride and partly walk down town daily to my office, and have occasional opinions to give, but more out of the State than in it; and then hasten up to my attractive home and office on Union Square, facing the lofty *jet d'eau* which is constantly playing before my eyes. The associations with this water are to me delightful. I was born on my father's farm in Putnam County, in the eastern part of the Highlands; and his farm was bounded by the Croton River, where I used to fish and to swim in my youthful days. God bless the stream! How would it have astonished my parents if they had been foretold, in 1770, that their eldest son would live in the midst of the City of New York, with that very Croton pouring its pure and living waters through the streets, and throwing its majestic columns of water fifty feet into the air! So you see how charmingly I am enabled to pass my evening days.

Although Chancellor Kent to his latest days retained an interest in public affairs and occurrences, that interest was, in his later days, not so absorbing and intense as at an earlier period. When seventy he wrote to his brother: "We have a good deal of

transitory visiting and calls, so that I don't see but
that we live quite as sociable and happy out in Eighth
Street as we did in Greenwich Street. You will always find a most welcome home here whenever it
suits your convenience to return. The trying crisis
of affairs at Washington renders the news and debates
in Congress interesting; but standing as I do near
the verge of human life, such scenes are not by any
means so engrossing as formerly; and though my
enthusiasm may not abate, yet the simple fact that
one has no further ambition or selfish calculations to
gratify, will inevitably cool the ardor of curiosity."

Again, a little later, he writes: "It is usual, but
not in the best taste, for old folks to be talking much
about their infirmities. I can say I have none, unless when I eat or smoke a little too much; but that
propensity is pretty well under check, and I have
reason to be thankful, and intensely so, for the discretion, prudence, and firmness with which I am furnished by Providence, to avoid excesses of all kinds.
It is in our power, by constant and unremitted bodily
and mental exertion adapted to our age and taste, to
smooth the descent down to the bottom of the hill of
life. I hope, my dear brother, you will never inter-
mit either, as long as you can move to act and see
to read, and I shall do all in my power to cheer and
comfort you, and I may shortly stand in need of the
same fraternal sympathy."

There was no one among Chancellor Kent's wide
acquaintance for whom he entertained more profound
respect than for Judge Story, of Massachusetts. There
is no record to show when and how the two first be-

came acquainted; but in 1836 the Chancellor, with
his wife, made a journey to Boston.   There he met
Judge Story, as he afterward related in a letter to his
son.

Chancellor Kent to William Kent.

July 4, 1836.

. . . Ruggles and I went on Saturday into Judge Story's
Circuit Court.   I was forced in, almost by duress, by Mr.
Charles Sumner, the lawyer.   The Judge was in the midst of a
law argument and giving his opinion on a point in the case.
The moment he saw me, he called out to me and came
down from the Bench to the Bar and shook hands with me
and introduced me to the lawyers who were there arguing.
Judge Davis, the district Judge, came from the Bench and
sat with me, and the cause went on.   There is attention
and honor for you !   I then went into the Supreme Judicial
Court of Massachusetts and the Judges were reading opinions.   I took a seat on the front counsel bench, though
invited to take a seat on the Bench.   When I went out the
Chief Justice Shaw, whom I never saw before, followed me
and got introduced to me.   In the afternoon we all went
to Cambridge, and with Judge Story to Mount Auburn.   I
admired and was awe-stricken with that beautiful and
interesting silent scene.   Last evening Ruggles and I
were at a party of lawyers, got up by Judge Davis for
me, and it was interesting, though I was too much the object of attention.   From Judge Davis' party we went to
another one after nine, at Judge Putnam's, and that was
in honor to me.   Upon the whole, the scenes of 1823, are
renewed with increased, rather than diminished, attention.
But Judge Story's power of conversation among the hills
and monuments and deep shady graves of Mount Auburn
was incomparable.   He lead Ma by the arm all the way,
and he was eloquence, and poetry, and pathos, and feeling

and tenderness, and anecdote, and boundless benignity, all personified in his identical person. I believe he is the most accomplished and ardent and enlightened intellect extant.

Three years later, in January, 1839, this visit was returned; for there appears in Chancellor Kent's notes, under that date, this entry: —

" January 11th. Judge Story called at my office; a fine chat. He looks thin and worn down, aged 57. He rises late, and does n't take enough exercise. He speaks highly of his law school. Has a poor opinion of the judicial spirit of the times, and of the moral degeneracy of the Bar. The English courts and Bar are thinking better of us, and study us. All the twelve judges are common men; Lord Abinger disappoints; Baron Alderson and J. Parks are the best Judges; Chief-Judge Denman, a clever, common man."

This memoir would be incomplete without the addition of the very charming letter sent by the Chancellor to Mrs. Story, on his learning of the death of the eminent jurist: —

Chancellor Kent to Mrs. Story.

NEW YORK, Sept. 17, 1845.

DEAR MADAM, — The death of your husband and my friend, Mr. Justice Story, has filled me with the deepest commiseration and sorrow. His image is constantly before me, and I respectfully beg leave to mingle my grief and sorrow with yours. He was one of the rarest and best friends I had the honor and happiness to possess. He has done more by his writings and speeches to diffuse my offi-

cial and professional character (far indeed beyond my de-
serts) than any living man. My obligations to him are
incalculable. Permit me to add my grateful sense of his
inestimable worth and value, in the purity of his life, his
domestic and social virtues, his generous and liberal feelings,
the inexpressible charm of his conversation, his varied accomplishments, his wonderful diligence, his profound learning, and his transcendent genius. The delightful recollection
of his life and character will, I trust and believe, console
and cheer you through the residue of your life. Believe
me, my dear madam, with the most respectful and affectionate regard,

Your friend and obedient servant,

JAMES KENT.

MRS. STORY.

In May, 1838, he was invited to be present at a
dinner, to be given by the Philadelphia Bar to the
Supreme Court of the State of Pennsylvania. This
invitation he declined, no doubt because he anticipated, in his presence at such a dinner, a fulsomeness
of laudation which would be distasteful. Again, when
in June, 1843, the Bar of Philadelphia tendered to
him a public dinner, he again declined.

Chancellor Kent to Committee of Philadelphia Bar.

NEW YORK, June 12, 1843.

GENTLEMEN, — I acknowledge with deep emotions of
sensibility and gratitude your letter of the 7th inst., in-
viting me on behalf of the members of the Philadelphia
Bar to a public dinner. To decline the acceptance of such
a spontaneous mark of respect for my services and character, from so respectable and enlightened a body of men
as the members of the Philadelphia Bar, is embarrassing to

my grateful feelings.   I receive the invitation, and the language in which you have been pleased to convey it, as a testimony of regard the most honorable and impressive that could have been offered; and it is with great regret that I am obliged to decline that distinguished honor.   I humbly trust that my excuse will be received with generous indulgence.

I am now on the verge of eighty; and I have for some time past thought it proper and expedient, from the gentle admonitions suggested by that period of life, to withdraw myself as much as possible from public duties of every kind, and to confine myself, while my life and health are permitted by Providence to continue, to domestic retirement and to the studies and pursuits to which I have been accustomed, and which are suitable to that tranquil position.

Be pleased to accept my ardent wishes for the continued honor and prosperity of the Philadelphia Bar, and for the continued elevation and improvement of our common country, on which our national character and liberties as well as personal security so essentially depend.

On the 31st day of July, 1843, when Chancellor Kent attained the age of eighty years, the members of the Bar of the State of New York, believing that in that manner better than in any other they could do him honor, presented to him an address, expressive of their profound respect and admiration for him as a man and as a jurist, and including an invitation to a public dinner.   After reciting the chief events of his long and useful life, the address closed in this eloquent strain: —

Address of the New York Bar.

. . . Although you have attained an age exceeding the ordinary term of human life, not only is your physical strength unsubdued and your mental vigor undecayed, but it is known that your sympathies are as warm, your feelings as vivid, your liberal curiosity as active, your pursuit of truth as earnest, your enjoyment of the charms of eloquence and poetry and your impressions of the beauties and sublimity of nature as deep-felt and genuine, as when with the high aspirations of youth you first entered on your long and honorable career.

You are, then, a living example of a certain and most important truth : that where the habits of the individual have been temperate and virtuous, and that serenity is enjoyed which the consciousness of a well-spent life can alone bestow, where the higher faculties of the mind continue to be exercised and the purer affections of the heart to be cultivated, age has no power over the intellect or the will; but while life remains both may continue to assert their independence and their supremacy. "Ita enim" — you will thank us for recalling the words of your favorite Cicero — "Ita enim senectus honesta est, si se ipsa defendit, si jus suum retinet, si nemini emancipata est, si usque ad extremum spiritum dominatur in suos."

But there are higher considerations which this topic suggests. How fitting is it that a life of strenuous and useful and most honorable toil should be followed by an old age such as you now enjoy ! How right that the mild glories of the sunset should affect our hearts more than the splendor of the day ! In the contemplation of an old age so cheerful and serene, so honored and beloved, to those who have minds to reflect and hearts to feel there is a moral grandeur that the physical sublime can never reach. It supplies a proof, deeply felt by those who are capable of understanding it, that the true reward of virtue, love, gratitude, and inward peace, even in this life, is not uncertain ; and in supplying this proof, it leads our thoughts with reverential hope to that more perfect and enduring reward which, as we trust, is to follow the crowning words, "Well done, thou good and faithful servant."

In July, 1846, Chancellor Kent was greatly gratified by the offer to his son, Judge William Kent, of the Professorship of Law at Harvard College. He earnestly advised his son to accept the position. "Judge Story has elevated the post," he wrote, "and given it luster, and this is a consideration you must think of for yourself. Upon the whole, though parting with you from my side gives me a pang, yet we shall see each other a great deal, that is certain, and I cannot be with you always. My tenure of life is short, and I would not, for the world, be responsible for the loss of that appointment. Upon the whole, it is probable it will give me vastly more pleasure than pain for the residue of my life. If you were to remain at the Bar, striving for business and laboring at the oar, my sympathies for you would destroy me. Now my sympathies will all be joyous. You would succeed, with such reputation, and write so well, so beautifully, so sensibly, and so eloquently, and perhaps favor the public with legal essays and commentaries *à la mode* Story. But we will talk more on these things when we meet, and God grant it may be in a few days and with auspicious health and joy."

The last journey which Chancellor Kent made was to Cambridge, to pay a visit to his son, Professor Kent. This was in May, 1847. On his arrival he wrote a lengthy letter to his wife, dated, "At William's Office, in the Dane Hall, Cambridge." He describes minutely the events of his journey, including a vivid description of the horrors of a night of insomnia

which beset him at a hotel in Springfield.   The letter
is written with all his old-time vivacity, but his health
was evidently declining.   He was now well nigh four-
score and four years of age, and the light of life was
flickering.   He had passed a long, useful, and honorable life.   He had reached the highest judicial positions in his native State.   Yale, Dartmouth, Columbia,
and Harvard Colleges had bestowed upon him their
highest honors.   His family, well and honorably settled in life, were about him.   He had nothing more
to wish.

It remains now only to trace the peaceful close of
this long and useful life.   It was some time after he
had attained the age of eighty years before even the
watchful eye of kindred affection could observe in the
Chancellor any evidence of declining strength.   He
had been so uniformly active and vigorous, his spirits
had been always so bright, and the hue of health was
so permanent on his countenance, that his friends had
anticipated that, when the end of life was reached, its
close would be sudden and unexpected.   It pleased
Heaven, however, to give to his bodily strength a
gradual and peaceful decline, while his mind retained
its clearness and power to the last.   Perhaps, in all
his long career, the last ten years of his life may be
selected as his happiest.   His external circumstances
were in every respect prosperous.   He had gradually
acquired, as the result of his legal and literary labors,
an ample competency of fortune, and was able, as he
was generous, to dispense assistance and comfort to
his children and dependents.   The wife of his youth
was, for sixty-three years, the affectionate partner of

every thought and faculty. His family was settled around him. His eldest daughter and her husband were the inmates of his house; his son, who had resigned his professorship to be near him, lived in an adjoining building; and his youngest daughter, returning from a temporary residence abroad, and being a resident of Brooklyn, completed, with their children around him, that affectionate circle, as he expressed it, of "Nati natorum et qui nascentur ab illis," with whom he lived in the daily interchange of offices of unbounded affection and confidence.

His labors as a lawyer, though gradually becoming less frequent, never ceased. Questions on points of law, family settlements, cases for arbitration, and inquiries as to general and constitutional jurisprudence were presented to him from all parts of the United States, and not infrequently from the British provinces, to the very end of his life. His readings on Law always continued; and his perusal of the English Reports and the decisions of the different States of the Union was unremitted, furnishing him with annotations for his Commentaries, which were going rapidly through successive editions, and became the depository of his vast legal erudition. His private affairs were conducted by him with singular ability, exhibiting an exact method, order, and discretion which never failed him in the fluctuating vicissitudes of pecuniary affairs, so marked in the United States during the ten years preceding his death.

The greatest and purest consolation of age was found in his literary readings, which were prosecuted at the age of eighty-four with the same ardor and

enjoyment as when, young in life, he first entered on
the study of the English classics.   In one respect his
taste was peculiar.   While he enjoyed all the branches
of English literature, and was indeed quite extraordinary in the extent and accuracy of his historical
knowledge, he was drawn toward Geography by a
taste innate and irresistible.   In his library, which
became very large and varied, the books of voyages
and travels become quite preponderant and encroach-
ing; and it was a source of amusement to his friends
to observe the enthusiasm with which he traced the
discoveries in Central Africa and Asia, and accompanied Parry and Franklin in their travels in the Arctic
circles.   He was quite insensible to all raillery on this
point, and drew maps of routes, islands, and prom-
ontories, showing the courses of the adventurous
travelers, which his descendants preserve as valued
and characteristic relics, though certainly not elegant
specimens of the topographical art.

As age drew on, he felt inclined to suspend the
annual tours which he had so often undertaken, and
so keenly enjoyed; and as a substitute, he purchased
in 1837 a cottage in the country, at a short distance
from New York, in Essex County, in New Jersey.   This
became, during the remainder of his life, his summer
retreat.   Nothing could be simpler or more unpretending than the establishment, which was seated on
the sloping side of a breezy hill, commanding an extensive prospect to the north and west of the Valley
of the Passaic, with villages, churches, hills, and dales;
and there, from his piazza, he used to watch, with his
family, and some friendly visitor from the city never

absent, the sun as it set behind the distant ridge of the Schooley Mountains.   It was a tranquil, solitary, and beautiful spot.

His winters were passed in the city.   The excitement of party politics had subsided with him.   The principles of what he deemed conservative statesmanship were indeed never abandoned, and he unswervingly supported, in all its contests and vicissitudes, the party which he believed most faithfully represented them.   But all acerbity of feeling was gone. He was ready to acknowledge honesty in political opponents, and reverted, in conversation, with hearty praise to George Clinton, Melancthon Smith, and the eminent leaders of the anti-Federal party, whom in his youth and early manhood he had strenuously opposed. Equally to him was the good feeling of the opposing party extended.   He was selected by them, as much as by his own party, as the umpire in controversies.

In his daily walks through the town, he was universally known; men liked to observe his elastic step, and graceful form, retaining far in age the qualities of youth, and to point him out as a remarkable example of protracted agility and strength.   It was a pleasant sight indeed to see his cheerful greetings of all he met, poor or rich, mechanic or merchant, and the kind salutation which he received from all.

Of his religious convictions but scant reference has been made in this Memoir.   His recognition of the indebtedness of man to the Father of all Goodness was often made evident in his correspondence.   But it was seldom that he wrote at length upon religious topics.   Indeed, on one occasion, when a correspondent, presuming upon a friendly letter from the Chancellor, forced upon him a long and elaborate sermon, in which he did not hesitate to call his friend to account, and to dictate a line of religious conduct repugnant to Mr. Kent's ideas of free thought, the Chancellor replied at once, vindicating his right of free selection, and of individual liberty of thought. But when in advanced life, he left with his children a message of faith, recorded by his son, which is in itself alone a sufficient statement of the aged Chancellor's belief.

"Shortly before my father's death," records Judge William Kent, " the conversation having turned upon the foreign custom of attending places of amusement on Sunday, my father said, ' I am by no means an ascetic in religion as you know, yet I was brought up strictly to regard the Sabbath, and I should like my children always to regard it.' "

His manner became serious, and after a few minutes he went on : —

" My children, I wish to talk to you. During my early and middle life I was, perhaps, rather sceptical with regard to some of the truths of Christianity. Not that I did not have the utmost respect for religion, and always read my Bible, but the doctrine of the atonement was one I never could understand, and I felt inclined to consider as impossible to be received in the way divines taught it. I believe I was rather inclined to Unitarianism; but of late years my views have altered. I believe in the doctrines of the prayer-books, as I understand them, and hope to be saved through the merits of Jesus Christ."

Some of the family coming into the room, he hastily added: " Go, my children. My object in telling you this is that, if anything happens to me, you might know, and perhaps it would console you to remember, that on this point my mind is clear; I rest my hopes of salvation on the Lord Jesus Christ."

The tidings of the death of the Chancellor were received by the public and by his many friends with every demonstration of regret and of grief. Resolutions were passed by the Bar, the New York Historical Society, and by other bodies. Personal friends, by letter, begged a share in the grief of the household. As expressed by Francis Lieber, in a letter to Judge William Kent, " He went to the grave as it is given to few men. Having spent a life of the highest usefulness, acknowledged at home and abroad, of an extent far beyond the common limits of human existence; loved, almost adored, by his family, and cherished with venerating affection by bands of friends; active almost to the very limit of his life, — he was allowed to depart in the arms of his own, leaving a name loved as long as they live, and honored as long as our nation shall exist. Are there many mortals who can compare with him? "

APPENDIX

CHANCELLOR KENT'S MEMORIES OF ALEXANDER HAMILTON

CHANCELLOR KENT'S MEMORIES OF ALEXANDER HAMILTON

NEW YORK, December 10, 1832.

To MRS. ELIZABETH HAMILTON:

DEAR MADAM, — You have requested of me "a detailed reply to the several queries subjoined," and you express a hope that you may not in that request "be regarded as asking more than my friendship to your father and husband would readily grant." I beg leave to assure you that it is sufficient that the application comes from the daughter of General Schuyler and the widow of General Hamilton, to make it command all the information within my power to impart, and I have only to regret that neither my memory nor the materials before me are sufficient to meet the extent of my wishes or to equal your expectations. The following are the questions you have proposed: —

1. "Your early acquaintance with my husband — when, and the circumstances of it?"

2. "His appearance and manners then?"

3. "Any facts connected with his history at the Bar before he went into the Treasury, or on his return from it?"

4. "Incidents connected with his services in the Convention at Poughkeepsie, and his last speech there?"

5. "Its effects on the decision of the Convention?"

6. "His characteristic manner of speaking; also the manner of Mr. Jay, Chancellor Livingston, and the principal opponents?"

7. "My father's agency in adopting the Constitution, and Judge Benson's?"

8. "Any anecdotes illustrative of his character or strong expressions?"

There are some points mentioned in those queries on which I have not the requisite information, but as you request me not to consider the inquiries as "limiting the answers," and as you suggest that my "information will relate mostly to his political and civil life," I cannot complain that you have not given me "ample room and verge enough." I shall therefore, with your permission, instead of a special and narrow reply to each question, return one general answer embracing the whole range of inquiry, and endeavor to give a brief but faithful detail of the professional and political life of your eminent husband, so far as the same came within my own knowledge or contemporary observation. It will be convenient, and will tend to give method and perspicuity to my recollections, if we divide the historical sketches of your husband's life in the following manner: —

1. From my first personal knowledge of General Hamilton, in 1782, to the call of the Convention in 1787.

2. His services in relation to the origin and adoption of the Federal Constitution.

3. His subsequent life.

I

My personal acquaintance with General Hamilton did not commence until some time after the conclusion of the American War, but I was not then ignorant of the character which he had long sustained, nor of the reputation which he had acquired by his talents and services. While I was a clerk in the office of Egbert Benson, the Attorney-General, as early as 1782, I heard it said that he was the author of some essays which had recently appeared in one of the public prints under the signature of *The Continentalist;* the purport of which was to show that the powers of Congress under the confederation were insufficient and ought to be enlarged. Those essays I never saw, but General Hamilton attracted my particular observation as early as July, 1782, when he was appointed a delegate in Congress from this State. The Legislature was then sitting at Poughkeepsie, where I resided, and there I saw him for the first time, though I was too young and too obscure to seek or to merit any personal acquaintance. He was in company with Mr. Benson and Colonel Lawrence, and his animated and didactic conversation, far superior to ordinary discourse in sentiment, language, and manner, and his frank and manly deportment interested and engrossed my attention.

In pursuance of that appointment he took his seat in Congress for the first time in the November following, and we there find him promptly and efficiently engaged in the promotion of measures calculated to relieve the embarrassed state of the public finances, and to avert the difficulties and dangers which beset the Union of the States. His efforts to reanimate the powers of the Confederation, and to infuse life, vigor, and credit into that languishing system, were incessant and masterly; and he was sustained in all his views and assisted in all his measures by his friend and illustrious coadjutor, James Madison, Jun. Other members of Congress at that period may have been entitled to an equal share of merit, but their services do not appear to have been equally conspicuous and distinguished.

The proceedings of Congress took a new and more decided tone and character while he was a present and active member, between November, 1782, and July, 1783. Within that period a series of active, intrepid, untiring, but fruitless, efforts were made to render the National Government under the Articles of Confederation adequate to the support of the Union. It is necessary that we should make a slight reference to the prominent proceedings in Congress, during the session I refer to, in order to perceive clearly and appreciate justly the high character of those efforts, which led on, step by step, to the renewal and consolidation of our Union, and to that rapid and glorious elevation of our country which distinguished the administration of Washington. Thus, on the 6th December, 1782, a motion was made by Mr. Hamilton and carried, that the Superintendent of Finance represent to the Legislatures of the several States, the indispensable necessity of complying with the requisitions of Congress for raising specified sums of money towards paying a year's interest on the domestic debt of the United States, and defraying the estimated expenses for the year ensuing; and to assure them that Congress was determined to make the fullest justice to the public creditors an invariable object of their counsels and exertion.

On the 11th of the same month he was chairman of a committee which reported the form of an application to the Governor of Rhode Island, urging in most persuasive terms the necessity and reasonableness of a concurrence on the part of that State in the grant to Congress of a general import duty of five per cent, in order to raise a fund for the discharge of the public debt. The application was to be accompanied with an assurance that such a grant was the most efficacious, the most expedient, and the most unexceptionable plan of finance that Congress could devise for the occasion; and that the increasing discontents of the army, the loud clamors of the public creditors, and the extreme disproportion between the current supplies and the demands of the public service were so many invincible arguments for the fund recommended by Congress; and that calamities of the most menacing nature might be anticipated if that expedient should fail.

So again, on the 16th December, Mr. Hamilton, Mr. Madison, and Mr. Fitzsimmons made a report of a very superior character in relation to the national finances, and in answer to the objections of the Legislature of Rhode Island against the grant of a general impost. The same discussion was afterwards renewed on the 30th January, 1783, by the report of a committee of which Mr. Hamilton was a member, in which it was stated that Congress had long been deeply impressed with the absolute necessity of taking measures to liquidate the public debts, and to secure the payment of interest until the principal could be discharged; and that the inability of Congress to perform its engagements with the public creditors, under the defective compliance of the States, was most apparent. Congress conceived it to be its duty to persevere in its intentions, and to renew and extend its endeavors to procure the establishment of revenues equal to the purpose of funding all the debts of the United States.

On the 20th March, 1783, Mr. Hamilton submitted a plan and recommendation of a duty of five per cent *ad valorem* on imported goods, and a land and house tax, to create funds for the discharge of the debts of the Union; for they had been created, as he observed, on the faith of Congress, for the common safety, and it was its duty to make every effort in its power for doing complete justice to the public creditors. He likewise, on the 22d of March, as chairman of a committee, reported in favor of a grant of five years' full pay to the officers of the army, as a commutation for the half pay for life promised them by Congress.

At last, on the 18th of April, 1783, Congress finally agreed to recommend to the States a grant of power for twenty-five years to levy specified duties on imported goods, to be applied exclusively to the discharge of the principal and interest of the debts contracted on the faith of the United States for supporting the War, and that other funds for the same purposes be supplied by the States. Mr. Madison, Mr. Ellsworth, and Mr. Hamilton were the committee who reported an address to the States, to accompany the resolution of the 18th of April; and it is rare that the records of the United States furnish the example of a document more replete with sound argument, or which equals it in pathetic and eloquent exhortations. But the exertions of Mr. Hamilton did not cease, nor was the patience of Congress exhausted, in suggesting and adopting measures to preserve the public faith and maintain the dignity and authority of the Government. The master spirits which animated and swayed the deliberations of Congress had the merit at least of unconquerable perseverance, and of preserving the national honor, while every other valuable attribute of power was lost.

On the 2d May, 1783, Mr. Hamilton moved a resolution calling upon the States in the most earnest manner to make such payments into the common treasury as might enable Congress to advance to the officers and soldiers of the army a part of their pay before they left the field, that they might return to their respective homes with convenience and satisfaction. He was also one of the committee which reported the resolution that the non-commissioned officers and soldiers enlisted for the period of the War be allowed their firearms and accoutrements, as an extra reward for their long and faithful services. Nor was this the only occasion in which Colonel Hamilton recollected the gratitude that was due for services in the field. On the 30th December, 1782, he was chairman of the committee which reported resolutions highly honorable to Major-General the Baron de Steuben. The sacrifices and services of that very meritorious officer, says the report, were deemed justly to entitle him to the distinguished notice of Congress, and to a generous compensation.

On other subjects General Hamilton, while he held a seat in Congress, showed equal solicitude for the preservation of the public faith, and the safety and authority of the Union. He was chairman of the committee which, on the 30th May, 1783, introduced the resolution calling upon the States to remove every legal obstruction under their local jurisdictions, in the way of the active and faithful execution of the fourth and sixth Articles of the Treaty of Peace; and that all future confiscations and prosecutions for acts done during the War should cease; and that the several States be requested to conform to the fifth article of the Treaty with that spirit of moderation and liberality which ought to characterize the measures of a free and enlightened nation. His anxiety to preserve the internal peace of the Confederacy was manifest by the resolution, which he seconded and supported, that the people of the district called the New Hampshire Grants — then, in point of fact, assuming to be an independent State — be desired to cease to molest the persons or property of those inhabitants who did not acknowledge their jurisdiction; and that, on the other hand, the persons holding commissions under New York also forbear to exercise any authority under the same, to the end that things might remain as they were until a decision could peaceably be made in the controversy. He was likewise chairman of the committee which stated the efforts which had been made on the part of Congress to suppress the mutinous proceedings of part of the troops of the United States, who had insulted Congress, and which eventually compelled them, from the want of sufficient protection from the executive council of Pennsylvania, to remove from Philadelphia to Princeton in New Jersey.

I have alluded to these documentary proofs as affording the most authentic and the most honorable testimony to the spirit and intelligence with which General Hamilton devoted himself, as early as the year 1782 and 1783, and at his own youthful age of twenty-five, to the support of the integrity and welfare of the Union. And it will abundantly appear, in the subsequent history of his life, that his zeal for the establishment of a national government, competent to preserve us from insult abroad and dissensions at home, and equally well fitted to uphold credit, to preserve liberty, and to cherish our resources, kept increasing; and that his views grew more and more enlarged and comprehensive as we approached the crisis of our destiny. It will hereafter appear, in the course of these narrative recollections, that he did more with his pen and his tongue than any other man, not only in reference to the origin and adoption of the Federal Constitution, but also to create and establish public credit, and defend the Government and its measures, under the wise and eventful administration of Washington.

Though I was not, at the time, conscious of the distinguished merit of General Hamilton as a member of Congress, yet his high character for genius, wisdom, and eloquence was everywhere known and acknowledged, and when, in the winter of 1784, his pamphlet productions under the signature of *Phocion* appeared, they excited a general sensation. They were addressed "to the considerate citizens of New York," and their object was to protect the rights of all classes of persons inhabiting the Southern District of the State; to put a stop to every kind of proscriptive policy, and to the creation of legislative disabilities and bills of attainder, as being equally incompatible with the obligations of the Treaty of Peace, the principles of the Constitution, and the dictates of policy. The appeal to the good sense and patriotism of the public was not in vain. It was unanswerable and irresistible. "The force of plain truth carried the work along against the stream of prejudice," and it overcame every obstacle.

A counter pamphlet, under the signature of *Mentor*, written by Doctor Isaac Ledyard, and representing the inhabitants of the Southern District who had remained within the enemy's lines as aliens, subject to penalties and disabilities in the discretion of the Legislature, was entirely demolished. A bill before the House of Assembly for putting various descriptions of persons out of the protection of government was abandoned. The rising generation, then just entering on the stage of action, readily imbibed those sentiments of temperate civil liberty and of sound constitutional law which he had so clearly taught and so eloquently inculcated. The benign influence of such doctrines was happily felt and retained through the whole course of the generation to whom they were addressed. I speak for myself, as one of that generation, that no hasty productions of the press could have been more auspicious.

In the summer of 1784 Colonel Hamilton attended the Circuit Court at Poughkeepsie, and I had then an opportunity, for the first time, of seeing him at the Bar as a counsellor addressing the court and jury. It was an interesting country circuit. Colonel Lawrence of New York, Peter

W. Yates of Albany, Egbert Benson (my revered preceptor, and who still lives, a venerable monument of the wisdom, the integrity, the patriotism, and the intrepidity of the sages of the Revolution), and some other gentlemen of the profession, whose names I do not now recollect, attended the court. I was struck with the clear, elegant, and fluent style and commanding manner of Hamilton. At that day everything in law seemed to be new. Our judges were not remarkable for law learning. We had no precedents of our own to guide us. English books of practice, as well as English decisions, were resorted to and studied with the scrupulous reverence due to oracles. Nothing was settled in our courts. Every point of practice had to be investigated, and its application to our courts and institutions questioned and tested. Mr. Hamilton thought it necessary to produce authorities to demonstrate and to guide the power of the court, even in the now familiar case of putting off a cause for the circuit, and to show that the power was to be exercised, as he expressed it, " in sound discretion and for the furtherance of justice." He never made any argument in court in any case without displaying his habits of thinking, and resorting at once to some well founded principle of law, and drawing his deductions logically from his premises. Law was always treated by him as a science founded on established principles. His manners were gentle, affable, and kind, and he appeared to be frank, liberal, and courteous in all his professional intercourse. This was my impression at the time.

General Hamilton was employed, while at that circuit, by Major Brown, to defend him on the trial of a suit in trover or trespass then pending, for seizing and converting to his own use British goods, under the pretence that they were the result of illicit commerce with the enemy. The country, towards the close of the American War, was exceedingly destitute of clothing and of all the comforts and conveniences which British manufactures had formerly afforded us. The high price of British goods of all kinds and the wants of the country rendered the temptation to illicit trade with the enemy almost irresistible. The Congress of the United States and the Legislatures of New York and some other States vainly endeavored, by ordinances and statutes imposing confiscations and penalties, to put a stop to the corrupt and pernicious traffic. The defendant in the case alluded to had been concerned in the seizure of goods alleged to be of that description, though it was understood at that day that there was generally as much of a predatory and lawless spirit in the persons who seized as in those who traded in the noxious goods. The cause became very interesting. Peter W. Yates, one of the leading counsel for the plaintiff, was subtle, acute, dry, and practical, and he exceeded my highest expectations; Colonel Lawrence was graceful, fluent, and ingenious; but Colonel Hamilton, by means of his fine melodious voice and dignified deportment, his reasoning powers and persuasive address, soared far above all competition. His pre-eminence was at once and universally conceded. He was pressed by his client to appeal to the feelings of the jury in favor of the poor and meritorious Whigs, against the secret enemies of their country in the character of traders in British goods. I heard him say, at the time, that he would never be found contending against the principles of *Phocion*, and that he told his anxious client that he could not gratify him to the extent of his wishes. He made, notwithstanding, in point of fact, whether he was conscious of it or not, an animated and powerful appeal to the passions and prejudices of the

jury. The audience listened with admiration to his impassioned eloquence, and they were almost ready to yield
to the truth of the suggestion which he threw into his
address, that a British statesman had remarked that the
true way to slacken the zeal and break down the stern
devotedness of the American Whigs was to open upon
them the flood-gates of commerce.

In January, 1785, I attended for the first time the term
of the Supreme Court at Albany and was admitted an
attorney; and I had the satisfaction to see General Hamilton come forward as an advocate on a much greater occasion, and with distinguished luster. The case I allude
to was the following: Chancellor Livingston claimed lands
lying on the south bounds of the lower manor of Livingston, and the claim was large in amount of property.
In an ejectment suit brought by Chancellor Livingston, as
plaintiff, against Hoffman, the cause was tried at the bar
of the Supreme Court at Albany, in October term, 1784;
and though Mr. Hamilton was one of the counsel for the
defendant, he was not one of the counsel assigned to sum
up the cause before the jury. The cause was tried with
great ability by Mr. Ogden of New Jersey and Mr. Benson, the Attorney-General, on behalf of the defendant.
Chancellor Livingston appeared at the bar as an advocate
in his own case, and his concluding address to the jury
was said to contain a boldness of illustration and a burst
of eloquence never before witnessed at our Bar. He rebuked severely the opposite counsel for their attacks on
the character of one of his ancestors, relative to the early
Grants of the Manor, and for "raking the ashes of the
dead in the presence of a great-grandson." He brought
his ancestor up from the grave and led him into court
to speak for himself, by a daring metaphor which sur-

prised and confounded the audience as well as the jury. He carried his cause, as it were, by a *coup de main* and obtained a verdict, rather by the weight of his character, and the charm and power of his eloquence, than by the force of evidence, or the merits of the case.

A new trial was moved for in January term, 1785, on the ground that the verdict was against the evidence. Mr. Benson, Colonel Lawrence, and Colonel Hamilton were in favor of the motion, and Mr. (afterward Chancellor) Lansing and Chancellor Livingston resisted it. I had the pleasure of being present at the argument, and was a witness of the contest of talent and eloquence between Chancellor Livingston and Colonel Hamilton, the brilliant and master spirits who controlled on that occasion. All the cases and reasons contained in the modern English decisions, and especially those which arose in the time of Lord Mansfield, and which are so well digested and elegantly illustrated in the third volume of Blackstone's Commentaries, were cited and urged in support of the motion. The Chancellor contended, on the other hand, that no single authority was to be found in support of the motion, in the case of a trial and verdict at bar in term time, and that the opposite counsel, in order to make out their case, were obliged to select parts from each of several cases, and to make up a piece of diversified mosaic, a motley compound, destitute equally of symmetry and law. He compared the efforts of his opponents to the construction of their father's will by Peter Martin and Jack in *The Tale of the Tub*, and who had found an authority for the use of shoulder-knots by picking out single letters in different parts of the instrument. He made a warm and declamatory eulogy upon trial by jury, and denounced with equal vehemence the judicial author-

ity of Lord Mansfield. He considered that the trial by
jury, with all the other great leading principles of English liberty, came from their German ancestors, and that
a disposition existed in the then Government of England
to undermine their Saxon liberties, and especially the inestimable trial by jury. No Englishman, he observed, was
found worthy of the task; a Scotchman must be selected,
who had the talents, subtlety, and love of power calculated to produce the effect; and the new-fangled doctrines of Lord Mansfield had enlarged and refined upon
the power of awarding new trials, so as at last to resolve
the trial by jury into the discretion of the court. Our
constitution had guarded against the dangerous innovation by declaring that the trial by jury as hereafter used
should be inviolate forever. And yet, no sooner had we
established our independence and organized our courts
than the pernicious doctrines alluded to were to be adopted
and called into action. " What would be the exclamation
of the Genius of Liberty, if she were now present in this
assembly, and saw the same gentlemen who had so honorably wielded the sword of war in her defence now
wielding the arbitrary decrees of Lord Mansfield for her
destruction."

The tall and graceful person of Chancellor Livingston,
and his polished wit and classical taste, contributed not a
little to deepen the impression resulting from the ingenuity
of his argument, the vivacity of his imagination, and the

dignity of his station. Mr. Hamilton had never before met
and encountered at the Bar such a distinguished opponent.
He appeared to be agitated with intense reflection. His
lips were in constant motion and his pen rapidly employed
during the Chancellor's address to the court. He rose with
dignity and spoke for perhaps two hours in support of his

motion.   His reply was fluent and was accompanied with
great earnestness of manner and emphasis of expression.
It was marked by a searching and accurate analysis of the
cases and a thorough and familiar acquaintance with all the
law and learning applicable to the subject.   He begged
leave to suggest, in reference to the same *Tale of the Tub*
that the Chancellor's interest had blinded his better judgment, and, like Peter's influence over his brother, had turned
the brown loaf into mutton.   He illustrated the fact that
the power of awarding new trials in the discretion of the
court had been recognized before the time of Lord Mansfield, and that it was a very reasonable and necessary power,
and a vast amelioration and improvement of the trial by
jury in property concerns.   Without such a salutary control,
the rights of property would be unsafe and at the sport of
ignorance and prejudice ; and trial by jury, instead of being
deemed a blessing, would excite the disgust and contempt
of mankind.   The court had no concern with the political
opinions of Lord Mansfield, but it was due to truth to say
that his profound learning, clear intellect, and admirable
judgment had elevated and adorned the jurisprudence of
England ; and by his wisdom and purity, while presiding
over the English administration of law, he had deservedly
gained the reverence of his own age, and his fame would
rest in the admiration of posterity.

It was some time before I had another opportunity of
hearing Colonel Hamilton speak.   I was as yet unknown to
him, and as I continued to reside for several years at Poughkeepsie, I did not usually attend the terms of the Supreme
Court, either at New York or Albany.   Mr. Hamilton was
called again into public life, on being elected a member of
the Assembly for the City of New York, in April, 1786.
The destinies of this country were at that time rapidly

approaching a crisis. The Confederation of the States was essentially dissolved, and at the session of the Legislature, in the winter of 1787, the active mind and intrepid spirit of Hamilton were displayed in various efforts to surmount difficulties and avert the dangers which surrounded us. The State of Vermont was then in the exercise of independent sovereignty, though not recognized in that capacity. His object was to relieve the State and nation from such a perilous state of things, and he introduced a bill into the House of Assembly, renewing the jurisdiction of this State over the territory in question, and preparing the way for the admission of that State into the Union. The owners of lands in Vermont, under grants from New York, considered their vested interests to be put in jeopardy by the bill, and they were permitted to be heard by counsel at the bar of the House in opposition to it. Richard Harrison addressed the House in a very interesting speech, in which he insisted that the State was bound to employ all the means in its power to recover and protect the rights and property of its citizens, and that, if it was deemed inexpedient to apply force, the State was morally bound and was abundantly able to indemnify its citizens for the loss of their property.

He excited great attention and respect by the perspicuity and strength of his argument, and the suavity of his manner and address. Mr. Hamilton promptly met and answered, in behalf of the House, all the objections to the bill, and he showed, with his usual ability and familiar knowledge of the principles of public law, that the case was one in which the State was dismembered by force without the power to prevent it. Remonstrances had been exhausted. It was in fact a revolution, and it was not the duty of the State, nor was she bound by the fundamental principles of the social compact, to engage in a crusade which must prove disastrous and fruitless, or to undertake to indemnify the claimants in a case of such magnitude.

In this same session Mr. Hamilton made great and manly efforts to prop up and sustain the tottering fabric of the Confederation, and the fallen dignity of Congress. In his comments upon Governor Clinton's speech, he sharply rebuked him for refusing to call the Legislature at the special and earnest request of Congress, to take into consideration their recommendation of a grant of an impost to pay the national debt. He regarded the refusal as heaping fresh marks of contempt upon their authority. He pressed upon the House the necessity of complying with the recommendation of Congress. His speech on that subject was taken down in shorthand by Francis Childs and published at large in his daily paper. It was received and perused with very great interest. I well remember how much it was admired, for the comprehensive views which it took of the state of the nation, the warm appeals which it made to the public patriotism, the imminent perils which it pointed out, and the absolute necessity which it showed of some such financial measure to rescue the nation from utter ruin and disgrace.

His argument was left unanswered, without an attempt to reply to it, and the proposition to accede to the grant to Congress of the impost was rejected by a silent vote. But a new era was at hand. The public mind had become prepared for a reorganization and enlargement of the powers of the National Government. General Hamilton was destined to display his exalted talents, and his ardent devotedness to his country's glory, on a broader theater and in a more illustrious course of public action. In this same session he was appointed one of the three delegates from this State to the General Convention recommended by

Congress to be held at Philadelphia in May, 1787. The sole and express purpose of that convention was to revise the Articles of Confederation, and report to Congress such alterations as should, when agreed to, render the Federal Constitution adequate to the exigencies of Government and the preservation of the Union.

II

THE second branch of the inquiry brings me to consider the services of General Hamilton in relation to the origin and adoption of the Federal Constitution. I never had any means of information respecting the extent and merit of those services, except such as were accessible to the public at large. It was a remark of the Hon. W. S. Johnson, who was a member of the Convention from Connecticut (and which remark was mentioned to me from a very authentic source about that period, though I cannot now recollect the precise time), that if the Constitution should prove to be a failure, Mr. Hamilton would be less responsible than any other member, for he frankly pointed out to the Convention what he apprehended to be its infirmities; and that, on the other hand, if it should operate well, the nation would be more indebted to him than to any other individual, for no one labored more faithfully than he did, nor with equal activity, to give the Constitution a fair trial, by guarding against every evil tendency, and by clothing it with all the attributes and stability requisite for its safety and success, and compatible with the principles of the republican theory.

This was the substance, though I cannot give the exact words of the remark, and it is confirmed by all our contemporary information. Mr. Hamilton's avowed object was to make the experiment of a great federative republic, moving in the largest sphere and resting entirely on a popular basis, as complete, satisfactory, and decisive as possible. He considered the best interests and happiness of mankind as deeply, and perhaps finally, involved in the experiment. He knew and said that no other government but a republic would be admitted or endured in this country. Experimental propositions were made in the Convention and received as suggestions for consideration, and he has stated himself that the highest-toned proposition which he ever made was that the President and Senate should be elected by electors chosen by the people, and that they, as well as the judges, should hold their offices during good behavior, and that the House of Representatives should be elected triennially.

But his opinion essentially changed during the progress of the discussions, and he became satisfied that it would be dangerous to the public tranquillity to elect, by popular elections, a Chief Magistrate with so permanent a tenure ; and toward the close of the convention his subsequent plan gave to the office of President a duration of only three years. He remained with the Convention to the last, though his colleagues, Robert Yates and John Lansing, Junior, had left it some weeks before ; singly representing this State, he heartily assented to and signed the Constitution. It appears to me, therefore, that his friend Gouverneur Morris did him great injustice when he represented him, according to the correspondence contained in Mr. Sparks' "Life of Gouverneur Morris," as having " had little share in forming the Constitution," and as " hating republican government, because he confounded it with democratical government." All the documentary proof and the current observation at the time, lead us to the conclusion that he surpassed all his contemporaries in his exertions to create, recommend, adopt, and defend the Constitution of the United States.

All his actions and all his writings as a public man show that he was the uniform, ardent, and inflexible friend of justice and of national civil liberty. He had fought for our republic during the American War. In his early production as *Phocion* he declared that " the noble struggle we had made in the cause of liberty, had occasioned a kind of revolution in human sentiment; we had the greatest advantages for promoting it that ever a people had; the influence of our example had penetrated the gloomy regions of despotism, and had pointed the way to inquiries which might shake it to its deepest foundations." That immortal work *The Federalist* is the most incontestable evidence of his fervent attachment to the liberties of this country, and of his extreme solicitude for the honor and success of the republican system. His recorded speeches in the State Convention, as taken down in short hand at the time by Mr. Childs, and written out by him in the evenings at my house, contain the same sentiments, coming fresh and fervent from his own lips. " I presume I shall not be disbelieved," he said, " when I declare, that the establishment of a republican government, on a safe and solid basis, is an object of all others the nearest and most dear to my heart."

General Hamilton confound republican with democratical government! It is contradicted by the whole tenor of his life. While he admitted that the petty republics of Greece and Italy were kept in a state of perpetual vibration between the extremes of tyranny and anarchy, he declared, in the 9th number of *The Federalist*, that " the efficacy of various principles is now well understood, which were either not known at all or imperfectly known to the ancients. The regular distribution of power into distinct departments; the introduction of legislative balances and checks; the institution of courts composed of judges holding their offices during good behavior; the representation of the people in the Legislature by deputies of their own election, these are means, and powerful means, by which the excellences of republican government may be retained and its imperfections lessened or avoided." If he doubted of its success, from his knowledge of history and his profound reflections upon the infirmities and corrupt passions of mankind, he was none the less anxious to meet those inherent difficulties, by a skillful and judicious structure of the republican machinery of government. Nor ought it to be forgotten that one of the last proofs which he gave of his inextinguishable devotion to the popular rights of his countrymen was his gratuitous and glorious forensic effort in favor of trial by jury and the liberty of the press.

At the October term of the Supreme Court at Albany, in 1787, I was, for the first time, personally introduced to Colonel Hamilton. I had the honor of dining at your father's house, in company with him and several other gentlemen, and as the new Constitution had just then appeared, it was of course the engrossing topic of conversation. I was a fixed and diffident listener, without presuming to intrude at all into the discussions of such sages. General Schuyler was full of lively, spirited, and instructive reflections, and he went into details, showing, in his usual calculating manner, the great expense and complicated provisions of our local financial systems, and the order, simplicity, and economy that would attend one national system of revenue.

Mr. Hamilton appeared to be careless and desultory in

his remarks, and it occurred to me afterwards how little did I then suppose that he was deeply meditating the plan of the immortal work of *The Federalist.* In the latter part of the same month of October, the essays which compose the volumes of *The Federalist* were commenced in the New York papers. Three or four numbers were published in the course of a week, and they were not concluded until nearly the time of the New York Convention in June, 1788. Those essays, as they successively appeared, were sought after and read, with the greatest avidity and constantly increasing admiration, by all persons favorable to the adoption of the Constitution. Colonel Hamilton was very soon and very generally understood to be the sole, or the principal, author. As the small and humble *Poughkeepsie Journal* was an incompetent vehicle for the republication of them, I undertook at first to make an abridgment, or abstract, of them for that paper, and it was the only newspaper then printed in this State, out of the cities of New York and Albany; but this was soon found to be impracticable, and that if it could be done they would lose all their interest and effect. The essays had grown in number sufficient for a small volume early in the spring of 1788, and the first part of them, to the extent of thirty-six numbers, were collected and reprinted, and a large number of the volumes were sent to me at Poughkeepsie for gratuitous distribution. My former master, mentor, and friend, Judge Benson, attended with me a county meeting in Dutchess, called for the nomination of delegates to the Convention, and the volumes were there circulated to the best of our judgments.

The essays composing *The Federalist* made, at the time, a wonderful impression upon reflecting men. The necessity and importance of the union of the States, the utter

incompetency of the Articles of Confederation to maintain
that union, their fundamental and fatal defects, the infirmities which seemed to be inherent in all ancient and modern confederacies, and the disasters which had usually
attended them, and finally, the absolute necessity of a government organized upon the principles, and clothed with
the powers and attributes of that which was then presented
to the judgment of the American people, — were all of them
topics of vast magnitude and affecting most deeply all our
foreign and domestic concerns. They were discussed in
a masterly manner, and with a talent, strength, information,
and eloquence to which we had not been accustomed.
The appeal to the good sense and patriotism of the country was not made in vain. It usually met with a warm
reception in frank and liberal minds, not blinded by prejudice, nor corrupted by self-interest, nor enslaved by party
discipline.

The New York Convention assembled at Poughkeepsie
on the 17th June, 1788. It formed the most splendid
constellation of the sages and patriots of the Revolution
which I had ever witnessed, and the intense interest with
which the meeting of the Convention was anticipated and
regarded can now scarcely be conceived and much less
felt. As I then resided in that village, I laid aside all
other business and avocations, and attended the Convention as a spectator, daily and steadily, during the whole
six weeks of its session, and was an eye and an ear witness
to everything of a public nature that was done or said.
The Convention was composed of sixty-five members, and
of them nineteen were Federalists, or in favor of the adoption of the Constitution, and forty-six were Anti-Federalists,
or against the adoption of it without previous amendments.
Not a member of that Convention is now living. The

remark will equally apply, as I believe, with but one exception besides myself, to every man who was then a housekeeper either in the village or its environs. That bright and golden age of the Republic may now be numbered "with the years beyond the flood," and I am left almost alone, to recall and enjoy the enchanting vision.

The Convention combined the talents, experience, and weight of character of some of the most distinguished men in the State. Most of them had been disciplined in the discussions, services, and perils of the Revolution. The principal speakers on the Federal side were Mr. Jay (then Secretary for Foreign Affairs), Chancellor Livingston, Mr. Duane (then Mayor of New York), Mr. Harrison, and Colonel Hamilton. On the other side they were the elder Governor Clinton, Mr. (afterwards Chancellor) Lansing, Mr. Jones (afterwards Recorder of New York), John Williams of Washington County, and Gilbert Livingston and Melancthon Smith, delegates from Dutchess. There was no difficulty in deciding at once on which side of the house the superiority in debate existed, yet in the ordinary range of the discussion, it was found that the dignity, candor, and strength of Jay, the polished address and elegant erudition of Chancellor Livingston, the profound sagacity and exhaustive researches of Hamilton, were met with equal pretensions by their opponents, supported by the simplicity and unpretending good sense of Clinton, the popular opinions and plausible deductions of Lansing, the metaphysical mind, prepossessing plainness, and embarrassing subtleties of Smith.

Mr. Hamilton maintained the ascendency on every question, and being the only person present who had signed the Constitution, he felt and sustained the weight of the responsibility which belonged to his party. He was indis-

putably pre-eminent, and all seemed, as by a common consent, to concede to him the burden and the honor of the
debate. Melancthon Smith was equally the most prominent and the most responsible speaker on the Anti-Federal
side of the Convention. There was no person to be compared to him in his powers of acute and logical discussion.
He was Mr. Hamilton's most persevering and formidable
antagonist.

But even Smith was routed in every contest. As Hamilton had been a leading member of the National Convention and a leading writer of *The Federalist*, his mind had
become familiar with the principles of Federal government
and with every topic of debate, and it was prompt, ardent,
energetic, and overflowing with an exuberance of argument
and illustration. The three principal topics of discussion
in which Mr. Hamilton was most distinguished and most
masterly, were: (1) On the importance of the Union, the
defects of the Confederation, and the just principles of
representation. (2) On the requisite tenure and stability
of the Senate. (3) On the power of taxation, and the reserved rights of the States. On each of these subjects he
bestowed several speeches, some of which were employed
in refutation and reply.

He generally spoke with much animation and energy and
with considerable gesture. His language was clear, nervous,
and classical. His investigations penetrated to the foundation and reason of every doctrine and principle which he
examined, and he brought to the debate a mind filled with
all the learning and precedents applicable to the subject.
He never omitted to meet, examine, and discover the strength
or weakness, the truth or falsehood of every proposition with
which he had to contend. His candor was magnanimous
and rose to a level with his abilities. His temper was spir-

ited but courteous, amiable and generous, and he frequently
made pathetic and powerful appeals to the moral sense and
patriotism, the fears and hopes of the assembly, in order to
give them a deep sense of the difficulties of the crisis and
prepare their minds for the reception of the Constitution.

The style and manner of Smith's speaking was dry, plain,
and syllogistic, and it behooved his adversary to examine
well the ground on which they started, and not to concede
too much at the beginning, or he would find it somewhat
embarrassing to extricate himself from a subtle web of sophistry, unless indeed he happened to possess the giant strength
of Hamilton, which nothing could withstand. Mr. Smith
was a man of remarkable simplicity, and of the most gentle,
liberal, and amiable disposition. Though I felt strong political prejudices against Governor Clinton, as the leader of
the Anti-Federal party, yet during the course of that Convention, I became very favorably struck with the dignity
with which he presided, and with his unassuming and modest
pretensions as a speaker. It was impossible not to feel
respect for such a man, and for a young person not to be
somewhat over-awed in his presence, when it was apparent
in all his actions and deportment that he possessed great
decision of character and a stern inflexibility of purpose.

The arguments used by Colonel Hamilton in the debates
in the Convention were substantially the same which he had
before employed in *The Federalist*. They could not well
have been any other, for he had already urged, in support
of the Constitution all the leading considerations which had
led to the plan of it, and which guided the skill of the artists.
The wisdom of the commentator was now repeated and enforced by the eloquence of the orator.

In his opening speech Mr. Hamilton preliminarily observed that it was of the utmost importance that the Con-

vention should be thoroughly and deeply impressed with a conviction of the necessity of the Union of the States. If they could but once be entirely satisfied of that great truth, and would duly reflect upon it, their minds would then be prepared to admit the necessity of a government of similar powers and organization with the one before them, to uphold and preserve that Union. It was equally so, he said by way of illustration, with the doctrine of the Immortality of the Soul, and he believed with Doctor Young that doubts on that subject were one great cause of modern infidelity; for to convince men that they have within them immaterial and immortal spirits is going very far to prepare their minds for the ready reception of Christian truth.

After pointing out the radical defects of the Confederation, and vindicating the popular basis of the new Constitution, he declared his convictions that the latter was a genuine specimen of a representative and republican government; and he hoped and trusted that we had found a cure for our evils, and that the new government would prove, in an eminent degree, a blessing to the nation. He concluded his first great speech with the Patriot's Prayer, "Oh, save my country, Heaven!" in allusion to the brave Cobham, who fell, "his ruling passion strong in death."

His two speeches on the organization, powers, and stability of the Senate were regarded at the time as the best specimens which the debates afforded of the ability and wisdom of a consummate statesman. They were made in opposition to a proposed amendment to the Constitution that no person should be eligible as a Senator for more than six years in any term of twelve years, and that they should at all times, within the period of six years, be subject to recall by the State Legislatures, and to the substitution of others. Mr. Hamilton on that occasion took large and philosophical views of the nature of man, his interests, his passions, his pursuits, his duties; and he drew his deductions from the end and design of government, the settled principles of policy, and the history of all other free governments, ancient and modern. He discovered equally an ardent zeal for the success of popular government, and a correct knowledge of those infirmities which had invariably attended it. Instability and a fluctuating policy were the prominent features in most republican systems, and the tendency of such vicious defects was to destroy all sense of pride and national character, and to forfeit the respect and confidence of other nations. He contended, therefore, that in all rational policy we ought to infuse a principle of strength and stability into the structure of our national government, by the creation of a senatorial branch, which should be comparatively small in number, and appointed for considerable periods of time, and inspired with a sense of independence in the exercise of its powers. Upon no other plan would the Senate, either in its legislative or executive character, be able to perform its functions, as the balance-wheel of the machine; or form on the one hand a salutary check to the mischiefs of misguided zeal and a fluctuating policy in the more popular branch, and on the other to the abuses and misrule of the President, in the exercise of the treaty and the appointing powers.

The tendency of federative governments, as all history taught us, was to weakness and dissolution, by gradual and steady encroachments of the members upon the national authority. Our own experience under the Articles of Confederation was a monitory example before our eyes of this fatal tendency. Local governments more readily concentrated popular sympathies and prejudices. The affections naturally grew languid in proportion to the expansion of the circle in which they moved.

Though Mr. Hamilton considered that amendment as tending to destroy the dignity and stability of the national Senate, and give the State Legislatures a fatal control in their discretion over the legislative and executive authorities of the Union, it was nevertheless adopted by a vote of all the Anti Federal members of the Convention, and it was one of the recommendatory amendments annexed to the ratification of the instrument. During the sitting of the Convention, information was received that New Hampshire had adopted the Constitution, and she made the ninth State that had adopted it. That great event wrought at once an important change in the situation of the United States, inasmuch as the Confederation thereby became *ipso facto* dissolved, and the new Constitution had become the lawful government of the States which had ratified it.

But the fact, however momentous, did not seem to disturb the tranquillity or shake the purpose of a majority of the Convention. Mr. M. Smith and Mr. Lansing both declared that the event had no influence on their deliberations, and the Convention continued their sharp debate for three weeks subsequent to that information and apparently regardless of it, and until all hopes of an auspicious issue to it seemed to be lost. It was in the midst of that gloomy period, and just before the clouds began to disperse and serene skies to appear, that Mr. Hamilton made one of his most pathetic and impassioned addresses. He urged every motive that he thought ought to govern men, and he touched with exquisite skill every chord of sympathy that could be made to vibrate in the human breast. Our country, our honor, our friends, our posterity were placed in vivid colors before us. He alluded slightly to the distress and degradation which dictated the call for a National Convention, and he portrayed in matchless style the characters of that illustrious assembly, composed undoubtedly of the best and brightest of the American statesmen, who could have had no motive but their country's good. They had lived in "times that tried men's souls." To discriminate might be odious. It could not be so to select Franklin, revered by the wise men of Europe, and Washington, "crowned with laurels, loaded with glory."

Soon thereafter information was received that Virginia had also adopted the Constitution. Colonel Hamilton read a letter to the Convention to that effect from Mr. Madison, and then a visible change took place in the disposition of the House, and led it to think of adopting the Constitution upon certain terms. A resolution to adopt it was before the House when Mr. M. Smith moved an amendment that it be ratified upon condition that certain powers contained in the instrument should not be exercised until a general convention of the States had been called to propose amendments. This proposition was discussed for some days, with increasing agitation and anxiety, and it was at last urged that the adoption of the Constitution would readily be received with that qualification annexed. Mr. Hamilton was strenuous and peremptory in his opinion and advice to the House, that such a conditional ratification was void, and would not and could not be accepted by Congress. All expectation from such a source he assured them would prove delusive. The members generally and gradually assumed a more conciliatory tone, and all vehemence in debate seemed to have ceased as by common consent. "We did not come here," said Mr. Jay, "to carry points or gain party triumphs. We ought not to wish it. We were without a national government and on the eve of an untried era. Everything demanded concession and moderation. The laurels of party victory might peradventure be bedewed with the tears or stained with the blood of our fellow-citizens."

Colonel Hamilton disclaimed the intention of wounding the feelings of any individual, though he admitted that he had expressed himself, in the course of the debates, in strong language dictated by ardent feelings arising out of the interesting nature of the discussions. On no subject, he observed, had his breast been filled with stronger emotions or agitated with more anxious concern. The spirit of the House was liberal and cheering, and at last Samuel Jones, one of the Anti-Federal members, had the magnanimity to move to substitute the words " in full confidence " in lieu of the words " upon condition." He was supported by Melancthon Smith, who had so eminently distinguished himself throughout the whole course of the session, and by Zephaniah Platt, then first judge of the County of Dutchess, who made a few observations expressing in a plain, frank manner, his sense of duty on that occasion and his determination to follow it. The members who came over from the Anti-Federal side of the House were twelve in number, being four members from Dutchess, four from Queens, three from Suffolk, and one from Washington, and, uniting themselves with the nineteen Federal members from New York, Westchester, Kings, and Richmond, they constituted a majority in the Convention, and the Constitution was ratified on the 26th of July.

I always considered that the gentlemen who made this memorable and unbought sacrifice of prejudice, error, and pride on the altar of patriotism and their country's welfare, were entitled to the highest honor. It was quite an heroic effort to quit such a leader as Governor Clinton, and such men as Yates and Lansing, who had been delegates to the General Convention, even though it was to follow their own convictions. It was understood that several other members were inclined to follow the same course, but they could not be brought to desert Governor Clinton, who remained inflexible. Had he consented to vote for the Constitution, the final ratification of it would probably have been unanimous. As it was, the spirit of harmony and conciliation with which the Convention closed was deemed most auspicious by all sincere lovers of their country. Considering the circumstances under which the Convention assembled, the manner in which it terminated afforded a new and instructive example of wisdom and moderation to mankind.

III.

THE third and last part of the history of General Hamilton to which you have requested my attention relates to his life subsequent to the adoption of the Constitution of the United States. After the Constitution went into operation, in the course of the year 1789, Mr. Hamilton was appointed to the office of Secretary of the Treasury. While the Constitution was in its progress to maturity, some of his friends had suggested in my hearing that the office of Chief-Justice of the Supreme Court of the United States would be in every way suited to the exercise of his discernment and judgment; and that he was well fitted for it by his accurate acquaintance with the general principles of jurisprudence. Of all this there could have been no doubt. But his versatile talents, adapted equally for the Bench or the Bar, the field, the Senate House, and the executive cabinet, were fortunately called to act in a more complicated, busy, and responsible station. I found myself by this time upon friendly and familiar terms with Colonel Hamilton. In the

winter and spring of 1789 he took a leading and zealous
part in the election of Governor. He was chairman of the
New York Committee of Correspondence, in favor of
Judge Yates as a candidate for Governor, in opposition
to the re-election of Governor Clinton, and he no doubt
was the author of some of the circular addresses from that
committee. / One of them was subscribed by his own hand
as chairman, and was circulated in a pamphlet form addressed to the Supervisors of each county. All the addresses of the New York committees on each side were
collected by me at the time and are now before me ; and
I cannot but be struck with the spirit of decorum which
characterizes their contents, in the midst of the most
earnest and the most animated competition.   In the
printed circulars the committees fairly reasoned before
the public the merits of their respective pretensions and
candidates.

I was in New York when the House of Representatives
was first organized in the beginning of April, 1789, and no
spectacle could have been more gratifying.   The City Hall
had been remodeled and fitted up in elegant style for the
reception of Congress, and all ranks and degrees of men
seemed to be actuated by one common impulse to fill the
galleries as soon as the doors of the House of Representatives were opened for the first time, and to gaze on one
of the most interesting fruits of their struggle, a popular
assembly summoned from all parts of the United States.
Colonel Hamilton remarked to me that, as nothing was
to be done the first day, such impatient crowds were evidence of the powerful principle of curiosity.   I felt another
and better apology in my own breast.   I considered
it to be a proud and glorious day, the consummation
of our wishes ; and that I was looking upon an organ

of popular will, just beginning to breathe the breath of life, and which might in some future age, much more truly than the Roman Senate, be regarded as the "refuge of nations." At any rate I dwell upon that recollection with some interest, for it has so happened that I have never since that day been present in the House of Representatives.

Colonel Hamilton filled the office of Secretary of the Treasury upwards of five years, and his official acts are all before the public, and do not come within the scope of my present inquiry. He resigned the office in January, 1795, after having raised the financial character of the Government to an exalted height, and finished those duties which appertained peculiarly to that department on its first institution. Those duties consisted in the establishment of a sound, efficient, and permanent provision for the gradual restoration of public credit, and the faithful dis- charge of the national debt. No man ever inculcated with more sincerity and zeal a lively sense of the obligations of good faith and the sanctity of contracts. In his view, the true principle to render public credit immortal was always to accompany the creation of debt with the means of extinguishing it. He demonstrated that the creation of a national bank was within the reach of the legitimate powers of the Government, and essential to the convenient and prosperous administration of the national finances. He made an able and elaborate report in favor of the encouragement of domestic manufactures, and he seems not to have entertained a doubt of the constitutional right of Congress to exercise its discretion on the subject.

He contended that the encouragement of manufactures tended to create a more extensive, certain, and permanent home market for the surplus produce of land, and that it was necessary, in self-defence, to meet and counteract the restrictive system of the commercial nations of Europe. It was admitted, however, that if the liberal system of Adam Smith had been generally adopted, it would have carried forward nations, with accelerated motion, in the career of prosperity and greatness. The English critics spoke at the time of his report as a strong and able plea on the side of manufactures, and said that the subjects of trade, finance, and internal policy were not often discussed with so much precision of thought and perspicuity of language.

During the time that Colonel Hamilton presided over the Treasury Department, the French Revolution was in action, and a fierce war broke out between Great Britain and the French Republic. He was one of President Washington's cabinet council, and a leading and efficient adviser of the President's proclamation of neutrality in April, 1793, declaring the neutral position of the United States, and his duty and determination, as the chief executive guardian of the laws, to preserve it. That proclamation was the index to the foreign policy of President Washington, and it was temperately and discreetly, but firmly maintained, under the sage advice and controlling influence of Hamilton, against the arts and intrigues of the French Minister to the United States, and against all the force and fury of the tempestuous passions of the times, engendered and influenced by the French democracy. He aided the great American policy of neutrality by his pen, in some fugitive pieces under the signature of *No Jacobin,* and in the more elaborate and elegant essays under the signature of *Pacificus;* and still more so by his opinion and advice in favor of the seasonable mission of Chief-Justice Jay to the Court of Great Britain, in the spring of 1794. That envoy was sent on purpose "to vindicate our rights with firmness and to cultivate peace with sincerity," and no one event was attended with more auspicious results, or contributed equally to establish and elevate the pacific policy of Washington, who, having "once saved his country by his valor in war, again saved it by his wisdom in peace."

Mr. Hamilton returned to private life and to the practice of the law in New York in the spring of 1795. He was cordially welcomed and cheered on his return by his fellow-citizens, and while he was gradually resuming his profession he felt himself called upon, by a sense of duty, to vindicate by his pen one great act of Washington's administration. Mr. Jay's treaty with Great Britain had been negotiated while he was in office, though it was not ratified by the President and Senate until the summer of 1795. It had honorably adjusted and extinguished the complaints and difficulties between us and Great Britain, and it contributed essentially to continue and strengthen the neutrality of the United States. But it was vehemently opposed and denounced by the party in this country which had originally opposed the Constitution, and which, from being formerly denominated the Anti-Federal, was then called the Democratic party; and it included, of course, all the devoted partisans of France and apologists for the violence and madness of the French rulers.

Mr. Hamilton vindicated the treaty in a series of essays under the signature of *Camillus*. They were written with vast ability, and in clear, strong, and elegant language, and disclosed a familiar acquaintance with all the grievances, claims, doctrines, and principles adjusted, ascertained, and declared by the treaty. Some of the essays are of permanent value, and will be read and cited as long as his name endures, as accurate and lucid commentaries on public law.

My acquaintance with Colonel Hamilton was revived after his return to New York, and it was enlarged and cherished, and eventually terminated in a warm and confidential friendship. Several of the essays of *Camillus* were communicated to me before they were printed, and my attention was attracted, by a single fact which fell under my own eye, to the habit of thorough, precise, and authentic research which accompanied all his investigations. He was not content, for instance, with examining Grotius, and taking him as an authority, in any other than the original Latin language in which the work was composed.

Between the years 1795 and 1798 he took his station as the leading counsel at the Bar. He was employed in every important and especially in every commercial case. He was a very great favorite with the merchants of New York, and he most justly deserved to be, for he had uniformly shown himself to be one of the most enlightened, intrepid, and persevering friends to the commercial prosperity of this country. Insurance questions, both upon the law and the fact, constituted a large portion of the litigated business in the courts, and much of the intense study and discussion at the Bar. The business of insurance was carried on principally by private underwriters, and as the law had not been defined and settled in this country by a course of judicial decisions, and was open to numerous perplexed questions arising out of our neutral trade, and was left, under a complicated mixture of law and fact, very much at large to a jury, the litigation of that kind was immense. Mr. Hamilton had an overwhelming share of it, and though the New York Bar could at that time boast of the clear intellect, the candor, the simplicity, and black-letter learning of the elder Jones, the profound and richly varied learning of Harrison, the classical taste and elegant accomplishments of Brockholst Livingston, the solid and accurate, but unpretending common-law learning of Troup, the chivalrous feelings and dignified address of Pendleton, yet the mighty mind of Hamilton would at times bear down all opposition by its comprehensive grasp and the strength of his reasoning powers.

He taught us all how to probe deeply into the hidden recesses of the science, or to follow up principles to their far distant sources. He was not content with the modern reports, abridgments, or translations. He ransacked cases and precedents to their very foundations; and we learned from him to carry our inquiries into the commercial codes of the nations of the European continent, and in a special manner to illustrate the law of insurance by the severe judgment of Emerigon and the luminous commentaries of Valin.

In the spring of 1798 Mr. Hamilton felt himself called upon by a sense of public duty to engage once more in political discussion. It will be recollected, as I once had occasion to observe in a brief review of his public life and writings which was published anonymously soon after his death, that France had long been making piratical depredations upon our commerce; that negotiation and a pacific adjustment had been repeatedly attempted on the part of this country without success; that one Minister had been refused an audience; that three Ministers Extraordinary had been treated with the grossest indignity, and money demanded of the United States on terms the most degrading. The doors of reconciliation being thus barred, we had no honorable alternative left but open and determined resistance. At that portentous period Mr. Hamilton published *The Stand*, or a series under the signature of *Titus Manlius*, with a view to arouse the people of this country to a sense of their impending danger, and to measures of defence which should be at once vigorous and manly.

The plan of this production was communicated to me by Mr. Hamilton before it appeared, and the very signature was a subject of discussion at my office. He wished for some appropriate name from Roman history, applicable to the stand which those ancient Republicans had made against the Gauls, and on examination the name selected was deemed by him the most suitable. In these essays he portrayed in strong and glowing colors the conduct of revolutionary France towards her own people and towards other nations. He showed that she had undermined the main pillars of civilized society; that she had betrayed a plan to disorganize the human mind itself by attempting to destroy all religious opinion and pervert a whole people to atheism; that her ruling passions were ambition and fanaticism; and that she aimed equally to proselyte, subjugate, and debase every government, without distinction, to effect the aggrandizement of the "great nation." All the States, even of the republican form, that fell within her wide-spread grasp — the United Netherlands, Geneva, the Swiss Cantons, Genoa, and Venice — had already been prostrated by her arms, or her still more formidable caresses.

He then gave a detail of the accumulated insults and injuries which the United States had received from France, and showed that her object was to degrade and humble our Government, and prepare the way for revolution and conquest. He concluded, as the result of his work, that we ought to suspend our treaties with France, fortify our harbors, defend our commerce on the ocean, attack their predatory cruisers on our coasts, create a respectable naval force, and raise, or organize and discipline, a considerable army, as an indispensable precaution against attempts at invasion, which might put in jeopardy our very existence as a nation. So undeniable were all these facts, so irresistible were the conclusions which he drew from them, that in the summer of 1798 those measures suggested by Mr. Hamilton were all literally carried into execution by Congress, and received the warm and hearty sanction of the nation. An honorable, proud, and manly sentiment was then enkindled and pervaded the continent; it reflected high honor on our national character, and that character was transmitted to Europe as a means of respect and a pledge of security.

It is well known that General Washington gave his decided approbation to all those measures of national resistance, and that he urged upon Government the employment of Colonel Hamilton in the military line. In a letter to President Adams, in September, 1798, he pronounced upon him a noble eulogy. He declared that Colonel Hamilton had been his " principal and most confidential aid; that his acknowledged abilities and integrity had placed him on high ground and made him a conspicuous character in the United States, and even in Europe; that he had the laudable ambition which prompts a man to excel in whatever he takes in hand; that he was enterprising, quick in his perceptions, and that his judgment was intuitively great." Upon the earnest recommendation of Washington, General Hamilton was appointed Inspector-General of the provisional army that was raised in 1798; but the time which he was necessarily led to bestow on his new military duties did not dissolve his connection with the profession and practice of the law. That military office was but temporary, and he soon resumed his full practice at the bar.

My judicial station, in 1798, brought him before me in a new relation, but the familiar friendly intercourse between us was not diminished, and it kept on increasing to the end of his life. At circuits and in term time I was called, in a thousand instances, to attend with intense interest and high admiration to the rapid exercise of his reasoning powers, the sagacity with which he pursued his investigations, his piercing criticisms, his masterly analysis, and the energy and fervor of his appeals to the judgment and conscience of the tribunal which he addressed. If I were to select any two cases in which his varied powers were most strikingly displayed, it would be the case of *Le Guen v. Gouverneur and Kemble*, argued before the Court of Errors in the winter of 1800, and the case of *Croswell ads. The People*, argued before the Supreme Court in February term, 1804. In the first of those cases the most distinguished counsel of the New York Bar were engaged ; but what gave peculiar interest to it was the circumstance that Gouverneur Morris, a relative of one of the defendants, gratuitously appeared as their counsel. The action had been originally commenced by Le Guen at law, upon the advice of Mr. Hamilton. The claim was very large in amount, and after expensive trials and the most persevering and irritating litigation, pursued into the court of the last resort. The plaintiff recovered upon technical rules of law strictly and severely applied.

The claim was a commercial one, and was in opposition to the mercantile sense of its justice. The success of it was thought at the time to be due in a very material degree to the overbearing weight and influence of General Hamilton's talents. The case I now allude to, in which Mr. Hamilton and Mr. Morris were brought into collision, was on an appeal from a decree in Chancery, in which relief on grounds of fraud had been afforded against the judgment at law. The zeal and anxiety which the cause enkindled had been increasing through the whole protracted controversy, and had become very intense at the period of this final review. Everything was calculated to tax to the utmost the powers of those two illustrious statesmen civilians. If the one was superior in logic and law learning, the other was presumed to be his equal in eloquence, imagination, and wit. The appearance of Mr. Morris was very commanding. His noble head, his majestic mien, the dignity of his deportment were all impressive. I have no notes or memorials remaining of the argument in the cause, but my memory serves me to say that it was a most beautiful and captivating display of the genius and varied accomplishments of those orators.

The questions of law involved in the case were indeed dry and technical, nor were the facts of a nature to excite much interest. It was the large amount of property in controversy, the character of the litigation, and, above all, the high reputation of the two leading counsel, that roused such ardent curiosity and anxious expectation. But any cause involving law and fact seems to be sufficient to afford aliment for the brilliant exhibition of minds of such high order and of such intellectual resources. There was, in that case, a mass of facts involving a complicated charge of fraud, and that was enough to command the exertion of the keenest sagacity, a critical severity, shrewd retort, and pathetic appeal. A Jewish house was concerned in the commercial transaction, and that led to affecting allusion to the character and fortunes of that ancient race. Some of the negotiations happened in France, and that produced references to that tremendous Revolution which was then still in its fury, and whose frightful ravages and remorseless pretensions seemed to overawe and confound the nations.

Mr. Morris and Mr. Hamilton equally resorted for illustration to Shakespeare, Milton, and Pope ; and when the former complained that his long absence from the bar had

caused him to forget the decisions, the latter sportively
accounted for it on another principle, and relied on the
poetical authority that—

> " Where beams of warm imagination play,
> The memory's soft figures melt away."

The other case I mentioned involved the discussion of
legal principles of the greatest consequence. Croswell
had been indicted and convicted of a libel upon Thomas
Jefferson, then President of the United States. The libel
consisted in charging Mr. Jefferson with having paid one
Callender, a printer, for grossly slandering George Washington and John Adams, the former Presidents; and the
defendant offered to prove the truth of the charge. But
the testimony was overruled by Chief-Justice Lewis, who
held the circuit, and he charged the jury that it was not
their province to decide on the intent of the defendant,
or whether the libel was true or false or malicious, and that
those questions belonged exclusively to the court. The
motion was for a new trial for misdirection of the Judge,
and those two great points in the case were elaborately
discussed before the Supreme Court, and they were considered by General Hamilton, who appeared gratuitously
for the defendant, as affecting very essentially the constitutional right of trial by jury in criminal cases, and the
American doctrine of the liberty of the press.

I have always considered General Hamilton's argument in that cause the greatest forensic effort that he ever
made. He had bestowed unusual attention to the case,
and he came prepared to discuss the points of law with
a perfect mastery of the subject. He believed that the
rights and liberties of the people were essentially concerned
in the vindication and establishment of those rights of the

jury and of the press for which he contended. That consideration was sufficient to arouse all the faculties of his mind to their utmost energy. He held it to be an essential ingredient in the trial by jury that, in criminal cases, the law and the fact were necessarily blended by the plea of not guilty, and that the jury had a rightful cognizance of the intent and tendency of the libel, for in the intent consisted the crime. They had a right and they were bound in duty to take into consideration the whole matter of the charge, both as to the law and the fact, for it was all involved in the issue and determined by a general verdict. On the independent exercise of the right of the jury in criminal cases to determine the guilt or innocence of the defendant, according to their judgment and consciences, rested the security of our lives and liberties. Nothing would be more dangerous to the citizens of this country than to place the trial by jury in such cases under the control and dictation of the court. The English history, in its dark and disastrous periods, showed abundantly by its records that the most dangerous, the most sure, the most fatal of tyrannies consisted in selecting and sacrificing single individuals, under the mask and forms of law, by dependent and partial tribunals. We could not too perseveringly cultivate and sustain the rights of the jury in all their common-law vigor, as the great guardians of liberty and life, equally against the sport and fury of contending factions, the vindictive persecution of the public prosecutor, and the " machinations of demagogues and tyrants on their imagined thrones."

On the other great question in the case he contended with equal ardor and ability for the admission of the truth in evidence to a qualified extent in justification of the libel. He showed that it depended on the motive and object of the publication whether the truth was or was not a justification.

The liberty of the press was held to consist in the right to publish with impunity the truth, whether it respected government, magistrates, or individuals, provided it was published with good motives and for justifiable ends. The hard doctrines under which his client was convicted came from the Star Chamber, that arbitrary and hated tribunal acting under the government of a permanent body of judges, without the wholesome restraints of a jury. He felt a proud satisfaction in the reflection that the Act of Congress of July, 1798, for preventing certain libels against the Government, and which Act had been grossly misrepresented, established these two great principles of civil liberty involved in the discussion. It declared that the jury should have the right to determine the law and the fact, under the direction of the court, as in other cases, and that the defendant might give in evidence in his defence the truth of the libel. He was as strenuous for the qualification of the rule allowing the truth of the libel to be shown in the defence, as he was for the rule itself.

While he regarded the liberty of the press as essential to the preservation of free government, he considered that a press wholly unchecked, with a right to publish anything at pleasure, regardless of truth or decency, would be, in the hands of unprincipled men, a terrible engine of mischief, and would be liable to be diverted to the most seditious and wicked purposes, and for the gratification of private malice or revenge. Such a free press would destroy public and private confidence, and would overawe and corrupt the impartial administration of justice.

There was an unusual solemnity and earnestness on the part of General Hamilton in this discussion. He was at times highly impassioned and pathetic. His whole soul was enlisted in the cause, and in contending for the rights of the jury and a free press he considered that he was establishing the finest refuge against oppression. The aspect of the times was portentous, and he was persuaded that if he should be able to overthrow the high-toned doctrine contained in the charge of the judge, it would be great gain to the liberties of his country. He entered, by the force of sympathy, into the glorious struggles of English patriots, during oppressive and unconstitutional times, for the rights of juries and for a free press; and the anxiety and tenderness of his feelings and the gravity of his theme rendered his reflections exceedingly impressive. He never before, in my hearing, made any effort in which he commanded higher reverence for his principles, or equal admiration of his eloquence.

Nor were his efforts on that occasion lost to his country. The fruit of them still exists and will remain with posterity, a monument of his glory, though the court was equally divided on the motion he discussed, and therefore decided nothing; yet in the following winter the Legislature of New York passed a declaratory statute, introduced into the House of Assembly by William W. Van Ness, his friend and associate on the trial, admitting the right of the jury in all criminal cases to determine the law and the fact under the direction of the court, and allowing the truth to be given in evidence by the defendant, in every prosecution for a libel; provided that such evidence should not be a justification, unless it should be made satisfactorily to appear that the matter charged as libel was published with good motives and for justifiable ends.

In April, 1804, I held the Circuit Court in the city of New York, and the most interesting interview which I ever had with General Hamilton was at his country seat at Harlem Heights, during the course of that month. He took me out to dine with him and I was detained at his house the next day.[1] We were assailed by a violent easterly storm the night I was there, and the house, standing on high ground, was very much exposed to the fury of the winds as they swept over the island from the " vex'd Atlantic." The solicitude of General Hamilton for my comfort, and his attention and kindness quite affected me. He visited me after I had retired to my chamber, to see that I was sufficiently attended to. In a memorandum which I made a day or two after that visit, and which is now before me, I state in allusion to it that " he never appeared before so friendly and amiable. I was alone, and he treated me with a minute affection that I did not suppose he knew how to bestow. His manners were delicate and chaste, and he appeared, in his domestic state, the plain, modest, and affectionate father and husband."

Gouverneur Morris was to have dined with us, but he sent an apology stating that " the Jacobin winds" had prevented him. We were consequently left to ourselves during the greater part of a day, and the conversation led to a more serious train of reflections on his part than I had ever before known him to indulge. His mind had a cast usually melancholy. The impending election exceedingly disturbed him, and he viewed the temper, disposition, and passions of the times as portentous of evil, and favorable to the sway of artful and ambitious demagogues. His wise reflections, his sober views, his anxiety, his gentleness, his goodness, his Christian temper, all contributed to render my solitary visit inexpressibly interesting. At that time he revealed to me a plan he had in contemplation, for a full

[1] *Supra*, p. 143.

investigation of the history and science of civil government, and the practical results of the various modifications of it upon the freedom and happiness of mankind. He wished to have the subject treated in reference to past experience, and upon the principles of Lord Bacon's inductive philosophy. His object was to see what safe and salutary conclusions might be drawn from an historical examination of the effects of the various institutions heretofore existing, upon the freedom, the morals, the prosperity, the intelligence, the jurisprudence, and the happiness of the people. Six or eight gentlemen were to be united with him in the work, according to his arrangement, and each of them was to take his appropriate part and to produce a volume. If I am not mistaken Mr. Harrison, Mr. Jay, Mr. Morris, and Mr. King were suggested by him as desirable coadjutors. I recollect that he proposed to assign the subject of ecclesiastical history to the Rev'd Dr. Mason, and he was pleased to suggest that he wished me to accept a share of the duty. The conclusions to be drawn from these historical reviews, he intended to reserve for his own task, and this is the imperfect outline of the scheme which then occupied his thoughts. I heard no more of it afterwards, for the business of the court occupied all our attention, and after the May term of that year I saw him no more.

I have very little doubt that if General Hamilton had lived twenty years longer, he would have rivalled Socrates, or Bacon, or any other of the sages of ancient or modern times, in researches after truth and in benevolence to mankind. The active and profound statesman, the learned and eloquent lawyer would probably have disappeared in a great degree before the character of the sage philosopher, instructing mankind by his wisdom and elevating his country by his example. He had not then attained his forty-eighth year, and all his faculties were in their full vigor and maturity, and incessantly busy in schemes to avert distant dangers and to secure the freedom and promote the honor and happiness of his country.

I knew General Hamilton's character well. His life and actions, for the course of twenty-two years, had engaged and fixed my attention. They were often passing under my eye and observation. For the last six years of his life he was arguing causes before me. I have been sensibly struck, in a thousand instances, with his habitual reverence for truth, his candor, his ardent attachment to civil liberty, his indignation at oppression of every kind, his abhorrence of every semblance of fraud, his reverence for justice, and his sound legal principles drawn by a clear and logical deduction from the purest Christian ethics, and from the very foundations of all rational and practical jurisprudence. He was blessed with a very amiable, generous, tender, and charitable disposition, and he had the most artless simplicity of any man I ever knew. It was impossible not to love as well as respect and admire him. He was perfectly disinterested. The selfish principle, that infirmity too often of great as well as of little minds, seemed never to have reached him. It was entirely incompatible with the purity of his taste and the grandeur of his ambition. Everything appeared to be at once extinguished, when it came in competition with his devotion to his country's welfare and glory. He was a most faithful friend to the cause of civil liberty throughout the world, but he was a still greater friend to truth and justice.

He wished the people to enjoy as much political liberty as they were competent to use and not abuse, — as much as was consistent with the perfect security of life and social rights, and the acquisition and enjoyment of property. He was satisfied, from profound reflection and from the uniform language of history, that all plans of government founded on any new and extraordinary reform in the morals of mankind were plainly Utopian. The voice of history, the language of Scripture, the study of the nature and character of man, all taught us that mankind were exceedingly prone to error; that they were liable to be duped by flattery, to be seduced by artful, designing men, to be inflamed by jealousies and bad passions; and he was satisfied that the greatest danger to be apprehended in this country was from the natural tendency of the organized and powerful State governments to resist and control the constitutional authority of the federal head. This I know from repeated conversations with him to have been one great ground of uneasiness and apprehension with him as to our future destiny. He knew that factions were the besetting evils of republics. They lead to the tyrannical oppression of minorities, of individuals under the mask and form of law; to the dangerous influence of cunning, intriguing, and corrupt leaders; to civil discord and anarchy, and eventually to an armed master. The fate of all former federative governments and the horrible excesses of the French democracy were before his eyes, and without the aid of his private reflections we can be at no loss, from the reasonings and sentiments in *The Federalist*, to know the quarter from which he apprehended danger and dissension, disunion and ruin to the nation.

I have thus endeavored, my dear madam, to the best of my ability, and with perfect candor and regard for truth, to satisfy your inquiries. And if what I have written shall afford you consolation, and shall contribute in any small degree to awaken in the present generation an increased attention to the history and character of your illustrious husband, I shall be amply rewarded for my effort.

I am, Madam, with the utmost respect and esteem,

Your friend and ob'd't serv't,

JAMES KENT.

Mrs. ELIZABETH HAMILTON.

INDEX

INDEX